TM

...FOR DUMMIES

BESTSELLING
BOOK SERIES

References for the
Rest of Us!™

Do you find that traditional reference books are overloaded with technical details and advice you'll never use? Do you postpone important life decisions because you just don't want to deal with them? Then our ...For Dummies® business and general reference book series is for you.

...For Dummies business and general reference books are written for those frustrated and hard-working souls who know they aren't dumb, but find that the myriad of personal and business issues and the accompanying horror stories make them feel helpless. ...For Dummies books use a lighthearted approach, a down-to-earth style, and even cartoons and humorous icons to dispel fears and build confidence. Lighthearted but not lightweight, these books are perfect survival guides to solve your everyday personal and business problems.

"...Dummies books consistently live up to their brand-name promise to transform 'can't into can.' "
— Ottawa Citizen

"...clear, straightforward information laced with a touch of humour."
— The Toronto Star

"...set up in bits and bites that are easy to digest, full of no-nonsense advice."
— The Calgary Herald

Already, millions of satisfied readers agree. They have made ...For Dummies the #1 introductory level computer book series and a best-selling business book series. They have written asking for more. So, if you're looking for the best and easiest way to learn about business and other general reference topics, look to ...For Dummies to give you a helping hand.

IDG
BOOKS
WORLDWIDE

8/99

SHOPPING ONLINE
FOR CANADIANS

FOR
DUMMIES®

by Fiorella Grossi, Marguerite Pigeon, and Joseph Lowery

CDG Books Canada, Inc.

IDG Books Worldwide, Inc.
An International Data Group
Company

Toronto, ON ◆ Foster City, CA ◆ Chicago, IL ◆ Indianapolis, IN ◆ New York, NY

Shopping Online For Canadians For Dummies®

Published by
CDG Books Canada, Inc.
99 Yorkville Avenue
Suite 400
Toronto, ON   M5R 3K5

www.cdgbooks.com (CDG Books Canada Web Site)
www.idgbooks.com (IDG Books Worldwide Web Site)
www.dummies.com (Dummies Press Web Site)

Canadian Cataloguing in Publication Data

Grossi, Fiorella

Shopping online for Canadians for dummies

Includes index.
ISBN: 1-894413-05-9

1. Teleshopping — Canada. 2. Shopping — Canada — Computer network resources — Directories. I. Pigeon, Marguerite.
II. Lowery, Joseph (Joseph W.). III. Title.

TX337.C3G76 1999   381'.1'0285467   C99-931671-0

Printed in the United States of America

1 2 3 4 5 IDGB 03 02 01 00 99

We acknowledge the financial support of the Government of Canada through the Book Publishing Industry Development Program for our publishing activities.

1O/SQ/QZ/ZZ/IN

Distributed in Canada by CDG Books Canada, Inc.

For general information on CDG Books, including all IDG Books Worldwide publications, please call our distribution center: HarperCollins Canada at 1-800-387-0117. For reseller information, including discounts and premium sales, please call our Sales department at 1-877-963-8830.

This book is available at special discounts for bulk purchases by your group or organization for resale, premiums, fundraising and seminars. For details, contact CDG Books Canada, Special Sales Department, 99 Yorkville Avenue, Suite 400, Toronto, ON, M5K 3K5; Tel: 416-963-8830; Email: spmarkets@cdgbooks.com.

For press review copies, author interviews, or other publicity information, please contact our Marketing department at 416-963-8830, fax 416-923-4821, or e-mail publicity@cdgbooks.com.

For authorization to photocopy items for corporate, personal, or educational use, please contact Cancopy, The Canadian Copyright Licensing Agency, One Yonge Street, Suite 1900, Toronto, ON, M5E 1E5; Tel: 416-868-1620; Fax: 416-868-1621; www.cancopy.com

 is a trademark under exclusive license to CDG Books Canada, Inc. from International Data Group, Inc.

 is a registered trademark under exclusive license to IDG Books Worldwide, Inc. from International Data Group, Inc.

About the Authors

Fiorella Grossi graduated from the journalism program at Ryerson Polytechnic University in 1991 and has been working as a journalist ever since. She spent several years as a magazine writer and editor specializing in business issues.

More recently, she made the move to television and has worked as a news and current affairs producer for both the Life Network and CTV Television. She refuses to live anywhere but the heart of Little Italy in Toronto, and maintains a deep and meaningful relationship with her cat Sol Goldberg, and Benito, the cheese salesman down the street. On her grown-up days, she fills her spirit with her nieces Cassandra and Julia.

Joseph Lowery has been writing about computers and new technology since 1981. He is the technical editor for *Selling Online For Dummies* and the author of *Dreamweaver 2 Bible* from IDG Books Worldwide. He's also the author of *Ten Minute Guide to Internet Explorer 4.0,* the co-author of *The HTML 3.2 Manual of Style,* and a contributor to *Special Edition Using Microsoft Word 97, Bestseller Edition* and *Microsoft Office 97 Small Business Edition 6-in-1.*

Joseph is a webmaster for a variety of clients, including a managed health care organization, an international public relations school, and a bar. Joseph and his wife, the dancer/choreographer Debra Wanner, have a daughter, Margot, who still doesn't understand that it's Daddy's laptop, even though all of her stuff is on it.

Marguerite Pigeon graduated from both journalism and philosophy at Carleton University, in Ottawa, in 1994. She started her career in daily news at CBC Radio, moved on to print reporting and photography at *The Elliot Lake Standard,* and ended up a senior television producer for CTV Television.

She now lives and works in Toronto as a freelance writer, having already begun work on two more titles for CDG Books. She spends the rest of her time droning on about the greatness of boxing, Blind River (her hometown), and her giant family (especially Mom), while harbouring dreams of literary fame.

ABOUT IDG BOOKS WORLDWIDE, INC. AND CDG BOOKS CANADA, INC.

Welcome to the world of IDG Books Worldwide and CDG Books Canada.

IDG Books Worldwide, Inc., is a subsidiary of International Data Group, Inc., the world's largest publisher of computer-related information and the leading global provider of information services on information technology. IDG was founded more than 30 years ago and now employs more than 9,000 people worldwide. IDG publishes more than 295 computer publications in over 75 countries (see listing below). More than 90 million people read one or more IDG publications each month.

Launched in 1990, IDG Books Worldwide is today the #1 publisher of best-selling computer books in North America. IDG Books Worldwide is proud to be the recipient of eight awards from the Computer Press Association in recognition of editorial excellence and three from *Computer Currents'* First Annual Readers' Choice Awards. Our best-selling *...For Dummies®* series has more than 55 million copies in print with translations in 31 languages. In record time, IDG Books Worldwide has become the first choice for millions of readers around the world who want to learn how to better manage their businesses.

In 1998, IDG Books Worldwide formally partnered with Macmillan Canada, a subsidiary of Canada Publishing Corporation, to create CDG Books Canada, a dynamic new Canadian publishing company. CDG Books Canada is now Canada's fastest growing publisher, bringing valuable information to Canadians from coast to coast through the introduction of Canadian *...For Dummies®* and *CliffsNotes™* titles.

Every one of our books is designed to bring extra value and skill-building instructions to the reader. Our books are written by experts who understand and care about our readers. The knowledge base of our editorial staff comes from years of experience in publishing, education, and journalism — experience we use to produce books to carry us into the new millennium. In short, we care about books, so we attract the best people. We devote special attention to details such as audience, interior design, use of icons, and illustrations. And because we use an efficient process of authoring, editing, and desktop publishing our books electronically, we can spend more time ensuring superior content and spend less time on the technicalities of making books.

You can count on our commitment to deliver high-quality books at competitive prices on topics you want to read about. At IDG Books Worldwide and CDG Books Canada, we continue in the IDG tradition of delivering quality for more than 30 years. You can learn more about IDG Books Worldwide and CDG Books Canada by visiting www.idgbooks.com, www.dummies.com, and www.cdgbooks.com.

John Kilcullen
President and Publisher
IDG Books Worldwide, Inc.

Steven Berkowitz
Chairman and CEO
IDG Books Worldwide, Inc.

Hart Hillman
President
CDG Books Canada, Inc.

Eighth Annual
Computer Press
Awards ≥1992

Ninth Annual
Computer Press
Awards ≥1993

Tenth Annual
Computer Press
Awards ≥1994

Eleventh Annual
Computer Press
Awards ≥1995

IDG is the world's leading IT media, research and exposition company. Founded in 1964, IDG had 1997 revenues of $2.05 billion and has more than 9,000 employees worldwide. IDG offers the widest range of media options that reach IT buyers in 75 countries representing 95% of worldwide IT spending. IDG's diverse product and services portfolio spans six key areas including print publishing, online publishing, expositions and conferences, market research, education and training, and global marketing services. More than 90 million people read one or more of IDG's 290 magazines and newspapers, including IDG's leading global brands — Computerworld, PC World, Network World, Macworld and the Channel World family of publications. IDG Books Worldwide is one of the fastest-growing computer book publishers in the world, with more than 700 titles in 36 languages. The "...For Dummies®" series alone has more than 50 million copies in print. IDG offers online users the largest network of technology-specific Web sites around the world through IDG.net (http://www.idg.net), which comprises more than 225 targeted Web sites in 55 countries worldwide. International Data Corporation (IDC) is the world's largest provider of information technology data, analysis and consulting, with research centers in over 41 countries and more than 400 research analysts worldwide. IDG World Expo is a leading producer of more than 168 globally branded conferences and expositions in 35 countries including E3 (Electronic Entertainment Expo), Macworld Expo, ComNet, Windows World Expo, ICE (Internet Commerce Expo), Agenda, DEMO, and Spotlight. IDG's training subsidiary, ExecuTrain, is the world's largest computer training company, with more than 230 locations worldwide and 785 training courses. IDG Marketing Services helps industry-leading IT companies build international brand recognition by developing global integrated marketing programs via IDG's print, online and exposition products worldwide. Further information about the company can be found at www.idg.com.

8/24/99

Dedication

For people like us, who are too busy and too optimistic to stand in line.

Authors' Acknowledgments

Who'd have thought we couldn't go shopping by ourselves? Turns out we couldn't have done it without the encouragement and persistence of Joan Whitman and Kim Herter at CDG Books, who guided us through the entire writing process, and Mike Kelly and Colleen Totz at IDG Books.

Along the way, we drew on the truly astounding knowledge of fellow e-com writer Rick Broadhead (who's been there and back), and held numerous consultations with ever-helpful Art Krzycki at VISA Canada.

Of course, it goes without saying that whenever you're absorbed in a writing project, family and friends will be forced to talk you down every time you think you're going to give up and chuck your computer out the window. We are grateful for their love, patience, and the occasional restraining hold.

Publisher's Acknowledgments

We're proud of this book; please register your comments through our IDG Books Worldwide Online Registration Form located at `http://my2cents.dummies.com`.

Some of the people who helped bring this book to market include the following:

Acquisitions, Editorial, and Media Development

Editor: Colleen Totz

Acquisitions Editor: Joan Whitman

Assistant Editor: Kim Herter

General Reviewer: Art Krzycki

Production

Project Coordinator: Regina Synder

Layout and Graphics: Amy M. Adrian, Angela F. Hunckler, Jill Piscitelli, Brent Savage, Janet Seib, Michael A. Sullivan, Maggie Ubertini, Mary Jo Weis, Dan Whetstine

Proofreaders: Nancy Price, Marianne Santy, Rebecca Senninger, Ethel M. Winslow

Indexer: Sharon Hilgenberg

Special Help
Michael Kelly, Michelle Vukas, Diane Graves Steele, Joan Simkins, Karen Robbins

---

General and Administrative

IDG Books Worldwide, Inc.: John Kilcullen, CEO; Steven Berkowitz, President and Publisher

CDG Books Canada, Inc.: Ron Besse, Chairman; Hart Hillman, President; Robert Harris, Vice President and Publisher

IDG Books Technology Publishing Group: Richard Swadley, Senior Vice President and Publisher; Walter Bruce III, Vice President and Associate Publisher; Steven Sayre, Associate Publisher; Joseph Wikert, Associate Publisher; Mary Bednarek, Branded Product Development Director; Mary Corder, Editorial Director

IDG Books Consumer Publishing Group: Roland Elgey, Senior Vice President and Publisher; Kathleen A. Welton, Vice President and Publisher; Kevin Thornton, Acquisitions Manager; Kristin A. Cocks, Editorial Director

IDG Books Internet Publishing Group: Brenda McLaughlin, Senior Vice President and Publisher; Diane Graves Steele, Vice President and Associate Publisher; Sofia Marchant, Online Marketing Manager

IDG Books Production for Dummies Press: Michael R. Britton, Vice President of Production; Debbie Stailey, Associate Director of Production; Cindy L. Phipps, Manager of Project Coordination, Production Proofreading, and Indexing; Tony Augsburger, Manager of Prepress, Reprints, and Systems; Laura Carpenter, Production Control Manager; Shelley Lea, Supervisor of Graphics and Design; Debbie J. Gates, Production Systems Specialist; Robert Springer, Supervisor of Proofreading; Kathie Schutte, Production Supervisor

Dummies Packaging and Book Design: Patty Page, Manager, Promotions Marketing

◆

The publisher would like to give special thanks to Patrick J. McGovern, without whom this book would not have been possible.

◆

Contents at a Glance

Cartoons at a Glance

By Rich Tennant

"Ronnie made the body from what he learned in Metal Shop, Sissy and Darlene's Home Ec. class helped them in fixing up the inside, and then all that anti-gravity stuff we picked up off the Web."

page 165

page D-1

"I don't care if you do have a coalition of kids from 19 countries backing you up; I'm still not buying you an ISDN line."

page 139

"Can someone please tell me how long 'Larry's Lunch Truck' has had his own page on the intranet?"

page 7

"It's a free starter disk for AOL."

page 237

"You're part of an 'Insect-Clothing Club' on the Web? Neat! Where do you get buttons that small?"

page 67

"Awww, jeez- I was afraid of this. Some poor kid, bored with the usual chat lines, starts looking for bigger kicks, pretty soon they're surfin' the seedy back alleys of cyberspace, and before you know it, they're into a file they can't 'undo'. I guess that's why they call it the Web. Somebody open a window!"

page 213

Fax: 978-546-7747 • E-mail: the5wave@tiac.net

Table of Contents

● ●

Introduction

● ●

*R*emember when people were afraid that computers would take over? Remember when people were afraid that calculators would ruin young minds? Well, we hope that in a couple of years people will be saying, "Remember when people were afraid to buy online?" And we hope that this book will serve to change the minds of a few folks.

Mention buying anything online and someone in the room invariably wonders if it's safe. It's your basic fear of the unknown, but that doesn't make it any less effective. If you're letting some unfounded apprehensions stop you from exploring the world of cybershopping, you're missing out on one exciting new experience.

If you think the Internet has exploded in the past couple of years, just wait until you get a look at shopping on the Web. Not only is there an enormous number of stores online, you'll also find an unbelievable variety of merchandise — if you know where to look. Stores from the smallest mom-and-pop shop to the largest name-brand department store are online and waiting for you to drop by. All you need is a computer, a connection to the Internet, and (all modesty tucked neatly away) this book.

Why a Book about Shopping?

Hmmm, a book on shopping? What's next, *Breathing For Dummies?* Isn't shopping one of the basic tenets of any society? And why tailor an entire book for Canadians — isn't the Net supposed to be building a *global* village? To answer these questions, let's start with the facts as we see them. We live in a country that's absolutely enormous geographically-speaking, but tiny when it comes to population, right? We're also very spread out and many of us aren't thrilled about trudging through the snow to shop during the winter. Okay. So what if we told you that if you learn to shop intelligently online, you can buy just about anything you want — from almonds to zebra-skinned cushions — without ever leaving your home? What if we also told you that some of the top Canadian brand names are available to you 24 hours a day, at good prices, whether you live in downtown Vancouver or rural Newfoundland? No snowshoes required! If any of this appeals to you, you've come to the right place.

Having said all this, we should also add that shopping *online* is a very different beast than shopping in an old-fashioned store. You look for bargains in a different way; you pay for goods differently; and the pitfalls you need to look out for are way different. As Canadians, we face some unique obstacles. To a great extent, Americans have been spearheading the e-commerce revolution. Take a good look around the Web and you'll find a truly astounding array of sites designed for American shoppers. If you want to take advantage of them as a Canadian, you're going to need to know the ropes.

To make the most of online shopping, you also want to be armed with knowledge about how to find Canadian Web sites and special shopping services that cater to you. Throughout the book, we've tried to balance our desire to give you as broad a picture of what's on the Web as possible, with our responsibility to you as _Canadian_ buyers. In other words, if we've found a particularly nifty service on the Web that has no Canadian equivalent, we've included it. As e-commerce blossoms here at home (and believe us, it's growing even as you read this page) you're going to find more and more shopping sites designed especially for Canucks. Quite honestly, though, nothing we're going to discuss in this book is rocket science — and if you're interested, you _can_ do it!

What's in This Book?

We think Internet commerce is going to attract a great number of people who have never been on the Web before, and at the same time, after Internet-savvy folks experience the convenience of online purchasing, they will begin to try out some of the more advanced telecommunication techniques. So while this book is generally organized from the basic to the more complex task — and you can certainly read it from start to finish — we kept the chapters very interest-oriented. So if you can't wait to get bidding in an online auction, by all means, turn to that chapter and jump in. If, however, you find yourself over your head, we've placed convenient cross-reference markers to chapters and sections that offer needed background.

Although a glance at the Table of Contents indicates that all of _Shopping Online For Canadians For Dummies_ is divided into seven parts, on closer inspection all is not equal. The first five parts cover the entire spectrum of the shopping online adventure — everything from the underpinnings of e-commerce security to placing a classified ad on the Web. While these five parts prepare you for any Web-based shopping eventuality, Part VI turns you loose in the global mall and gives you the guidance to explore the best stores online. The final Part of Tens boils it all down for you in easy, digestible tidbits. Here's the blow-by-blow breakdown:

Part I: Shopping Online Basics

We think of Part I as a big cheerleading teacher who moonlights as a cop. By the end of this part, you'll be bolstered in your desire to shop online by a look at an overview of the advantages and opportunities of Web buying. You'll also be reassured by the real skinny on Internet security: what the dangers are and how you're protected. Finally, Part I also offers a complete Internet primer for those who have never surfed the Web fantastic but have always had the desire.

Part II: What You Can Find Online

The exploration of buying online begins in earnest in Part II. A category-by-category overview of the shopping potential on the Internet is combined with the techniques necessary for exploring the sites. Thus, a discussion of the eclectic one-of-a-kind products available online leads into tips and tricks on how to best surf the Net.

Part II moves from the large, polished structures of online malls and catalogues to the down-home, next-door-neighbour openness of the electronic classifieds, where bargains are king and pitfalls are plenty. The final chapter in this section describes one of the Internet's booming businesses: information and information technology. In this chapter, you discover the different software and document categories and how to research almost anything on the Net. Downloading and installing software can be daunting for the novice; this chapter aims to make it simple and fun.

Part III: How Do Ya Wanna Pay?

Whereas Part II was more concerned with online *shopping,* Part III is the nitty-gritty side of online *buying.* Each chapter offers a detailed analysis of electronic transactions. Each of the payment systems now available works a little differently, and this part gives the pros and cons of them all. Chapter 9, in particular, spells out everything we Canadians should know, whether we're buying at home or outside of Canadian cyberspace.

Part IV: Bargain Hunting on the Web

While appealing to your more mercenary instincts — getting a bargain — Part IV is also an exploration of the specialness of online buying. Because computers are supposed to make our lives easier, why shouldn't computers make our shopping easier, too? Chapter 11 examines how programmers are developing electronic tools to enhance the online shopping experience.

Chapter 12 covers a specialized form of shopping that is exploding on the Web: the auction. In addition to bringing what can be an elite experience to the masses, online auctions can save the savvy shopper a lot of money. Chapter 13 is dedicated to covering the latest "push" technology, including a nifty concept called *subscriptions.* Who cares about news and sports information on your desktop when you can get the inside scoop on a sale?

Part V: When Bad Shopping Happens to Good People

If you plan on shopping online, you'd better know what to do when the Information Superhighway gets a little bumpy. Part V is a reference guide aimed at helping the shopper-in-need. The various chapters describe how to use the online customer service systems for tracing everything from back-ordered goods to overnight deliveries. You also find out how to track online orders when someone makes a mistake. Finally, we offer advice on online buying's roughest patches: bad-faith promises, non-existent vendors, and credit-card fraud. When shopping goes awry, don't get mad. Turn to Part V and get your money back.

Part VI: The Online Shopping Directory

The Online Shopping Directory is one big playground. When you're ready for a break, or you just want to try out some of the techniques explained in the book, take a stroll through the sites listed in Part VI.

Part VI covers a wide range of categories each with the very best of the Web, both Canadian and around the globe. Research has shown that many savvy Net surfers use the Web to shop for major purchases like vacations, automobiles, and real estate. Next come life-style selections such as electronics and flowers. You'll find listings for Web stores in these and many more categories in this section.

The Online Shopping Directory uses a different layout so that we can pack in more sites for your browsing pleasure. You'll also find a series of handy-dandy mini-icons gracing each listing so that you can tell at a glance if a given site has what you need. The mini-icons are explained in detail at the start of Part VI.

Part VII: The Part of Tens

Give it to us straight, Doc. We can take it. Part VII gives it to you super-straight. You discover why you should be shopping online and what's easier or cheaper to find online than off. No excess verbiage. Just the inside scoop in a concise, dinner party-quotable format.

What's with All the Margin Icons?

Throughout this book, every so often you'll encounter a paragraph or two marked with a special symbol called an *icon*. As the song goes, every little icon has a meaning all its own. Okay, maybe that's a different song, but it still holds true in this case. Now just what are those icons and their meanings? Well, we've gathered them all together for your viewing pleasure:

It's not like we expect you to defuse a bomb or anything. The Warning icon appears whenever we need to point out a potential stumbling block or possible misstep.

We try to keep the jargon down to a bare minimum, but every now and then, we gotta speak geek. When we do, we'll toss a Technical Stuff icon up so you can cover your eyes in the nick of time.

To make it easy to find the material you need, we use the Cross-Reference icon whenever we refer to a topic that appears elsewhere in the book.

Want the skinny, the real deal, and the inside story? Keep an eye peeled for the Tip icons because every time you see one, you're sure to find one of the secrets of the universe — and a little something that will help you in your shopping spree.

Part I
Shopping Online Basics

The 5th Wave   By Rich Tennant

"Can someone please tell me how long 'Larry's Lunch Truck' has had his own page on the intranet?"

In this part . . .

We're sure you've heard the old saying, "A journey of a thousand miles begins with a single step." But when you're just starting out, how do you know the direction in which you should begin stepping? So it is with Part I that we give you all the direction you need to get going. Even if you're starting at the very beginning and are going online for the very first time.

Other basics are covered here aside from answers to "How do I . . ." type questions. Fundamental issues — and fears — especially concerning Internet security need to be addressed before you can begin to shop online with confidence. No one can expect you to take out your wallet in a figuratively unsafe neighborhood; we think that by the end of Part I, you'll feel just as safe as a gold bar in Fort Knox.

As important as Web security is, we think a better understanding of the variety of what's available in the Internet storefronts is essential. After all, you won't be compelled to shop where there's nothing you might buy. We have no qualms about assuring you from the outset that you have never seen the diversity of goods and services now for sale online. What starts our heads spinning is the fact that — as overwhelming as the range of online merchandise is today — it's really just beginning. And you're ready to take that first step on a fabulous journey.

Chapter 1

Shopping: The Online Way

· ·

In This Chapter

▶ Checking out the advantages of shopping online

▶ Investigating who's opened an Internet storefront, and why

▶ Going on a virtual shopping spree — for free

· ·

A man leans out of his shiny new convertible and says to the pedestrian passing by, "What do you think of my new wheels? I bought 'em online!" The passerby takes a look up and down and says, "Pretty snazzy, but everyone buys stuff on time." The driver says, "No, not on time. Online — you know, over the Internet!" The pedestrian takes a really long look at the car, shakes his head, and mutters, "Man, that baby must have taken you MONTHS to download!"

Everybody's talking about shopping online. Whether you call it Web shopping, e-commerce, or going down to Ye Olde Cyberstore, buying online definitely is starting to catch on. But, like any new twist on a familiar experience, people have many questions and misconceptions about using the Internet as a shopping mall. From the most basic, "Is it safe?" to the more esoteric, "How do I know whom I can trust?" to the downright thrifty, "How much can I save?", many people have legitimate concerns about spending their hard-earned loonies on the Internet.

Not only can you get very tangible benefits (read as bargains, freebies, and what-a-deals) from this somewhat intangible entity, but you can also become more technologically savvy, culturally enriched and, broadly communicative in the process. (Not to mention better looking!) The computer is a fabulous tool — as long as you're using it to do something. The more you approach the computer in a task-oriented fashion, the more you'll get out of it. And if your task is shopping, hooo boy, are you gonna get a lot out of it!

Why Buy Online?

Okay, so you can shop in the neighbourhood, you can go to the mall, you can order through a catalogue, you can pick up the phone while watching the The Shopping Channel and order just the right doohickey for the mantle —

there's lot of places to buy things, so why do you need to shop online? What can the Internet possibly bring to the shopping experience that isn't already available in more familiar, cozy ways?

Glad you asked.

We're open 24/7!

The Internet never closes. It is convenient 24 hours a day, 7 days a week, 365 days per year. You shop when you want to shop, you take as long as you want comparing products (why do you think they call it a browser?), you hunt for the best deals, and then you buy when you're good and ready, by golly! This concept of time shifting first hit the mass-market mentality when VCRs made their widespread 12:00-flashing appearance. For the first time, you could watch a movie on your schedule, not one set by the local PayPerView. The same concept holds true — in spades — for shopping over the Web.

From the very beginning, the Internet has always been about accessibility. The first computers to form the backbone of the Internet were connected so that information could be available on a continuous, as-needed basis. Internet computers don't sleep, don't take vacations in August or close for the holidays, or hang out a Gone Fishin' sign when the mood hits them. The Internet was founded so that university research scientists could share experimental data that would, hopefully, one day save hundreds of thousands of lives, but is that really more important than finding a terrific deal on round-trip airfare to Hawaii?

Clearly the Internet is becoming the field of dreams for more and more shops and merchants, who are taking their stores online for this very reason: To make it easier for you to give them your money — and get something in return, of course. (Are you hearing the whisper, "If you build it, they will come?") Naturally, it doesn't hurt that the online stores can be available every moment of every day. Moreover, online stores can serve hundreds, if not thousands, of customers at a time — all without having to spend one thin dime on sweeping the sidewalk out in front of the store or having to pay property tax while waiting for the customer doorbell to chime.

One of the first real Web-burning success stories is an online bookstore called Amazon.com (www.amazon.com). An excellent Canadian example of such success is Chapters.ca, the bookseller's Net store for consumers (www.chapters.ca). (People love books, what can we say!) As you can see from the home page shown in Figure 1-1, Chapters.ca offers millions of books every waking moment of every day — and then delivers them to your door in a timely fashion.

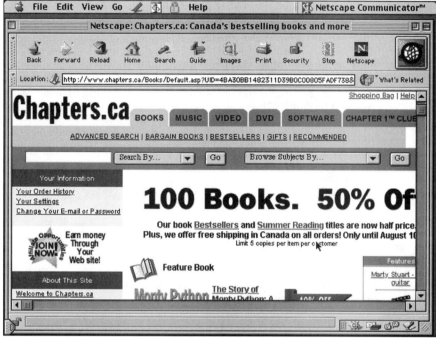

Figure 1-1:
One of the best online bookstores, Chapters.ca, enables you to search its virtual shelves for any title, author, or subject matter under the sun.

Speaking of timeliness, we should mention that shopping on the Web is a blend of instant gratification and waiting on the big delivery truck. Increasingly, you can download more and more products directly from the Web storefronts: software, reports, pictures, videos, and music. True, we're not quite at the "Click the 'Mortgage' button to download your new house" stage (although there are places where you can now apply for a mortgage online!), but the potential of the Internet has companies looking for innovative ways to satisfy you, the customer, like never before.

One of the things we enjoy most about shopping online is taking our time. We love nothing more than poring over facts about this computer or reading reviews for that digital camera. We can download feature charts by the dozens; we can ask the stupidest questions imaginable of hundreds of the savviest shoppers around; we can comparison shop 'til we drop. And not once will we hear the throat-clearing "ahem" of one salesclerk. Now *that's* a reason to shop online.

Parlez-vous White Sale?

Another major selling point for online buying is built right into the Web's full name: the *World Wide* Web. One of the way-cool experiences is surfing Web sites that are pretty close to home and then — blink! — you're transported to a site on the other side of the globe. Now apply that concept to shopping and you've got yourself a global marketplace where any storefront anywhere in the world is just a click away.

With online shopping, you're no longer limited to which malls are in driving range or how long you can stand the hold music as you wait for customer service to get around to you — which is a good thing especially for you, Mr., Mrs. or Ms. Online Shopper, since Canadian merchants are trying to catch up to the rest of the world in getting a shopping address in cyberspace. Got a hankerin' for a nice Chianti to go with those fava beans? Surf on over to Castello di Monterinaldi (www.monterindaldi.it) for some authentic Italian vino. Maybe you'd like some Azerbaijanian caviar exported from the Czech Republic (www.caviar.tic.cz) to go with those fabulous French truffles you dug up on the Web at the village of Sainte Alvére in Perigord (www.sainte-alvere.com).

If you spot a commercial Internet address (also known as a *URL* — pronounced *you-are-ell*) with a suffix other than .ca or .com, chances are it isn't from around here. A common identifying mark for international Web addresses is a period followed by a two-letter abbreviation, such as .it (Italy), .fr (France), or .cz (Czech Republic).

Shopping on the Web means that every boutique, mom-and-pop shop, major chain, and super-mall savvy enough to open a storefront on the Internet is at your beck and call. (Of course, because you're connecting to the site through the Internet, it's a local call to boot!) In most cases, you can pick the delivery option — whether it's gotta-have-it overnight or no hurry, no worry ground service.

Of course, you don't have to go far to buy something online. Web sites with a local delivery emphasis are just beginning to crop up in Canada. While the choices right now are somewhat limited and often restricted to metropolitan areas, go to any of these Web sites and time and again, you'll read that the company is planning to expand its service area. In some places in Canada, you can even cross off items on your grocery list — and you'll get it all delivered right to your door.

The key point to keep in mind is that you can shop for almost anything almost anywhere in the world online.

The science of ElectroShopology

One of the coolest reasons to do your shopping with a computer is that you're using a computer! And, as we all know, computers can do some things a wee bit faster than us carbon-based life forms. By now, you're beginning to get the idea of the vast enormity of the world of online stores. How can you possibly search the Web to find that one perfect gift for Aunt Harriet that says, "I love you, but stay outta my hair and don't forget me in the will"? We've got an idea, let's tell the 'puter to do it!

In addition to sophisticated search engines (which you get to explore in Chapter 3), computer programs are now available that are designed specifically to help you find the right item at the right price. These little beasties — that like to be called shopping agents — take your shopping list and in a wink (well, maybe a wink and a half) come back to you with a screen or more full of recommendations, prices, and contacts. (These programs unfortunately don't scan for Canadian Web sites or they certainly don't return products from a site in Canadian dollars. Again, this is another growth area predicted by Internet experts and you can read all about them in Chapter 11.)

How would you like to have your computer call you when an especially worthy sale is going on? The advent of push technology (as opposed to pushy salespeople) lets you sign up with all kinds of vendors who notify you whenever a new tchotchke that you just gotta have comes on the market. Just say the magic word and you can get everything from an e-mail reminder to a guy jumping up and down on your desktop to tell you about a bargain you don't want to miss.

The online auction houses are a true hotbed of Internet buying and selling as well as some of the most innovative technology. Not only do some of the auction Web sites let you program their system to bid for you with a minimum and (thank goodness!) a maximum bid, but you can even tell the computer to page you should another bid top yours. Want a cheap thrill? Drop into an online auction site like Bid.com (`www.bid.com`) and watch two automatic bidding machines try to outbid each other. Ooohhh, goosebumps all over our nerdy selves!

There's plenty more about Web site auctions in Chapter 12.

The Ever-Expanding Marketplace

Never before has the push toward getting Canadian merchants online been so urgent. Many are predicting that it will be during the 1999 Christmas shopping season that online shopping in Canada will go through its Big Bang Phase. (You know, the theory that the universe started from a relatively small collection of gases and matter and then exploded with growth.) The number of stores and businesses on the Web has been increasing in the past number of years. Truth told, it was really difficult finishing this book. Just when we thought we had found very major online store peddling a certain widget and could, therefore, sign off on a chapter, a new site would put up an Open For Business sign in cyberspace — and force us into revisions!

The number of stores that can coexist online has no clear ceiling. Virtual space, unlike mall storefronts or downtown parking spaces, is limitless. So what sort of growth are we talking about? Try these numbers on for size:

✔ One of the leading search engines, Yahoo! Canada, lists nearly 100 Canadian categories encompassing more than 15,500 sites. These categories include:

   • Home and Garden, with 362 sites. Cocooning, here we come.

   • Internet Services, with 266 sites. Big surprise.

   • Computers, with 1,605 sites. Another no-brainer.

   • Travel, with 822 sites. Where do you want to go today?

✔ When recently queried about shopping malls in Canada, Yahoo! Canada responded with 95 sites. These include Web sites for land malls as well as virtual malls.

✔ Canadians spent about $668 million online in 1998, an increase of 156 percent over the previous year, according to study commissioned by IBM Canada Ltd. and the Retail Council of Canada.

✔ People who try shopping online, like it — and they keep coming back. According to a study by A.C. Nielsen, 84 percent of those surveyed who made a purchase online said they "probably" or "definitely" would do so again.

✔ Business-to-business sales are very big on the Internet. Businesses sold $4.6 billion to each other online in 1988, compared to $1.5 billion the year previous.

✔ One of Canada's leading auction sites, Bid.com, announced a 652 percent increase in revenue to $20.1 million in 1998, up from $2.7 million in 1997.

✔ Padinox Inc., a manufacturer of upscale Paderno cookware, believed the potential of online shopping so great that the firm opened its shelves to consumers on the Net — thereby competing with the manufacturer's primary source of business: retailers! Now, about 10 percent of Padinox's sales come from the Net.

✔ Videoflicks.com, the online sister to the VHS/DVD movie rental chain of stores across southern Ontario, offers more than 65,000 titles for sale, for which the site experiences 14 million hits a month. Ouch.

A *hit* is one click from a visitor's Web browser. While not the best figure to indicate the number of visitors a site receives, since folks can hit a Web site many, many times in one visit, hits do indicate the amount of interaction involved. (For more on browser, head over to the section "Making the connection" in this chapter).

The great Web Rush of the '90s

Ask yourself, when was the last time you saw an advertisement on TV or in the newspaper that didn't offer a Web address in teeny-tiny print somewhere?

In the mid to late '90s, shops around the world including Canada were rushing to stake a claim on a part of this virtual gold mine. What got everyone so excited? The potential of doing business on the Web — which experts were predicting would overtake mail-order shopping.

Firms in the financial services industry in Canada have been the leaders in moving from brochure-like sites to more engaging, interactive displays. You have noticed the ads for online trading and banking, haven't you?

There's good news and bad news when it comes to Canadian online retailers. Let's start with the bad news, since we like ending things on a good note. Canadian shops have been much slower coming out of the gate in the race to cyberspace shopping, for a number of reasons. Surprisingly, many companies don't hold the Internet up as a high priority in their business strategy. The good news? We, as others, predict that will soon change. Why? Two factors: The push for competition and the fact that folks are actually beginning to buy items over the Web.

The pressure to set up a checkout counter online has never been greater than now. Just how much Canadians spend online depends on who you ask — the figures vary with the firm conducting the study, but it's clearly in the hundreds of millions. That should be good news, except for the fact that the vast majority of those Canadian dollars were spent outside the country. Clearly, Canadians are beginning to feel comfortable shopping on the Net.

Big retailers are taking heed, setting up shop on the Net. Many of the most familiar Canadian retailers already have a shopping presence in cyberspace and many of them continue to improve their sites, making them more user-friendly and providing visitors with more than just their core product. One example is Indigo Online (`www.indigo.ca`). The bookseller unveiled a far more feature-packed site in the summer of 1999, as shown in Figure 1-2. It has what you'd expect — books, books, and more books — but it also includes real video and audio events as well as a chat area where fellow bookworms can chat about their favourite titles.

Figure 1-2:
Sure, the
Indigo
Online store
let's you buy
books but it
also gives
you a
chance to
connect
with other
bookish
types and
keeps you
informed of
major
literary
happenings.

So what other major players are online that you may have heard of? Take a look at Table 1-1 for a partial list of the usual suspects — now accessible to you 24 hours a day over the Web.

Table 1-1	Online Shopping Bonanza
Retailer	*Web Address*
Sears Canada	www.sears.ca
Budget Rent a Car Canada	www.budget.ca
Home Depot	www.homedepot.com
Birks	www.birks.com
President's Choice	www.pcbaskets.com
Future Shop	www.can.futureshop.com
Tilley Endurables	www.Tilley.com
Second Cup	www.monctonlife.com/second cup
Sam's CDs	www.samscd.com

For a more exhaustive, but never exhausting, exploration of other retailers available online, check out Chapter 4.

Virtually safer

Until now, the primary stumbling block to everyone jumping into the online buying pool has been good ol' fashioned fear of the unknown. Many people were understandably nervous about passing their credit-card information over the Internet.

At the same time, some merchants were just as nervous about setting up their online stores. Not only did they have to worry about being responsible for passing a whole lot of valuable information over the Web, there was no way to verify who they were dealing with. Why offer the dishonest few yet another way — in addition to telephone and mail orders — to use someone else's credit cards?

To ease jitters for both buyers and merchants, a lot of other people have been working on ways to make sure that your Web buying trips are completely secure. These "other people" include consortiums of companies such as Visa and Microsoft; one of the security methods they've developed is *Secure Electronic Transactions, or SET.*

Recently, both Visa and MasterCard have offered a significant edge to any merchant willing to open an online store using the new SET technology. Usually, when a customer denies that he or she made a particular purchase, the credit-card companies insist that "the customer is always right" and the store must absorb the cost of the disputed merchandise; this is called a *chargeback.* Chargebacks are a huge cost for stores that sell goods in any way other than face-to-face.

The companies behind SET — which uses a form of ID card called a digital certificate — are saying SET makes online shopping safer than telephone or mail orders. Digital certificates can authenticate the buyer for the merchant, sort of like an electronic "mother's maiden name" test. Visa and MasterCard are so confident that SET is a better way to go that the companies are waiving the chargeback for any SET-enabled merchant.

Just how many store owners will decide to leap into the Internet Age because of this new no-chargeback policy isn't clear. However, with all the other advantages that selling online offers merchants, putting dollars back in the store owner's pockets can be the one item that makes an online store a no-brainer.

Your First Online Shopping Trip

Awright, enough jawing, let's get shopping!

For your first online shopping experience, how about a little freebie? The Web offers many opportunities for sampling wares — from shareware to virtual test-drives. If you know the right places to look, you can find a great number of free experiences and goods on the Net.

A nice little innovation emerged from the student laboratories at MIT: electronic greeting cards. The Web makes it possible for you to send your loved one, your boss, or even yourself a personalized, full-color greeting card, if they're online. You can even send your creation to your unenlightened relations and friends who haven't discovered the joys of online life. Not only can you go shopping on the Web and get something for nothing, but you can also brag about it at the same time!

So here's the road map you're going to follow on your shopping trip:

1. Get online.
2. Search for a greeting card company.
3. Go to an online greeting card store.
4. Pick out a card.
5. Personalize it.
6. Send it!

If you've never gone online before, look over Chapter 3 before you begin this adventure. There, you get a basic understanding of the Internet and figure out how to use a browser.

Making the connection

A great number of different companies can connect you to the Internet, but there really are only two access roads: the *browser* or the *Internet Service Provider.* Both are ultimately necessary to make the connection, but your journey begins with one or the other.

The *browser* is the software that interprets the signals coming over the Web and converts them into images on your monitor; it's the software complement to your modem. The two best-known browsers are the Microsoft Internet Explorer and the Netscape Navigator. Both are excellent programs and one works pretty much like the other.

The *Internet Service Provider* also goes by the acronym *ISP.* Whazzat, you say? ISPs are the cable companies of the World Wide Web. They provide you (for a monthly or hourly fee) with a connection to their computer, which, in turn, connects to the Internet. Thousands of ISPs are vying for your business these days. Some of the larger ones are Sympatico and Internet Direct, as well as some of the U.S. long distance companies that have set up shop in Canada, such as Sprint Canada. The major online services, such as AOL Canada and @Home, include an ISP as part of their service so you can access the Internet through them.

Depending on your setup, you either double-click the icon for your ISP or your browser first. Usually, one automatically starts the other. Some of the older systems require that you start your ISP connection program first and then, after all the modems have had their say, manually start your browser.

After you make the initial connection, your browser loads what is known as your *home page* or *start page.* Now you're ready to begin your hunt for just the right online gift.

Searching . . . searching . . .

Given the vastness of the Web, you may wonder how you ever find anything, much less something you're looking for. In this case, the Mother of Invention brought about a special type of Web site called a *search engine.* A search engine indexes and catalogs all the other Web sites and pages and makes it possible for you to find the proverbial needle in a haystack.

A substantial number of search engines is available, such as Excite, Lycos, and HotBot, as well as those geared to Canadian content, including AltaVista Canada and Yahoo! Canada. In this exercise, we'll use the Canadian version of one of the oldest and most popular search engines, Yahoo! This search engine pioneered the concept of letting people search by categories; it also enables you to search by keyword or phrase.

Follow these steps to switch to Yahoo! Canada:

1. **Select the URL address at the top of your browser.**

2. **Type the Internet address for the Yahoo! Canada site into the Address text box:**

   `http://www.yahoo.ca` (which automatically changes to `www.ca.yahoo.com`)

   Depending on your particular browser, you may be able to get away with typing less than the full Internet address. For instance, in the Netscape browsers, all you have to type in the above example is `yahoo.ca` and the browser fills in the rest. With Internet Explorer 4.0, the trick is to press Ctrl+Enter instead of just the Enter key after you've typed the company name. Some older browsers require that you type `www.companyname.com` or `www.companyname.ca` but allow you to leave off the perplexing `http://` portion.

3. Press Enter.

After Yahoo! Canada loads, look for the Search text box at the top of the screen; all search engines have something similar that lets you type in some keywords to search for.

4. Click once on the Search text box and type "greeting cards", **including the quotation marks.**

By surrounding your keywords with quotation marks, you're telling the search engine that you're interested in a specific phrase, not a couple of keywords. (When you press on the Canada only radio button, you'll limit your search to only Canadian sites. That would give us a pretty meager selection, so for our purposes in this exercise, we'll keep it as world-wide as possible.) Your screen should look something like Figure 1-3.

5. Click the Search button on the Yahoo! Canada screen.

After Yahoo! Canada chews over your search request for a bit, you see what it found. If a particular category has a lot of sites, Yahoo! returns a breakdown of categories first. When we submitted the "greeting cards"

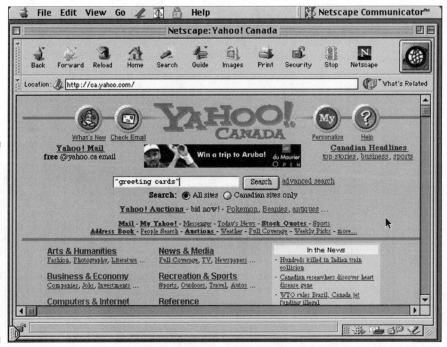

Figure 1-3: The Yahoo! Canada Web site is a massive search engine that lets you search by keyword, phrase, or category.

request, we got back six different categories. (You may get a different number because the Web is always adding and losing sites.) This is how Yahoo! Canada lets you narrow your search.

Notice how each time you pass your cursor over any of the blue, underlined phrases, the pointer turns into a hand. This is your browser's way of telling you that what you are pointing to is a hyperlink, or a connection to another Web page.

You can use many tricks of the trade when it comes to search engines. For a more in-depth look, check out the section "Teaching Your Computer to Fetch: Search Engine Basics" in Chapter 3.

6. **In the category listings, select Business and Economy: Companies: Gifts and Occasions: Greeting Cards.**

   Each listing starts with a broad category and then gets more specific. For example, Companies is a subset of Business and Economy, Gifts and Occasions is a subset of Companies and — you get the idea.

   Next, you see another listing with a few general categories up on top followed by a whole bunch of individual sites. All of the sites listed have something to do with "greeting cards" — and this is where a lot of the fun, and frustration, of surfing the Web comes in. Because you don't know what lies on the other side of any link until you select it, you can go through a fair amount of trial-and-error. You can also have what we call a "happy accident" as you take a turn off the beaten path and stumble into a wondrous garden of a site.

   If you're playing along at home, you can see that there are a terrific number of greeting card sites. Scroll down until you find a name you recognize. Ah, there's one — Hallmark!

7. **Select the Hallmark link.**

   Now, you're on your last Yahoo! Canada page. Hallmark is big enough to have its own subcategory after "Greeting Cards," and Yahoo! Canada now shows these listings.

8. **Select the blue underlined line that reads just "Hallmark."**

   Now you leave the warm and cozy confines of the search engine and are off into the World Wide Web. Surf's up!

Choices, choices, choices

Most Web sites have a front door known as the site's *home page.* Your click on the Hallmark link in Yahoo! Canada brought you to Hallmark's home page. Getting to the home page of many Canadian Web sites is often a two-step process since we are a bilingual nation. You know how automated phone systems will ask you to press a number if you want to proceed with English or French? Well, the same thing has taken hold on the Net. When you enter the site's URL, the first page you see is often simply a page that asks you to select whether they want to read the Web site in English or French before displaying the *real* home page.

Each Web site is different in its design and the way in which you navigate or get around the site. Most sites have a series of buttons or words directing you to different sections of the Web site. Feel free to explore any path that looks interesting to you; you can always return to where you were by clicking the Back button on your browser.

To visit Hallmark's Electronic Greetings section, click the Shopping Online link on the left side of the Web page. Hallmark's online store appears and you'll see a section called Electronic Greetings (hey, we'll take easy navigation of a site over creativity any day!). Click on View All Categories. After you find a category that appeals to you, browse through the subtopics and click on one you like to view the available cards under the topic. As you can tell from Figure 1-4, we chose "Pet Lovers" — but you can choose whatever you like. For our introductory purpose, we're looking for cards that are marked "Free!"

The layout of the online shelves is very similar to many other electronic stores. Each item is marked with a code, a price, and a bit of other information. Selecting the associated link — sometimes the link is a picture, sometimes it's text, sometimes, it's both — generally takes you to another screen

Figure 1-4: Many online stores have a myriad of selections; these Hallmark electronic cards are among more than 1,000 available.

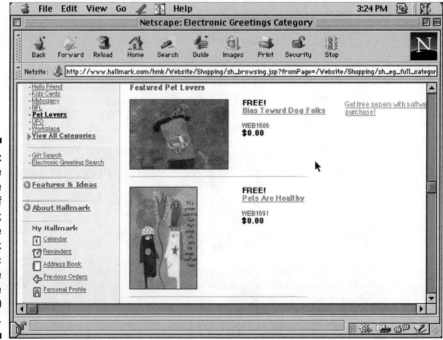

with more detailed information about the item. In your case, the link for a card you fancy brings a slightly bigger image of the card and a chance to personalize it.

Making it your own

Interactivity is a key factor in the online shopping experience. Not only can you take in various bits and pieces of information — okay, a flood of information — but you can often also shape the product to your personal satisfaction. Being able to interact with an online store — to say, in effect, "Make it like-a this!" — is a real added value that keeps customers coming back for more.

In your greeting card adventure, you now get to add a personal message to the card you're buying. Here's a chance to show your creative stuff. Go ahead and write . . . we'll wait. Done? Okay, now it's time to start moving toward the checkout aisle. Most online stores strive to make it easy to get around and order from them, so you often see the same basic layout for a store repeated throughout the site. Enter the name and e-mail address of that special someone you'll be surprising with this card. Be sure to check the box underneath to save the information in your address book — next time you get the itch to reach out and byte someone, the info is already there. Finally, select a delivery date, as shown in Figure 1-5. The best online stores have special features like this to add value to their products and outgun the competition.

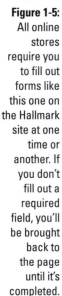

Figure 1-5:
All online stores require you to fill out forms like this one on the Hallmark site at one time or another. If you don't fill out a required field, you'll be brought back to the page until it's completed.

You're almost done with your shopping adventure. At the bottom of the page, click the "Add to Shopping Cart" button. When you shop online, most stores provide you with a virtual shopping cart so you can pick up an item and then shop some more. When you finish, you have a chance to change your mind about any of the items you have picked up along the way. Many online stores let you even change the quantity of any of the items in your shopping cart at checkout. Try that at your local grocery store!

Completing the transaction

After you decide that you've got all the cards you want, you are in the final stages of the checkout process. Here you have a chance to delete a single item, remove them all, continue shopping, or just check out. During the checkout process, you may be asked to verify some of the information you previously entered, especially your e-mail address. This step is because most online stores send an e-mail confirmation with every order. Verification cuts down on order mistakes and gives you a written record of the transaction — much like a credit-card receipt.

Once you've decided you have everything you need, click on Check-Out. The next task is to become a member. Many sites do something similar to make it easy for you to come back. Most use a "user name" and "password" combination to protect your information. And many, like Hallmark, will go the extra step of assuring you that they won't sell your information to other companies — a major benefit in the age of electronic junk mail, also known as *spam*.

Follow the prompts to fill out your membership information and click on the Place Order button. Be sure to note the User Name and Password you entered — pick something accessible and memorable. Write it down where you won't forget it.

After you give the final go-ahead click, the order gets submitted and you receive a tip o' the hat and, of course, a chance to continue shopping.

With the exception of entering any credit-card information — and actually spending any money — this greeting-card shopping spree is a good model for what online buying is all about: Searching, selecting, ordering, and enjoying.

Chapter 2

The Big Question: Is It Safe?

*T*he one scene that everyone remembers from the movie *The Marathon Man* was the one between Dustin Hoffman and the dentist. Laurence Olivier who played the dentist, a Nazi war criminal with a degree in orthodontics, and he went after our hero, Dustin, tooth-and-drill in one of the most chair-squirming scenes ever filmed. And what did Dr. Larry want to know? What was the one question he kept asking, molar after molar?

"Is it safe?"

Of course, Larry the Dentist was actually Larry the Nazi war criminal so he wanted to know if it was safe to walk around without wearing his nose-and-glasses disguise. You — and a whole lot of people like you — are asking the same question about buying over the Internet: Is it safe? Well, keep your air drills in your pocket and we'll tell you.

Yes.

Okay, satisfied? Nah, we wouldn't be either. You've probably heard too many scary predictions about shopping online to dismiss your concerns so easily. So in this chapter, we're going to give you an overview as well as some down-and-dirty details as to why we and a few million others think that buying online is A-OK.

The Way Things Work

When Fiorella was in university, her dad often showed up on her doorstep asking her to type up some last-minute business forms (there's always some kind of pay-back involved when parents pay for tuition!). One day, rather than pulling out her typewriter as per usual, she fired up her computer. Her father, who'd only seen computers in movies (where they usually were out to kill people and/or take over the world) . . . er, FREAKED! Fiorella typed away to the chorus of her dad's doomsday predictions. He stopped in mid-sentence when Fiorella had it printed out in black and white for him. Amazed, he managed to ask, "How did you do that?" which eventually led to "Can we type everything in that box?"

Internet security is still in that "fear of the unknown" stage that personal computers were in back in the early '80s. Ask most people on the street how the Internet works and, after a few hundred "I dunnos," you may get an answer along the lines of "computers talk to each other over the phone." So we're going spend a few moments clearing away some of the shrouds of mystery that surround both the World Wide Web and buying online. If nothing else, imagine how you may feel as you walk around tomorrow and think, "Hey — I know how the Internet works! Ah ha!" Ah, a geek is born.

How the Internet works

You've probably heard the term the *Internet* about 90 zillion times in the last couple years. But what does it mean, and why should you care? Well, why you should care is your own business, but we can tell you what the term means.

Basically, the Internet is a really big network of computers around the world. The simplest network consists of two computers talking to one another, sometimes over the phone and sometimes over special cables; the Internet has thousands of computers in its network. The main Internet computers act as traffic cops to send the right signals in the right direction.

Here's what happens, in order, after you sign on to the Internet and start surfing wildly:

1. You start your browser program.

2. The browser wakes up the modem and tells it to dial a number.

3. When the modem connects, you hear your computer's modem talking to your Internet Service Provider's (ISP) modem. They're haggling over what speed to talk at. It sounds like two cats on the back fence doing Elvis knows what.

4. After the connection is solid, your computer sends a request to your ISP's computer. The request says, "Deliver me to this address, please." The address in question is the Internet address of your system's start or home page.

5. Your ISP unfolds its network road map and finds the quickest way to get to your requested Internet address.

6. The request gets on the Internet and travels from one computer to another until it reaches its destination, the computer that is hosting your start page.

7. "Can you show me the Web page at this address, please," asks the nice request of the host computer.

8. The host computer, unless severely depressed (or "down" in computer lingo), complies happily and sends the information back down the Information Superhighway — although not necessarily the same way that it came — to your computer.

9. Your computer begins translating the message and throwing it up on-screen. After all the words and images transfer to your machine, the Web page is complete.

10. Each time you click a link, it happens all over again, starting from paragraph four of this list, where the request first gets made.

The aspect of this process that scares folks the most is all the different computers that the information passes through to reach its final destination. Even if you know and trust both your ISP and the organization with which you're ultimately communicating, you may think to yourself, "Who are all those middlemen?"

So the first thing to realize is that grabbing any information off the Internet is no trivial task. You can easily rule out 99 percent of the folks with pantyhose over their heads who'd like to separate you from your money. Internet crime is definitely *not* a no-brainer.

But what about the super-genius hacker? The twitchy boy (or girl — I'm an equal-opportunity offender) who speaks FORTRAN, dreams in Assembler, and lacks what are politely called social skills? Can't such a person capture your credit-card number as it goes whizzing by?

Well, we admit that this scenario *is* a remote possibility. Illicitly intercepting a credit-card number over the Internet takes a lot of knowledge, a load of skill, and a ton of perseverance. But you can see in the following section what our clever hackers actually can catch during an Internet transaction and whether it really does them any good.

A typical online transaction

Buying anything online is a hair more involved than just surfin' the Net, dude. Stands to reason — you've got more people with their fingers in the pie: you, the shopkeeper, the credit-card company, and the bank. That's a lot of sticky fingers. Because more folks are passing valuable info back and forth, security is very important for all concerned.

Now follow along as we describe a typical, everyday online purchase, from the spark in your brain that says, "I want that thingie now," to the bundle of heaven delivered to your door:

1. You're cruising the virtual malls and your eyes light on the perfect gift for yourself. You click the Buy Me button and drop the item into your Webified shopping cart.

2. Trundling up to the online checkout counter (where every line is express), you notice that the little open-lock symbol on your browser is now closed. You just entered "The Security Zone," where all the information that passes between you and the shop is scrambled 50 ways to Sunday.

3. Next, you're asked the inevitable question: "Paper or plastic?" No, sorry, it's the other inevitable question: "How ya gonna pay?"

4. You whip out your electronic wallet and select Visa. Hit that Pay with Visa button and your credit-card number as well as your digital ID pass to a Web server using a special high-security standard called *SSL*. (We cover that item in detail in the section called "Tales of Crypto Keys and Digital IDs" later in this chapter.)

5. The shop computer strips off the order info and passes the heavily encrypted money matters — without peeking — to the merchant bank over secured phone lines.

6. The bank checks your digital driver's license (no ugly picture) and a similar one for the merchant to make sure that everybody is who he (or she or it) says he (and so on) is.

7. The bank gives the online shopkeeper a thumbs up. And the shopkeeper gives you a thumbs up. (Could you hold this glass vase, please? We're all thumbs.)

8. The merchant sends you an independent verification via e-mail. The whole shooting match up 'til now lasted maybe 15 seconds. Now, all you need to do is wait for the nice delivery person to honk his horn.

9. Your couldn't-pass-it-up-doodad arrives the next day via overnight delivery. After all, what's the point of gratification if, like coffee, it's not instant?

If you were watching carefully, you noticed that, after the good stuff — the credit-card info and the like — started to pass along the Internet, the doors and windows started slamming closed in a hurry.

So what about Harry and Henrietta Hacker? What did they manage to grab with all their skullduggery during this transaction? Well, they either got a whole lot of nothing because they couldn't crack into the dedicated, secured phone lines that the banks use for transmitted financial data around the globe, or they picked up some gobbledegook. At least, that's what it's going to look like to them for the next 40 quadrillion years as they try to break the code that scrambled your credit-card info.

These, then, are the basic building blocks of Internet security: encrypted messages, secured phone lines, and digital IDs.

Tales of Crypto Keys and Digital IDs

With so much business at stake, a few folks out there are willing to stake their reputations, not to mention next year's bonuses, on creating a secure online environment in which you can spend your bucks. For example, research scientists from MIT have developed secret code technology so top-drawer that the U.S. government has labeled it a state secret and won't allow anyone to export it. Netscape Communications designed its own Internet security protocol known as *Secure Socket Layer* (*SSL*). Adopted by thousands of online storefronts, it protects both merchant and buyer. And Visa and MasterCard co-developed the *Secure Electronic Transaction* (*SET*) method for making sure that *they* get their money — so you *know* that it's ironclad.

The basis for much of Internet security comes from a science known as *cryptography*. No, not the study of above-ground burial places. You know, coding and decoding. James Bond. Secret Squirrel. So take a brief spin through the neighborhood of scrambled messages and secret decoder rings in the following sections and see whether you can raise your online shopping comfort level a notch.

Encryption keys

Speaking of secret decoder rings, why don't you go get yours? We'll wait. . . . Oh, back already? Okay, here's the code: Remember the HAL 9000 Computer from *2001: A Space Odyssey*? Use your decoder ring to tell us what company HAL represented.

Need a clue? Here's the key — substitute each letter of HAL for the next one after it in the alphabet. So your decoder ring should turn the *H* into an *I*, the *A* into a *B*, and the *L* into an *M*. Which gives you . . . IBM! Congrats — you just mastered the secrets of Internet Encryption 101.

Cryptography is a science that became vitally important during World War II when the Allied and Axis forces were trying to read other's secrets. In fact, one of the determining factors of the war was that the Allies used some of the first computers to make their secret codes so complex that no one could break them — and used the same computers to crack the German and Japanese codes like so many eggs.

Modern-day encryption for the Internet took a big leap forward in 1997 after three MIT scientists — Ronald Rivest, Adi Shamir, and Len Adleman — created what's now known as the *RSA public-key encryption method*, the basis for the majority of the encryption systems in use today. What's RSA stand for? Take a look at the first initials of the inventors' last names. Ah ha! Codes within codes.

RSA employs a technology known as *public-key encryption*. What the technology really should be known as, however, is *public-key, private-key* because that's really what's involved. You use a pair of software "keys" — really a code — to pass secure information back and forth on the Net. One key you offer to anyone who wants to send you a message through his or her own computer (the public key), and the other you keep in a little tiny box underneath your hydrangea bushes. (That's the private key — and that's Marguerite's hiding place, so don't look there!) Actually, your private key's stored in your browser or security software.

Whenever anyone wants to send you some super-private info, such as a credit-card number, the software they're using locks the information, or *encodes* it, by using the public key — which they got from you. After your software encodes a message, anyone trying to read it sees only a bunch of meaningless gobble de gook. (Unless, of course, that person also has your private key.) Now the only computer in *da World* that can unlock this message is yours — by using your private key.

So how does one actually make a key pair? To find out, just trundle over to Virtual Locksmiths of Canada, Inc. (for anyone about to input the name in their search engine, we're joking!), and take a step-by-step tour:

1. **Fire up your handy-dandy encryption program by double-clicking its icon.**

   An excellent example of such a program is Phil Zimmerman's PGP — which stands for Pretty Good Privacy — and is available for free from `www.nai.com/asp_set/products/tns/intro.asp`, shown in Figure 2-1. Click on PGP Freeware.

   If this is your first time "getting" software from the Net, check Chapter 7 for the lowdown on downloading.

2. **If you're using PGP, choose Keys⇨New Key to start the process. After you've read the opening Wizard screen, select the Next button — as you will after completing each step.**

3. **In the text boxes on-screen, enter your name, e-mail address.**

4. **Choose the type of keys you would like to make.**

   You'll be told that most users of PGP keys will be expecting the Diffie-Hellman/DSS key pair, since RSA is the "old style" PGP key. Anyone using a Diffie-Hellman/DSS pair won't be able to use your key if you choose RSA.

5. **Choose the level of complexity of encryption, which you measure in bits.**

   The current freeware version of PGP offers key pairs ranging from 1,024 bits to 4,096 bits. The rule here is that, the larger the value, the more secure, but slower, is the transaction. PGP recommends a value between 1,024 and 2,048 bits.

6. **Decide if and when your keys expire by selecting the appropriate option.**

   This step is the equivalent of changing all the locks in your house every year. Not a bad idea, but making all those sets of keys for the kids every time is a chore.

7. **Enter a pass phrase in the text box.**

   You use the pass phrase like you do a password — to keep your information for your eyes only. The longer and more complex the pass phrase is — that is, the higher its mix of letters and numbers — the more secure it is.

   Encryption keys generate prime numbers based on random data. (You remember what a prime number is, don't you? A number divisible only by itself.) Finally, PGP cuts the keys, and you can send your public key via e-mail or incorporate both the public and private keys for use into certain e-mail programs, like Qualcomm's Eudora.

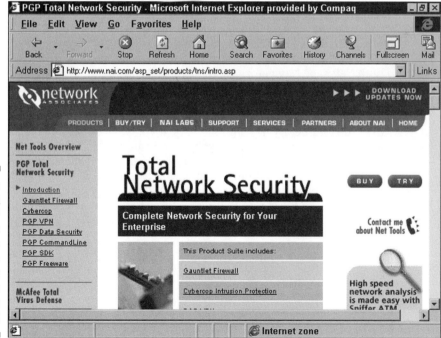

Figure 2-1: Click the PGP Freeware link to download the encryption program PGP.

You're just dying to know what an encryption key looks like, aren't you? Basically, a key is just text — but what text! Take a look at Figure 2-2 to see what Joseph's public key came out to be the first time he signed up.


```
-----BEGIN PGP PUBLIC KEY BLOCK-----
Version: PGPfreeware 5.5.2 for non-commercial use
<http://www.pgp.com>

mQGiBDS9oSoRBAD8VoAWnyTH6A2CEREoix2YjS60gdjyR+IeFFMHx3UgBCsS9Nnq
9wDv3T1JtLEgZszuM9Yyaornh92e+p40VaGuzOVietiy6ruNVPx2qmae6WEmjkE2
L9OIrhshFZM92iRsztpg1D4dIFwjMjuPoUhvUV2DK/F6i6sSt7aKW5WFTwCg/5jn
gH94uOyerIvqtzPiQyTy5GED/RAz7uiqgf99FU8J148xYYGQWFTA/1XL+U5TZUK4
dl3s7YmQOtvWtHyKaR20D7wTudyCjS3LtLgEjRGA6TTZqPNGGRLgR7/4ExWmyU3w
YSN9Mjxm3RzlszmiOOBZnQEAyXiC5Tq/HKxA5xIIDCsrCqXQBCy5sTRB9nY3kHH+
RH0NBADEChdZQ+lxWYkxYi9/DPutc+B35xTvu5hPr68hfDWhTK5i5S453Kp63/KH
dFKfT8T967ihaOGyC1aYryQDw9z2YHzY5k/ZDKpoRw79nCqaPX3eGWwTqlJyq2Xo
qOu0p+45Vlfv0RnInnORtEq/Z1Jrm5t6sjTRi5xwkIMls/tkYrQhSm9zZXBoIExv
d2VyeSA8amxvd2VyeUBpZGVzdC5jb20+iQBLBBARAgALBQI0vaEqBAsDAgEACgkQ
2BpBuhbV0/uPvwCfbCI4PoLgo4H+fuREkJdY5+uq1QUAnR2G/0mcPv6xITx2o4vW
3VaLE585uQINBDS9oSsQCAD2Qle3CH8IF3KiutapQvMF6P1TET1FtvFuuUs4INoB
p1ajFOmPQFXz0AfGy0Op1K33TGSGSfgMg7116RfUodNQ+PVZX9x2Uk89PY3bzpnh
V5JZzf24rnRPxfx2vIPFRzBhznzJ2v8V+bv9kV7HAarTW56NoKVyOtQa8L9GAFgr
5fSI/VhOSdvNILSd5JEHNmszbDgNRR0PfIizHHxbLY7288kjwEPwpVsYjY67VYy4
XTjTNP18F1dDox0YbN4zISy1Kv884bEpQBgRjXyEpwpy1obEAxnIBy16ypUf2Zaf
q9AKUJsCRtMIPWakXUGfnHy9iUsiGSa6q6Jew1XpMgs7AAICCACCUrES+JUAKwhS
jVv6k3rwdZxKnWJHq8mH+oL3bBY+UHOSXgTYyqdmyvrSMT2QwJ3D3CHY33kznZSf
9gpn4KmgCqjz582ulDZ2eV9fd28PBVHKqycPRQj/mbyhaofN4CNCjQUEFzEr6XyQ
E6fwVkAlMOhbPwPU6naNMoqn8So0AMG2Bsr3WbV/mL5hgx2pSH0ozq3oWXME08oT
bwEzsxx/eut4rD5wr15QZMuWvh210FBCbJnFy6nGzJpVERQeAoqJsdyvZSGeiMR/
SNIAgRdAvyP58wqAN0QirDaJjY+BEyrSuue3oH5wAxkFVWJULnJCqu4/Afve0zdE
E+JmK67uiQBGBBgRAgAGBQI0vaErAAoJENgaQboW1dP7IWwAnRHFnhWNiMd2Ib2Q
eoeSwVa0a9gfAJ960wQNChNZ2e8/wZre9XmW6I73Aw==
=3gLl
-----END PGP PUBLIC KEY BLOCK-----
```


Figure 2-2: Here's an example of a public key, as generated by PGP.

SSL

Don't get the idea that you've got to go around locking and unlocking every transaction that you initiate on the Web. The Web already has its own underlying foundation of security that uses the public-key encryption method called *Secure Sockets Layer* — known as *SSL* to those in the know. SSL was originally devised by Netscape Communications, the company that first popularized Internet browsers with its Netscape Navigator series. (SSL is used in both Netscape Navigator/Communicator 2.0 or higher or any version of Microsoft Internet Explorer.)

SSL is a computer-to-computer technology that encrypts the information sent over the Internet by using public keys. If you've made any forays into the world of online shopping, you've probably already encountered SSL. Anytime you see the words *Secure Server,* that's a reference to SSL. Many shopping pages offer you the option of placing your order by using their regular Web server or their secure server. Some older browsers didn't support SSL, so you had to use the server that did nothing to protect your information. Given the choice, which one do you think is a better way to go? Secure or insecure? Secure, we're sure!

You can tell whether your browser is linked to a secure server in two ways. First, in most browsers, a small padlock symbol appears in the status bar if you're visiting a secure Web site. (Older versions of Netscape Navigator showed a complete key if you'd connected to a secure server as opposed to the usual broken key.) Second, if you take a peek in the Address line, the normal http:// has changed to https://. The extras s is for *secure!*

Digital signatures

A second, *major* advantage to the public-private key pair concept addresses another vexing Internet commerce problem: How do you know with whom you're dealing? The Web is basically an anonymous communication medium, based on user names (or domain names, for that matter) that can change at the drop of a preference box. How can you justify sending your hard-earned money to someone if you're not sure that the person's who he (or she) says he (or it) is? (Cue the spooky music. . . .)

One way is by using our new friend, the public-private key pair. You've already seen how the key encryption scrambles and protects your messages. Now look at how your private key can act as your digital ID card.

Say that you encode a message by using your private key and send it off to the Grand Poobah of Upper Echelon. The Grand Poobah then picks up his public key ring, with thousands of public keys on it. (He is, after all, the GP.) Trying any other public key but yours can't unlock the coded message; yours is the only one that works. This limitation proves that the message had to have come from you. That key becomes, in fact, a *digital signature.*

Digital certificates

Although the digital signature *implies* your identity, the *digital certificate* states it. Digital certificates are another major reason why the Web is now "open for business." Digital certificates are primarily used in business-to-business transactions — a store exchanging information with a credit card's member financial institution, such as a bank, for example. Digital certificates come from trusted third parties whose business is to make sure that you're who you say you are. There are a number of these companies, called *certificate authorities* or *certificate signers,* but the primary issuer of certificates is VeriSign, Inc. (www.verisign.com).

As we mentioned, there are a number of certificate authorities — but like everything involved when buying online, you want to make sure the company you use is legitimate. One place where you can find a dependable one is *in* your Netscape or Microsoft browser. They each have a built-in list of certificate authorities which Netscape and Microsoft have checked out and accepted for online transactions.

If you're using Netscape Communicator 4.0 or higher, click on Security button in the toolbar and then click on Signers under Certificates to view its list. From the menu bar with Internet Explorer 4, choose View⇨Internet Options. Now click the Content tab and then click on the Authorities button.

After a company completes the VeriSign application — which includes business information such as a Dun and Bradstreet reference or other documents that enable VeriSign to verify the company is legitimate and registered with the proper government authorities — VeriSign generates a public-private key pair along with the digital certificate it issues for the organization. All this procedure takes place over the Internet, and the browser does the actual installation of the digital certificate in the company's system. Then, whenever a secure system asks to see some ID, the company's browser presents the digital certificate. Think of it as an electronic driver's license that you store in your browser.

You can get your own personal digital certificate from VeriSign if you want. The key benefit right now is that you can exchange secure e-mail with other digital certificate holders. Soon, however, you'll be running into more and more Web sites requiring that you have a personal digital certificate for online purchases as more secure technologies develop. One such technology, called *Secure Electronic Transaction*, is already on its way, and, naturally, we cover it later in this chapter (in the following section, as a matter of fact).

For personal use, VeriSign offers a *Class 1 ID* certificate that verifies your e-mail address and personal identify and offers up to US$1,000 coverage in case of corruption, loss, or misuse (by some other disreputable party) of your digital certificate — it's good for a year and, as of this writing, costs US$9.95. (If your employees, partners and customers chat via the Net and you want to control just who gets into your intranet or extranet, check out VeriSign's *Pre-purchase Multiple Digital IDs.*)

If you're already comfortable with surfing on the Net, just go get that digital certificate!

Hey, put that wallet away — your money's no good here. VeriSign offers a 60-day trial Class 1 ID certificate (sans the insurance, natch) for free.

Chapter 3 gives you all the Internet basics that you need. If you want to go there for some online information before continuing on here, go ahead. We'll still be here after you're done.

Here's a road map to getting your own personal digital certificate:

1. **Crank up that browser and log on to the Internet.**

2. **Go to** `http://www.verisign.com/clients/index.html`, **which takes you directly to VeriSign's Personal Digital ID page.**

3. **After you read all the literature and poke around a bit, click the Get Your ID Now button.**

4. **Choose the ID you want by clicking on the Enroll Now button below the Class 1 description.**

5. **Enter your personal data where indicated in the text boxes.**

   A good idea is to enter your e-mail address in your certificate so that you can send and receive secure e-mail. You probably also want to personalize your certificate with birthday information and gender to ward off confusion with other folks who may have the same name as you.

6. **At the bottom of the info page, enter a challenge phrase in the text box.**

   This phrase is not a password for your e-mail but rather something such as your mother's maiden name that VeriSign customer service can use to verify that you're actually who's calling.

7. **Choose whether you'll buy or try out the Class 1 ID buy clicking on the radio button options.** (Keep in mind that the trial version isn't fully stocked up.)

8. **Enter your billing information, including your credit card number.**

   (If you're fingers at this point are a little twitchy, just look at the locked padlock. Rest assured, you're safe!)

9. **After you read all the legalese at the very bottom of the form, click the Accept button to proceed.**

   Now VeriSign tells you (and your browser) that it accepts the application, and it turns over the public-key generation process to the browser. Your browser then asks you for a password to open your secure e-mail.

10. **Enter the same password in each text box to confirm. Click the Submit button to go on.**

    After your browser finishes its computational encryption, it sends a notice to VeriSign.

    VeriSign then fires off an e-mail to you — we're not kidding, it's there right now! — that contains a PIN number necessary for you to collect your digital certificate. Because the PIN is a very complex series of letters and numbers, the best thing to do is to copy it to your Clipboard.

11. **Use your mouse to highlight the PIN number in the e-mail and then choose Edit⇨Copy to copy it to your Clipboard.**

    In the same e-mail, you also see a link to the VeriSign Web page, where you can pick up your ID.

12. **Just click the link to VeriSign and go there.**

13. **After you reach the VeriSign pickup station, click into the Digital ID PIN text box and paste your PIN number by choosing Edit⇨Paste as shown in Figure 2-3.**

    Why all this back-and-forth? This confirms to VeriSign that the person applying for the ID uses the supplied e-mail address. This way, no one can apply under your e-mail address and get your digital certificate.

    Dot's it! VeriSign transfers the digital certificate and everybody shakes hands and goes home smiling.

All right, so where's the T-shirt that says, "My computer went to VeriSign and all I got is this lousy digital certificate!"?

Your browser maintains your digital certificate, and — just 'cause you've been good — we're going to show you what one looks like. Figure 2-4 shows you a typical digital certificate, complete with a serial number and a certificate fingerprint that certifies that this certificate is unique! You can view your certificate any time by checking out the security information on your browser.

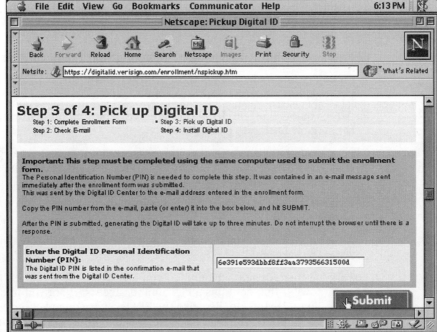

Figure 2-3: The steps involved to get to The VeriSign ID Pickup Center ensure that you are who you say you are.

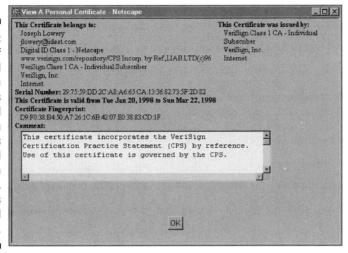

Figure 2-4:
A sample of digital certificate contains personal information as well as encoded identification information, such as a digital fingerprint.

Now that you've made sure others can rest assured that you are, in fact, who you say you are, how can you ensure that the merchant you're dealing with is who he says he is? Simple. Once you're ready to buy at a Web site, choose View⇨Page Info or Document Info from the menu bar if you're using the Netscape browser. Those of you surfing with Internet Explorer 4.0 or higher, choose File⇨Properties from the menu bar and then click on the Certificates button. In both cases, you'll be able to see the site's certificate, informing you of the owner of the site and the certificate signer.

Ready, SET, go!

As we mentioned already, the SSL encryption system already makes online buying safe. Nonetheless, there is one drawback with the system: online merchants can't tell if the credit card number used on their site, in fact, belongs to the person using it.

That's where *Secure Electronic Transaction,* or *SET* comes in. It's an up-and-coming technology intended to raise the online-shopping comfort level for pretty much the entire universe. Credit card giants like Visa, along with mega players in the computer biz, including Netscape and Microsoft, began developing SET in 1996. At the time of this writing, the technology was just coming out of the gate and in trials around the world.

SET is a set . . . er, collection of Internet security standards designed to protect customer and merchant alike. In fact, SET's goal is to make online shopping as safe as purchases made by phone or mail-order.

SET uses a combination of all the security technologies that we discuss to this point in this chapter: encryption methods, digital certificates, digital signatures — the whole kit and kaboodle.

In addition to encryption methods and digital signatures, SET provides two more layers of security between you and a crook. First, everyone involved in a SET transaction must have a special digital certificate — the merchant, the customer and your credit card's member bank. In this way, SET verifies that everyone is the real McCoy (or Marguerite Pigeon or Fiorella Grossi or . . . you get the picture). Clicking on the Buy Me Now button at a merchant's Web site sends your digital ID along with your credit card number to the merchant. Then, the merchant sends its digital ID along with your information to the bank. The bank receives all that information and, if everything checks out, clears the transaction.

Hold on, there's more. Digital IDs also protect you because your credit card information is encrypted or scrambled. So a merchant can't see your credit card info — nor can a hacker breaking into a merchant's Web site!

Credit-Card Guarantees and Other Truths

Okay, time to play that fabulous new game show, *Worst Case Scenario.* On the phone is Tracy from Trenton, Ont. Tracy just went shopping on the Internet and actually used her credit-card number online to buy some flowers for her little sister's baby shower. What's the Worst Case Scenario? Please choose from among the following possibilities:

A. Hackers from hell swipe Tracy's credit-card info and go on a spending spree in the South of France. Tracy's now in debt to the tune of $3,547,994.17, with a 17.5 percent interest rate, no less.

B. The online flower store turned out to be a front for the Venusian Liberation Army, and it delivered Tracy's bouquet in a bomb-shaped vase to the Canadian Forces Base in Trenton. The Military and the Department of Defence are holding Tracy responsible.

C. The florist delivers baby's breath mixed in with the roses — strictly against Tracy's instructions because Tracy's sister is allergic to them. The sister has a sneezing attack, the baby makes an early appearance (it's a boy!), and Tracy refuses to pay. The credit-card company backs Tracy because it got a copy of her e-mail with the order instructions.

And the answer is . . . **C!** We're sorry, but that's the worst that could happen. Thank you all for a great show — see you next week on *Worst . . . Case . . . Scenario!*

Standard credit-card policy

Bottom line? You're protected online just as much as you are offline — and, in some cases, even more. Credit-card companies want you to shop online — you did notice who was spearheading the SET standards, right? So, listen up: You are no more on the hook for the cost of a fraud that occurs when buying online (whether you card number was stolen or the merchant you happen to deal with turns out to be a fraud) than you would be if your card is stolen or if, say, a waiter copies your number and starts buying every gadget from Canada to Timbuktu. Read the fine print of your credit card application and you'll find out that you're only liable for the first $50 should your credit card be used fraudulently. You can even refuse and dispute charges.

The combination of digital certificates and encrypted information, to some people's way of thinking, actually makes online shopping a tad safer than shopping by telephone or by mail order — even in a real-life bricks-and-mortar store. And as we note in Chapter 1, many credit-card companies are willing to put their money where their thoughts are by waiving that liability if a customer denies the charge. (Usually, it's the online merchant who sold items to the crook in the first place that's on the hook for the charge.) Credit-card companies are willing to do so because online transactions generate a pretty significant paper trail, making the situation much harder for a customer to say, "Nope, didn't happen," if it really did.

Chapter 3

Shopping Around the Web

· ·

· ·

*Y*ou almost certainly have a bargain-crazy relative or a friend whose motto is "Never Pay Retail" — someone from whom you've gathered buying tips and a working knowledge of what to look out for while shopping. Shopping online is a fairly new experience in Canada, however, so you don't have many role models or advice columnists around to get you going. What if you're a complete novice not only to online buying but also to computers in general and the Internet in particular? Where can you turn? Ahem. Shall we begin?

Getting Online from the Get-Go

Because you're into shopping — ya got this book, didn't you? — you've *got* to love modems these days. As a pure shopping commodity, modems are hard to beat. How many other products do you know that are:

✔ Better (faster, more powerful, and so on) than last year's model.

✔ Easier to use than ever.

✔ Offering more features every season.

✔ Constantly getting cheaper.

If someone asks us whether now's a good time to buy a modem, we chant our mantra — "Better, faster, cheaper; better, faster, cheaper" — which, loosely translated, means: "No matter when you buy, you can always get a better, faster, cheaper model next year. But not until next year." Picking up a modem today is one time that an impulse buy is amply rewarded.

Now, *what* kind of modem you buy is a different question. As do so many questions in life, this one, too, *depends*. Specifically, the question depends on what you want to use your modem for. We're going to put on our psychic turban and hazard a guess: Online shopping? Okey-dokey — time to see what you can get in the ol' shopping cart.

If you already have your system (a computer complete with modem) and you're raring to go online, skip to the section, "Setting up an ISP account," later in this chapter.

Getting the hardware you need

A modem is the one essential piece of computer hardware that you need for going online. Because modems connect your computer to the telephone line and onto the outside world, ya gotta have one. Most new computer systems sold these days come with a modem included. If yours didn't and you're in the market for one, however, read on.

In case you're into deep geek arcana, *modem* is short for *MO*dulator-*DEM*odulator, which is what the device does to the signals leaving and approaching your computer.

External and internal modems

The best advice that we can give you in buying a modem is to "Buy the fastest that you can afford." You measure the quality of a modem by the amount of information that it can transfer per second. *Information* in this case you gauge in thousands of bits, or *kilobits*, abbreviated as *Kb*s and shortened even further to just the single letter, *K*. With modems, the higher the Kbs number, the better the modem. The common speed used to be 28.8K, later replaced by 33.6K, but you'll have a tough time finding those on the shelves anymore. The standard has now become 56K. But not all Internet Service Providers (ISPs) offer this high speed connection, so make sure you ask an ISP before signing up with its service.

Cable modems

A couple modem options currently on the horizon threaten to blow ordinary modems out of the ballpark. The first is *cable modems*. Under the brand name WAVE, which is offered by a number of cable companies across the country, cable modem service uses the same network as your television cable to connect your computer to a much faster delivery system. In fact, they send and receive data around 100 times faster than can a regular 28.8K modem.

It will end up costing you slightly more than if you simply installed a normal modem (the price tag for WAVE service is about $40, not including installation), but the real issue is availability. Cable systems are just now beginning to connect communities around the country with two-way cable-modem capabilities. Give your local cable company a call and see whether it's now cable-modem ready.

ADSL connections

A new player in the field speeds up Internet access through the regular telephone line. Promoted by Canada's telephone companies, *ADSL* (short for *Asymmetrical Digital Subscriber Line*) brings users a constant, always-on connection to the Internet via your existing phone line. So you can chat with your mother about what you put in the mail to her for Mother's Day at the same time that you're ordering something for her online.

ADSL may not be as fast as cable modems, but practically speaking, you probably won't notice the difference once you're zipping through the virtual aisles. The cost is about the same or slightly higher as cable modem service (currently Sympatico offers one of the least expensive rates, but that may change soon as other ISPs try to compete in this market). However, like cable, ADSL isn't widely available yet. So call your local phone company to see whether its available in your community.

Both cable and ADSL have just gotten out of the gate, so attempting to call one the winner in the race to your computer is rather premature at this point. One thing's for sure — the World Wide Web isn't going to remain known as the "World Wide Wait" for too many more years.

The software side

After you install your modem, it's still just a fancy doorstop until you add some software into the mix. As we mentioned in Chapter 1, two basic software components are essential for the online experience: The dial-up connection and the browser. The first gets you (and keeps you) online, and the second gives you something to do. Sometimes, you find the two combined into one package, as is the case if you're working with an online service such as Sympatico. If you're working with an independent ISP, however, you're more likely to need to install both the dial-up software and the browser individually.

After you install the software, you commonly find that the two programs work together quite well. You can start the dial-up software, and after the connection is made, the browser also starts. Or you can just click the icon for the browser, and the dial-up software kicks in first. As more and more folks go online, the drive is to make the connection process as much of a no-brainer as possible.

Online services such as AOL Canada offer their own proprietary software, which bundles everything that you need in one package. To stay competitive, all online services now offer a complete Internet connection in addition to their special members-only areas.

If, on the other hand, you're using an ISP, you can probably just use your browser of choice. The two leading contenders among browsers are, of course, Microsoft's Internet Explorer and Netscape Communicator. Both are very similar in design and overall use. Which one you prefer definitely comes down to a personal choice — neither of these browsers really offers an over-whelming advantage over the other.

Setting up an ISP account

The Internet Service Provider biz has become a growth industry, so quite a few companies have jumped in the pool. You can find providers that either service just your area, or larger companies that provide nation-wide access, such as Istar Internet and Netcom Canada. The local telephone service companies sell access through the Sympatico service, while U.S. phone companies that have set up shop in Canada to sell long distance have also jumped into the ISP fray, including Sprint Canada. Consequently, you have some choice in the ISP vendor decision.

Connection fees can vary, but generally, you can find providers that offer unlimited monthly service for a flat monthly rate of around $20 to $25. You can find providers that offer lower rates for more restricted time (such as $9.95 for the first 5 or 10 hours), but if you go over that number of hours, you're going to find yourself dishing out far more than the price tag for an all-you-can-surf deal. You can also find providers that offer packages for frequent use at rates below those for unlimited service, such as $15 for the first 60 hours of service a month.

Some ISPs provide service only for computers equipped with certain operating systems, like Windows 95, so make sure you are specific about your computer with the ISP you are checking out. And if you're a rank beginner at this Internet biz, one criterion to look at in shopping for an ISP is its technical support. Make sure that someone competent is always available to answer your questions and get you over the rough spots.

Personal info

How you pay for your Internet service also varies. Many will simply bill you, but you may run into providers that require a monthly deduction from your chequing account or a credit card to sign up, like Sympatico or AOL Canada. You also need to pick what's known as a screen name and a password. Usually the ISP software comes with a screen name/password combo just to get you online, and after you're in, you need to pick your own.

A screen name can be as close to or as far away from your real name as you want. Many people go for a "first initial-last name" combo, such as *mpigeon* — notice that there are no spaces or wacky characters. (Marguerite is enough of a wacky character without any.) Depending on how many customers your ISP is already serving, however, your first choice may already be taken. You can also add in an underscore character or a hyphen to give yourself a bit of distinction: m_pigeon and m-pigeon, for example, are both valid screen names. Of course, you can always go for something a bit more unique, such as, oh, say . . . *picklepicker*. But only if you're name isn't Peter Piper.

You enter your password every time you log on. Most systems provide some method for the computer to remember your password so that you don't need to enter it every time, but you should still pick one that's easy for you to remember but difficult for others to guess. Generally, any combination of letters and numbers longer than eight characters is good.

Pick a number

As your computer calls your ISP, it's dialing an access number. Although just a regular phone number, the access number directly calls your ISP's computer. If you should call on a regular phone, you're greeted with a high-pitched faxlike tone.

You shouldn't have a problem finding ISPs that offer a local access number — that is, in your own area code. In addition to the monthly ISP access fees, you also must pay for the telephone connect time. But that should only be a concern to you if you travel and plan to go online while you're away. Luckily, some providers, particularly the large ones, offer access numbers across Canada and the world.

Not all access numbers are created equal. Check the number to make sure that it can handle the fastest speed that your modem supports. Be on the lookout especially if you own one of the 56K modems. These access numbers should be clearly marked.

After you pick your access number (or numbers — some software enables you to pick a backup number as well), that number's automatically written into your dialer so that you don't need to input it each time you connect to your ISP.

Okay! You've cleared the first hurdle toward that great shopping mall in the cyberspace — now move on to your next stop, Browserville.

Browser 101

The older science-fiction movies always had a device invariably called the "Universal Translator" — which turns an alien race's bleeps and squawks into human speech. Browsers are something like that imaginary device; a browser takes in all the different type of Internet communication — no matter what machine makes it — and presents that information in a visual, comprehensible manner.

Browsing the Internet is really pretty simple after you get the hang of some basic concepts. Going from site to site or "surfing the Net" is a fundamental skills as well as just being fun. Figuring out how to return to favourite sites requires a tad more savvy — but nothing to keep you up at night. In fact, what does tend to keep many people up at night is not the difficulties they face but the joy they find in exploring the fascinating information sphere called the Web.

As we mention earlier in "The software side," the two main browsers available today come from Microsoft and Netscape. Most of these browsers' features function the same — in many cases, even the names for the buttons are identical. In those cases where you may encounter significant differences between the two programs, we diligently point 'em out.

The lay of the screen layout

The first time that you take a look at your browser window, it can seem a little on the overwhelming side. You've got menus and buttons for the main program as well as different menus and buttons for each Web site that you visit. The key to quickly mastering the browser is to pay attention only to those items that you need and — for the time being — ignore the rest.

In this section, you take a peek at two leading browsers and how they look after you first log on to the Internet. After your browser first connects to the Web, it loads what's known alternatively as your *start* or *home page*. The folks who got you the software generally sponsor a home page that you see after you first log on — if the browser came straight from the manufacturer, for example, it most likely has the manufacturer's home page as its default (the Netscape or Microsoft home page). If you're using software that your ISP provides you, nine times out of ten, you first log on to your ISP's home page.

Whatever the home page you start with, you're certainly not stuck with it. In fact, you can make any page on the Internet your home page. You can name your poison through your browser's preferences.

Quite often the home page has a way for you to begin exploring the Internet by using search engines or offers suggestions for cool sites to visit. Here's a real sign of the times: Both Netscape and Explorer now offer shopping areas, which are essentially online stores.

Take a look now at Figure 3-1, which shows a current version of Netscape's Home Page, sitting pretty inside the Netscape Communicator browser. For the moment, just pay attention to the four items we've marked for you: the Back and Forward buttons, the Home button, and the Address text box.

If you now look at Figure 3-2, you see the equivalent setup for Microsoft's Internet Explorer browser and its home page. We've marked the same four buttons on this browser for your viewing pleasure.

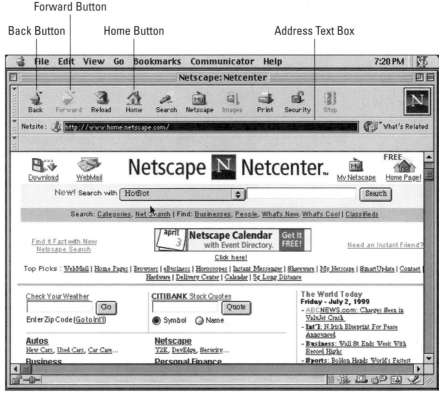

Figure 3-1:
The home page of Netscape Communicator offers a clean listing of current topics and more.

Why have we singled out these four items? They're the basics — the "reading, writing and 'rithmetic," so to speak — of browsers. So what do they do? Glad to oblige your inquiring mind; just check out the following list:

✔ **Address text box.** Better known as your launch pad into cyberspace, the Address text box has two functions: First, it displays the current Web page you're on. Second, the Address text box is where you enter a new Internet address that you want to visit.

Netscape Communicator calls this text box by different names (Go To, Location, or Netsite) depending on whether you're opening a file on your hard drive or visiting a Web site, but the feature serves the exact same function regardless of your current action or its current name.

✔ **Home page.** As you may suspect, clicking this button brings you back to your home page! Use it whenever you find yourself surfing the Web in the wilds of Borneo or you're not quite sure where you are. This button becomes extremely useful if you've chosen a new, more relevant Web site as your home page.

Forward Button

Back Button   Home Button   Address Text Box

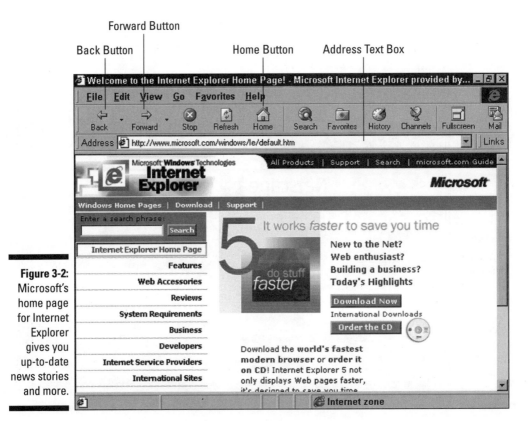

Figure 3-2:
Microsoft's
home page
for Internet
Explorer
gives you
up-to-date
news stories
and more.

✔ **Back button.** Very often, you find yourself following a link on a Web page and then deciding you'd rather go back to where you were before. That's the Back button's function — to return you to the page you were just on. Luckily, the Back button is not limited to just one page — you can go in as deep as you want into a site and then Back button your way out of it. Other, faster ways of backtracking on the Web are possible, but for right now, the Back button is just your speed.

✔ **Forward button.** The Forward button is Back's good ol' buddy and partner in navigating the Web. Selecting the Forward button returns you to the page you were on before you hit the Back button.

Okay, got those four key elements fixed firmly in your mind? Time to go use 'em.

Going online for the first time

Each time you start your browser, your home page loads in the main window. On-screen, you see a mixture of text and graphics begin to appear. Usually, the text loads in much more quickly than do any graphics — although some pages are set up not to display anything at all until all the pictures transfer from the remote computer to your computer. The general term for any type of file transfer is *downloading*.

After the remote computer completes its transfer of files, you see a message in the status bar of the browser (along the bottom of the screen) that indicates that the document is complete (or *done*).

A third element that blends in with the text and graphics is the page's *links*. A link is text or a picture that, after you click it, opens another Web page. You can identify links by the following two main visual cues:

- ✔ Text that's been made into a link is usually underlined and often blue in color. Sometimes you even see a phrase such as "Click here."
- ✔ The real indicator of a link is your mouse pointer. As you move around in the browser, most of the time that the pointer is over the Web page, it's in the shape of a text cursor: the I-beam. If your pointer moves over a link, however, the I-beam changes into a pointing hand.

To show you what to look for, take a look at Figure 3-3, a screen shot of the Canadian version of AltaVista, a fairly new launchpad for Web surfers. Although you can't tell that the underlined text links are blue, most are. We've placed our mouse pointer over one of the links and, as you can see, the pointer has changed temporarily into a pointing finger. That's a link, all right.

Jumping to a Web site

So how do you start surfing? Well, paddle out slowly. . . . Oh, sorry, wrong ocean. Remember the Address text box that we pointed out? That's your gateway. Here's the simple, three-step process:

1. **Click once anywhere in the Address text box.**

   The entire Internet address already in place (most likely your home page) is highlighted.

2. **Type the Internet address for the Web page that you want to visit.**

   Most modern browsers don't require you to type in the full address, with all the `http://` prefix and so forth, but for now, use the entire address to avoid any complications.

3. **Press the Enter key.**

   If you're working with a Macintosh, you press the Return key.

Zoom! You've made the leap into cyberspace. "Houston, we have liftoff."

Figure 3-3: You can identify a link on a Web page by the way your mouse pointer changes into a hand as it passes over one.

Pointer as Hand

Can't wait to start exploring? Following are some *URLs* (short for *U*niform *R*esource *L*ocator, the technical name for *Internet address*) to get you started. We're not going to tell you where they lead you — instead, why don't you discover what they are for yourself? (If your browser doesn't automatically supply the http:// prefix for each URL, you'll have to add it yourself.)

- ✔ www.cdplus.com
- ✔ www.indigo.ca
- ✔ www.beaconmall.com
- ✔ www.autodepot.com

Remember that you can always retrace your jumps around the Net by clicking the Back button at the top of your browser window.

Once you get the hang of surfing and selecting links at various Web sites, you'll likely find yourself scratching your head and muttering to yourself, "Where the heck am I?" Netscape makes retracing your steps a little easier. Say you want to return to a Web site you visited earlier but can't remember the exact URL. If you select the Back button without letting go of your mouse, a drop down menu appears listing the recent Web sites you've visited in alphabetical order, as shown in Figure 3-4.

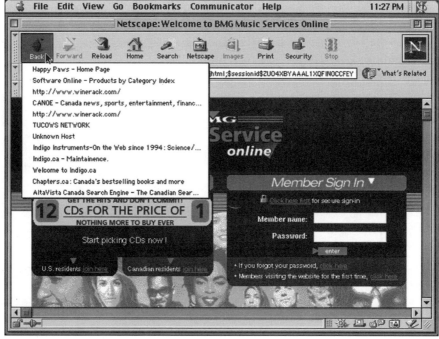

Figure 3-4:
Netscape
makes
retracing
your steps
easy. Hold
down your
mouse on
the Back
button and
then scroll
down to the
URL of site
you'd like to
revisit.

Investigating a Web site

So you made it to your first Web site — now what? What did Armstrong do
after he landed on the moon? Okay, after the speech and the flag thing? He
looked around. But how, exactly, do you look around a Web site?

All Web sites are different, with different information (the online buzzword is
content) and, especially important for a novice to know, different ways of
moving from page to page, or *navigating* the site. Because you can never
know exactly what to expect after you arrive at a new Web site, you must
keep an eye out for certain clues and recurring structures.

Many Web designers, for example, include a strip of buttons called a *navigation bar* along one side of the page. Although these buttons vary wildly in
appearance from site to site — they can look like cows, folders or just plain
words — they're all links to other pages on the Web site and generally have
some descriptive text attached. Figure 3-5 shows a typical site with the type
of navigation bar we're talking about. Although this site has its buttons on
the left side of the page, you can also find them on the right side or along the
top and bottom of a Web page.

Figure 3-5:
You can
reach any of
the major
sections
of the
Ticketmaster
site by
clicking on
some of the
navigation
buttons on
the left side
of the
screen.

Web pages almost always consist of far more than meets the eye, at least initially. A Web page has no real limit to its size as does your computer screen. If a Web page is longer than your screen is tall, a *scroll bar* appears at the right side of your browser window — just as one does if you're working on a long letter in your word processor. You can view the rest of the Web page by clicking and dragging the scroll bar to a new position, by clicking the up and down scroll arrows, or you can press the Page Down and Page Up keys to get around. Web pages can also be wider than your screen, although far less commonly so, and so a horizontal scroll bar appears along the bottom of your browser window if that's the case with a particular Web page.

Not only do you find links to other Web pages in a special area of the page, such as in a navigation bar, but you can also find them within the text. Links embedded in the text may appear as the heading of a story or article or in the words of the text itself. Text links are almost always underlined and are usually (but not always) colored blue. Remember, however, that you can always tell a link by the way that your pointer changes into the fickle finger of fate . . . er, we mean into a pointing hand . . . as it moves over one.

Every so often, you stumble into a Web page that takes forever to load. Maybe the delay's the result of the page's enormous graphics or the song playing in the background, but sitting and waiting for a Web page to load isn't usually how you want to spend your day. Click the Stop button to interrupt the downloading and then select the Back button to get the heck outta Dodge!

Another feature on many Web sites is a page devoted to nothing but links. Quite often the designer of such a Web page uses the word *link* to describe (and act as a link to) these pages, but not always. We've seen some link pages referred to as Other Sources, Resources, Further Information, Like-Minded Folks, and, Joseph's favourite, the Jolly Jump Station. What these pages all have in common is that, although they're part of the current site you're visiting, almost all the links on the pages take you to yet another Web site. Judicious use of the Back button is called for whenever you explore any page of links.

We think that's the bottom line in exploring any Web site: Follow your instincts, don't be afraid to click anything, and always keep your Back button at the ready.

Returning to favourite pages

Okay, say that you're starting to get the hang of this Web-surfing fandango, and — wait, what's *this* Web page all about? Ah, it describes the perfect present for our publisher's birthday (so who said a little brown-nosing doesn't get you anywhere!). We want to come back later to get this item. We've got to write down this Web address!

BLAAATTT! Wrong. Or at least not the easiest way to remember a Web page — and you *do* want easy, don't you? You have absolutely no reason to try to jot down the URL of that site or remember how you navigated your way to that fabulous Web page — because your computer can do the job for you. Its memory is *much* better than yours, after all, in retaining such minutiae as an Internet address.

Both major browsers have a similar feature to keep track of Web sites that you want to revisit. Explorer refers to these Web pages as *Favorites* — hey, you use a U.S. browser, you're stuck with American spelling — while Netscape calls them *Bookmarks*. The process for recording a page's address is a little different in each browser, but the effect is exactly the same.

The Netscape approach

Suppose that you stumble across a Web site with great bargains on ocean cruises, and you want to come back later and fully investigate the site — and maybe book that two-week vacation you've been dreaming about. To mark the page in Netscape, follow these steps:

1. **Make sure that you're on the exact page to which you want to return.**

   Bookmarks apply to a Web page, not a Web site. If you're interested in the entire site, you need to select the Web page's home button to return to that particular page.

2. **Bookmark the Web page in Netscape by using one of the following two methods:**

   • Click the Bookmarks button on the Location bar and then choose Add Bookmark from the menu that appears.

   • Use the keyboard shortcut: Ctrl+D (in Windows) or Command+D (on the Macintosh).

   No matter which method you choose, the same thing happens: The title of the selected Web page appears in the dynamic (that is, changing) Bookmark list. In our cruising example, maybe something such as "Oceans-R-Us" would appear in the list.

Now, whenever you want to check back in at that particular Web page, all you need to do is click the Bookmark button and select the newly added title. Bang, zoom!! — you're whisked back to your selected site. Figure 3-6 shows what happens to your Bookmark file if, like Fiorella, you have no life.

The Microsoft way

If you're working with Microsoft's Internet Explorer, you can easily keep track of all the Web pages to which you want to return — Microsoft calls them *Favorites.* Follow these steps to begin your collection of favorite Web pages:

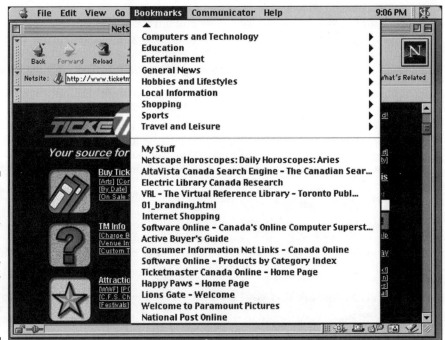

Figure 3-6:
Netscape's Bookmark system enables you to easily revisit any Web site that you mark.

1. **Make sure that you have the Web page that you want to remember showing on-screen.**

   As with Netscape, Microsoft keeps a list of favorite Web pages, not Web sites.

2. **Use either of the following methods to designate a Web page as a Favorite:**

   • Choose Favorites⇨Add to Favorites from the menu bar.

   • Use one of those special keyboard shortcuts. As in Communicator, it's Ctrl+D (in Windows) or Command+D (on the Macintosh).

   You find the title of your Web page tacked onto the bottom of your Favorites list, which you can access by (surprise, surprise) choosing Favorites from the menu bar.

Going back to that newly added page is very straightforward: Choose Favorites from the menu and then choose the listing for the page you want to visit. The browser takes the hint and serves up that page — no problem.

Teaching Your Computer to Fetch: Search Engine Basics

After you get over the hump of just getting online, the bigger challenge is actually finding something that you want online. For every nugget of valuable information or link to an excellent bargain, a mountain-high volume of related but unwanted Web sites blocks your view. How do you find your way to the good stuff?

Naturally, the usual means are still available: A friend passes you a don't-miss Web address, or you spot an URL in a magazine ad. If all else fails, you can always look up what you want. Better still, you could have someone else look it up for you — for free. We're referring, of course, to *search engines*.

Search engines are the Yellow and White Pages of the Internet combined — and then some. As with the Yellow Pages, you can use a search engine to look up an item by category. And as with the White Pages, if you know a company's name, you can locate its address directly by using a search engine. But Web search engines can do something that no telephone book on earth can do: You can hunt down a topic on the basis of key words or phrases. We're great believers in search engines, especially since more and more of them are taking the fingerwork out of finding online stores by launching their very own Shopping areas with listings of merchants that let you ca-ching at their sites. Bless 'em.

A new wrinkle with Internet Explorer 4.0 and higher Favorites

If you're using Internet Explorer 4.0 or later versions, an additional — and very zippy — method of Favorites control is available to you: the Favorites Explorer. Select the Favorites button from the main toolbar, and you see your browser window split in two parts. On the right is the Web page that you're currently viewing but with scroll bars added, if necessary, so that you can still view the entire page. On the left, you now find the Favorites Explorer with a full list of all your custom listings. You can still click any Favorite listing to visit the page, but the difference is that both the Web page and your Favorites listing are on-screen at the same time, as shown in the following figure! This feature enables you to quickly review as many Favorites as you like without going back and forth to the menu. If you want to see the Web page in all its glory, just click the Favorites button on the toolbar again or click the Close button (the X) at the top right-hand corner of the Favorites Explorer.

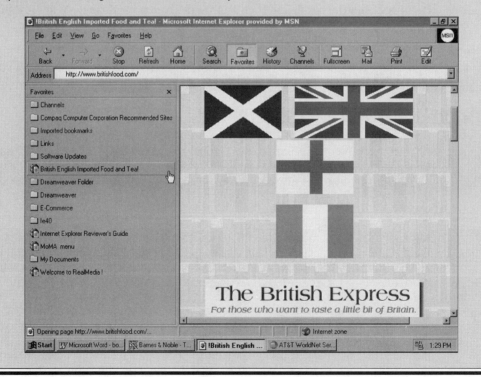

Looking for a specific company, but don't know if it has a Web site? Try the poor man's search engine — type the company name directly in the Address text box (without any prefixes or suffixes), press the Enter key, and see what comes up. Very often you strike gold the first time. If not, give the regular search engines a whirl.

Because search engines are one of the more successful types of Web sites, you find quite a number of them on the Web, each trying to carve out a slice of the Internet pie. Before examining specific search engines more closely to get the most out of them, we're going to perform for you a sample search that would work on any of them.

Simon's simple search session

As you start looking at the various search engines, you see a lot of differences. But, by and large, they all have one thing in common: a quick and easy way to conduct a simple search. All the search engines have a text box into which you can enter your keywords and a button nearby to start the search. Here's the blow-by-blow to basic online searching:

1. **Type the Web address of your favourite search engine in the browser's Address text box.**

   For demonstration purposes, we're going to use the URL for Yahoo! (`www.yahoo.com`) — but in the following section, "The searchers," we'll show you the Canadian version.

2. **Press the Enter or Return key after you type the full address.**

   The search engine's main page appears on-screen, showing the various available categories, some news of the moment, and lots of links. Near the top of the page, you can see the Search text box, as shown in Figure 3-7.

3. **Type a keyword or a phrase into the Search text box and click the Search button.**

   After a moment, the search engine returns the results — which could vary from zero to tens of thousands of links, depending on your search criteria. (Try typing the keyword computer into the Search text box if you've got an idle week or two to kill.)

   The results page consists of a list of links, often with a brief description of the Web site presented in order of relevance — the sites that match your search criteria most closely are listed up front. As you go down the list, you'll find that the links are less relevant.

4. **Click any of the resulting links to go to that particular Web page.**

5. **If that Web page isn't what you're looking for, click the Back button to return to the results from your search and try clicking another link.**

Text Box

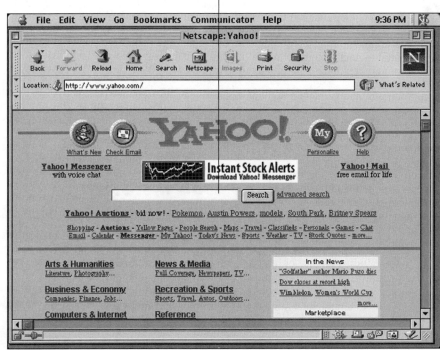

Figure 3-7:
Enter your
keywords or
phrases
directly into
the Search
text box on
your search
engine's
main page.

Internet Explorer 4.0 has a search-engine link built in. Get online and then click the Search button in the main toolbar. The Search Explorer opens in only part of the main screen, much as the Favorites Explorer does. What the Search Explorer opens, however, is a Web page on the Microsoft site that displays a rotating series of search engines — and the results of your search show up in the browser window on the right. Very cool. If you're the kind of person that has to have the latest and greatest of any item, download Explorer 5.0 for its new set of search functions. One of the dandiest of its innovations is the way the browser has integrated the most popular search engines to save you time (excluding, unfortunately, Canadian versions). Say you don't like the results one engine gives you? You just click the Next button to pass your exact query along to the next engine. Extremely cool.

The searchers

After you first start using search engines, you quickly see that the problem isn't finding something on your topic; it's finding the *right* "something." Lots of secrets and tricks can narrow your search so that you can find just what you want and no more. There are a number of U.S.-based search engines like Excite and Infoseek that offer special shopping areas or searching functions. But you'll have a hard time finding inventory in Canada so that you can avoid nasty exchange rates and duck the hand of the mighty cross-border taxman (more on that in Chapter 9).

Well, don't fret — that's why we're here. We'll show you some of the ways on the Internet that make your travels in CyberCanada easy. We're actually quite grateful for the growth of the Internet biz in Canada, because it's spawned only-in-Canada search engines or inspired U.S.-based search engines that have seen such a great opportunity in our neck of the woods to launch Canadian spin-offs or versions. Each search engine behaves a little differently, however, so you're best off taking a close look at a few of them to pick up the nitty-gritty details. The following sections do just that.

Yahoo! Canada

You had a chance to meet Yahoo! in Figure 3-7 in the preceding section, the granddaddy of popular search engines started way back in 1994 by a couple of Stanford University yahoos. Now we're pleased to present to you — drum roll please — its grandchild, so to speak, Yahoo! Canada (we're afraid that the exclamation mark is part of the trademarked name, so we're stuck with it).

Yahoo! Canada has a fairly clean, uncluttered interface, which contributes to its ease of use. Yahoo! Canada uses the same database of Web sites as the main Yahoo! site, so don't expect to be privy to any different information if you choose the Canadian engine. But with Yahoo! Canada, you can find made-in-Canada sources quicker.

How, do you ask? Simple. If you're starting a search using key words on the main page, click on the "Canadian sites only" radio button under the search text box, as shown in Figure 3-8. Your results then will be restricted to only Canadian sites. It doesn't get any easier than this folks.

Yahoo! Canada is based around the *category concept.* After you first drop in on Yahoo! Canada, you find a two-column list of about 15 main categories — everything from Arts & Humanities to Society & Culture. This categorization goes a long way toward cutting down the extraneous hits that you may get from searching the entire Internet.

Selecting any one of these main subjects takes you to a page of all the category's subtopics. Here is where the search engine makes things a little more exciting. At this point you can select one of the subtopics, which will take you into the next level of even more subtopics . . . and so on. Your results page will display Canadian sites first, flagged with, er, a miniature Canadian flag, as shown in Figure 3-9.

The steps we've just given you have one drawback: After clicking on subtopic after subtopic, you may discover that there aren't any Canadian sites within the topic you're searching! Did someone say, "Hello? Are you deliberately trying to give me computer rage?" (Boy, you guys are tough!) There is another option. Once you select a category and are taken to the page of subcategories, you can then restrict your search to all things Canadian by clicking on the Canadian sites only button, as shown in Figure 3-10. From there, you'll then be taken to subtopics that include — you guessed it — only Canadian sites.

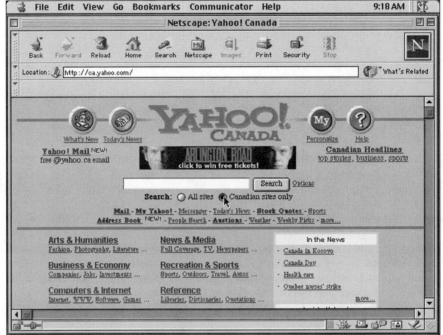

Figure 3-8:
Yahoo!
Canada
helps you
narrow your
search
to only
Canadian
sites.

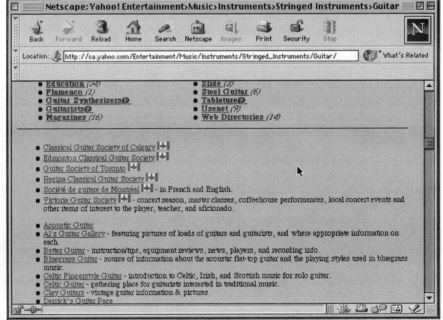

Figure 3-9:
Yahoo!
Canada
will list
Canadian
sites first
in results
page, sitting
awfully
proud next
to a
Canadian
flag.

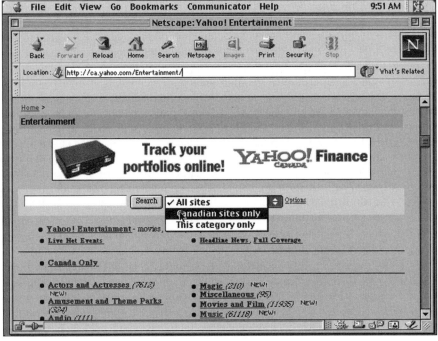

Figure 3-10:
You can save yourself a lot of time at Yahoo! Canada by selecting either one of the options the search engine gives you to scour subtopics for Canadian sites.

Following are some other hints that can help your Yahoo! keyword search:

✔ Use quote marks to turn key words into key phrases. Typing **"stereo equipment"** as a phrase gets you the results you want with fewer misleading links than typing just the two separate keywords.

✔ Add a plus sign in front of a keyword to make it required for a match. You can find a better buy on a stereo, for example, by using the following syntax in your search: **+stereo +inexpensive.**

Notice that there are no spaces between the plus sign and the keyword.

✔ Add a minus sign in front of a word to filter it out of the search. By the same token, if you don't want to get taken in your hunt for the best stereo deal, you can try typing the following series of keywords: **+stereo +inexpensive -cheap -steal.**

But we want to shop. Well, you know that online buying has arrived if the big boys want a seat at the table. At the time of this writing, Yahoo! Canada, in conjunction with Visa, was locked behind closed doors working to launch a Canadian shopping guide similar to the one on the main site called Yahoo! Shopping. In keeping with the Yahoo! category theme, the Canadian shopping guide will be category rich in shopping items so that you can avoid any zigs and zags in your beeline to the checkout counter.

Maple Square

Another site that catalogues Canadian Web sites — but is much smaller than Yahoo! Canada — is Maple Square. You can enter your search terms in its text box or simply search through subject categories. Maple Square gives you the option of searching the entire Web, but searches Canadian Web sites only by default, as shown in Figure 3-11.

The syntax to follow when searching this site is different from what Yahoo! Canada requires. With Maple Square, you don't need to use quotation marks to turn key words into phrases. Also, use the word AND between keywords to find Web pages that contain both words, with the following syntax: **stereo AND cheap**. Note that there are spaces around the world AND. To exclude a word in your search, insert the word NOT before the keyword. Say you don't want price to be an issue when looking for a site selling stereos. You'd then use the following syntax: **stereo NOT cheap**.

AltaVista Canada

So far, we've discussed search engines that look for *Web sites* that match your query. But the most common type of search engine out there are those that read millions of *Web pages* and presents to you those pages that include your search words. Keep in mind, a Web site can include dozens and dozens of Web pages. So, don't be surprised when one of the search engines we're about to discuss presents a results page that lists a number of different Web pages from the same site.

At the top of the heap in Canada is AltaVista Canada, a spin-off of the U.S. search engine AltaVista. Launched in January 1998, it was born out of a partnership between TELUS Advertising Services (TAS), a wholly-owned subsidiary of Edmonton-based TELUS Corporation, and AltaVista Search Service, which is owned by Digital Equipment Corporation.

Like Yahoo! Canada, AltaVista Canada, shown in Figure 13-12, draws from the same database as its American cousin and searches through Web pages located in Canada as well as those that include Canadian content but are rooted outside our borders. The bad news is that AltaVista Canada doesn't include any nifty categories to help you narrow your search. The good news, however, is that you can select the radio buttons above the text window after you've entered your keywords to narrow your results to Web pages in AltaVista Canada's Government Index or News Index. And you can also search in specific languages.

Two quick AltaVista Canada tips: First, use capital letters if you're looking for information on a proper name — for example, the *Montreal Canucks*. Second, if you're looking for Web pages that contain two keywords (although not in a phrase), insert a plus sign before both words. The syntax to follow would be: **+stereo +equipment**.

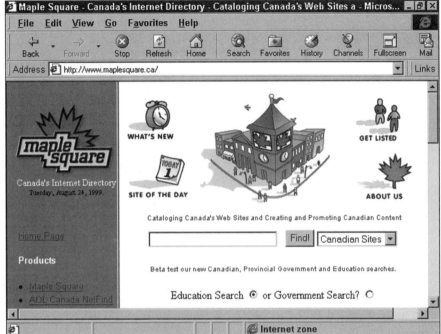

Figure 3-11:
Maple
Square
automatically
searches for
Canadian
Web sites.

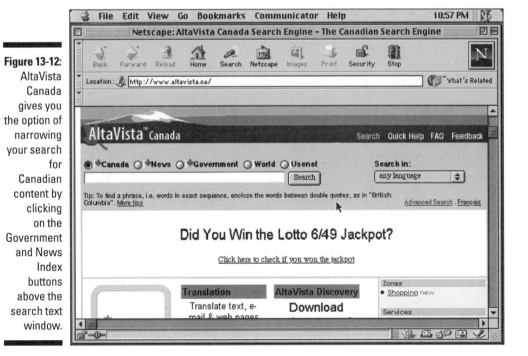

Figure 13-12:
AltaVista
Canada
gives you
the option of
narrowing
your search
for
Canadian
content by
clicking
on the
Government
and News
Index
buttons
above the
search text
window.

If you take a closer look at Figure 3-12, you'll notice an AltaVista Canada innovation that is of special interest to the online buyer — the Shopping zone. Selecting it will take you to more than 25 categories, from auctions, to music and video, to travel — each listing a number of merchants' links. Scroll down and click on a merchant and you're taken to its Web site where you can buy directly from that merchant.

Most of the merchants are U.S.-based, but AltaVista Canada made up for it by flagging those merchants that ship within Canada and bill in Canadian dollars, as shown in Figure 3-13.

AltaVista Canada also offers a very strong support mechanism for finding your purchase in an offline (that is, a regular) store — just type in the sort of business your looking for in the Yellow Pages section of the Web page. Now, type in your city name and click on the Start Search button and you'll get a listing of stores, from which you can find the one nearest you — including a phone number of the store to help you find the place.

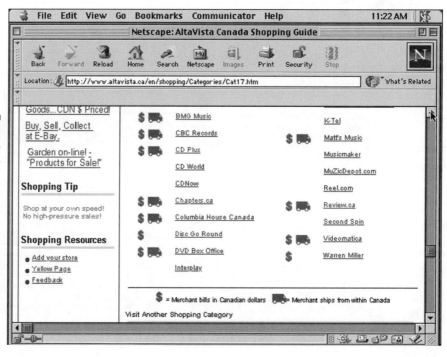

Figure 3-13: You know instantly which merchants in AltaVista Canada's shopping zone ship within Canada before you get to the order form.

Canada.com

Another search engine fairly new in cyberspace this side of the border is Canada.com, launched by the Southam Inc. newspaper chain. You can't help but get excited by this site. In one scroll, you can check out how the markets are doing, what the top headlines are, and what the weather's like in your province.

By default, this search engine will look for only Canadian sites. Ironically though, Canada.com will only search through those sites that have URLs ending in `.ca`, as shown in Figure 3-14. You can also switch your search to the World Wide Web and receive results that identify Canadian Web pages that match your query with a Canadian flag — is this starting to sound familiar?

Canada.com has also made the search for Canadian online stores a heck of a lot easier. It has a shopping section that lists more than 100 online stores grouped under categories, from auctions, to health, to wines, as shown in Figure 3-15. Scroll down to the category of choice, click on the merchant's name and you'll be linked to its Web site. If you still can't find what you're looking for in Canada, you can always browse through the search engine's U.K. and the U.S. shipping sections.

Figure 3-14: Select the bar near the text box at Canada.com to limit your search to Canadian Web sites with URLs that end in ca.

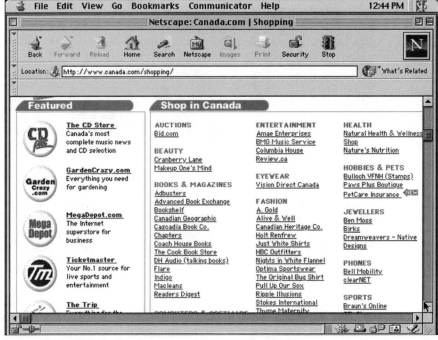

Figure 3-15:
Canada.com
automatically
gives you
listings that
are only
Canadian-
based
merchants.

Lycos

While it doesn't offer a Canadian version of its service, the U.S.-based Lycos search engine can help you shop online in Canada. On its home page (at www.lycos.com), click on Canada under the engine's regional zone. You'll find nearly 40 subcategories, and guess what — one of them is shopping with a number of links to online stores in Canada. And it goes one further by providing a list of Web sites — hand-picked by Lycos's volunteer editors — that can give you more ideas. You can do the same at the home page of the Hotbot search engine, which is part of the Lycos network.

In Chapters 4 and 5, we discuss some of the nifty online offerings from Internet services like AOL Canada and Sympatico. But you've got enough here to get your fingers wet. So what are you waiting for — an engraved invitation? (Oh, did we forget to talk about the Engraved Invitation button? Maybe next chapter. . . .)

Part II
What You Can Find Online

The 5th Wave

By Rich Tennant

"You're part of an 'Insect-Clothing Club' on the Web? Neat!
Where do you get buttons that small?"

In this part . . .

We're beginning to think that we were Sherpa guides in a past life. You know, one of those escorts who helped the first intrepid adventurers find their way up the Himalayas? We get so excited when we get the opportunity to introduce anyone to unexplored territory that we feel we were born to it. And we've got some pretty great trails to lead you on in our quest for the hottest Web stores.

Part II takes you on a worldwide, whirlwind tour of the best in online shopping. From the eclectic, truly electronic boutiques featuring the offbeat and the unique to online-shopping malls, you'll soon see that virtually everything is up for grabs in the virtual world. Suddenly, distance has disappeared as a deterrent for shopping. Oh, don't want to hop on a jet and pick up some shoes in Milan? Hop on the Web instead and find 'em online.

The Web has room for everyone from the largest international manufacturer to your cousin Lionel who's decided to finally put his train set up for sale. Can't find what you want through any of the regular venues? Or better yet, don't want to pay retail? Try the online classified market where anyone — including yourself — can put anything up for sale. We'll even show you how.

The final land we help you explore in Part II is the golden realm of electronic information. Information can take the form of business reports that can make you shine in your job or software that can make your work zoom by. All kinds of electronic information can be bought online — and delivered right to your computer, over the Web. Come on, we can't wait to show it to you. . . .

Chapter 4

Electronic Boutiques and Beyond

. . . .

. . . .

*R*emember when you were a kid and you tried to count the stars? The more that you concentrated, the more your eyes adjusted to the darkness — and the stars just kept appearing. Tracking shops on the Internet is a bit like that; the more you look, the more online shops you find. We can just hear Carl Sagan now: "Bill-yuns and bill-yuns of Web stores."

Just as you can see different kinds of stars in the heavens, you also can find many types of virtual storefronts on the Internet. You won't have any problem finding what your heart and wallet desires if you're willing to shop across the border and around the world. But we want to shop Canadian! True, online shopping here is in its infancy, and you may be surprised at how many large and small retailers and manufacturers don't offer a cyber checkout line. But — there's always a "but" when it comes to online shopping on the Net — you will still be astounded by what you can find on the Net, whether it's the online version of a store that's already a household name, or a small entrepreneur with a nifty idea. Follow us.

One-of-a-Kind Stores

You hear a lot about how the Web is creating a new multinational community of communicators, where no one government or opinion holds sway. Inhabitants of this new realm even have a name: Netizens. The same enabling force that allows folks from all around the world to share their research, experiences, and visions has given birth to a new breed of storefront — the truly electronic boutique.

> ✔ **Earthlore Ltd.** (www.earthlore.mb.ca): In the mood to take your kids on an archeological dig — in the play room? Order one of the I Dig Dinasours kits and you and your kids can chip away at sandstone to unearth model bones from 65 million years ago. You got your Tyrannosaurus-Rex, your Velociraptor, even a Triceratops egg nest.

Once you open your browser's borders, there's virtually no end to the diversity of shops online. One of our favourite U.S. spots is the Spam site (at www.spam.com). If you have a particular fondness for the Spam luncheon meat logo or a picture of the can and would love it on your boxers, mouse pad or cups, look no further than here.

How can such a variety exist and why do you see literally no limit to its growth? The following section tackles these hard questions and delivers some pretty zippy answers.

Why such a variety?

In the first phase of Internet growth, major companies and corporations around the world rushed to reserve their domain names and establish their Web sites, many for no better reason than to have a www.our-company.com or www.our-company.ca on their business cards. Now, the next virtual gold rush is under way as electronic commerce takes off and customers begin to spend some currency, as well as time, on the Web.

From a business owner's perspective — especially that of the small business owner — why is selling online such a good idea? Three key factors: investment, access, and support.

Low startup costs

The fixed costs for getting and staying online, especially for small start-ups with even smaller budgets, are considerably smaller compared to opening and maintaining a real-world storefront. It's very much like an entrepreneur setting up a self-employed venture in his or her kitchen, rather than shelling out hundreds, if not thousands, of dollars in monthly rent and a two-year lease in Anywheresville, Canada (read: overhead).

After a business secures a location (and what start-ups can afford to pay don't get them the prime spots), it still faces the matter of outfitting the store with shelves, displays, and other fixtures — and don't even get us started if the store needs a major overhaul. We'd wager that the only reason most of us know the term "store fixtures" is because that's what we see on the Going Out of Business signs.

What does the virtual store owner need in terms of making the storefront attractive? Hiring a graphic designer for a week or so to create an interesting,

Creating a store that specializes in one item or theme is a great concept that's very hard to realize in the everyday world. Store owners tell each other that the three most important keys to success are "location, location, and location." Unless you locate your shop in a major metropolitan area that can draw from a wide population, the narrower your store idea, your audience could approach zero. Which is why malls were invented.

Putting your storefront on the Internet, however, opens up a planet of possibilities. On the Web, a store's focus can be as narrow as you can possibly imagine and still be accessible to the largest possible group. Consider the followings examples:

- **Crochet Creations** (www.crochetcreations.com): The ultimate gift catalogue for crocheted items. You'll be hooked (!) by such items as crocheted fridge magnets, crocheted scrunchies, and crocheted wedding doll dresses. Think we're making it up? Check out Figure 4-1.

- **Movie Poster Warehouse** (www.movieposter.com): A virtual emporium of movie viz. You have access to more than 1 million titles of movie posters and 5,000 photographs of movie stars. Whether you're a movie buff and collector or just want a cheap wall to decorate the walls, you can view more than 7,000 posters from classics like *King Kong* to current fare like *Braveheart*.

Figure 4-1: If you're into the '70s retro scene, you'll feel right at home ordering any number of crocheted items from Crochet Creations.

fun-looking place to shop. There's no question that a huge store will be faced with an equally huge initial layout of cash to get a world-class site up and running, from hundreds of thousands to even millions dollars. For example, it cost $9 million to set up ChaptersGLOBE.com, one of Canada's largest Web sites geared toward book-lovers seeking information on authors and news of the literary world. (This site is not to be confused with its sister site, Chapters.ca, focused on the general book reader, as well as videos, DVDs, CDs and software.) Costs, while relatively less than those slapped on opening a bricks-and-mortar store, have certainly made some shops hesitate to open their doors on the Net.

That's changing now, particularly for the small outfits. Bringing together all the elements involved in setting up a successful e-commerce site is no cakewalk — the costs for the start up and maintenance of a site can be hefty for the entrepreneur who already has a real world shop. In fact, cost has been one of the main obstacles in front of retailers opening their doors in cyberspace. But that is all changing. The job has become a do-it-yourself type with the number of new software packages on the market that can help a entrepreneur to get up a Web site virtually overnight. For not much in the way of an investment, a small online start-up can, with a little creativity, look as good as the largest corporation.

Now to the real advantages of a Web storefront. First, you have your stock. A walk-in store owner must have a product on the shelves or in the backroom so that it's there right when a customer walks in — or else the customer walks out, empty-handed. That's a lot of capital to invest in just sitting around wishing and hoping and dreaming. The Web-savvy shopkeeper, on the other hand, can keep only the hottest items in-house for immediate shipment and pull in the rest on an as-needed basis. ChaptersGLOBE.com has access to more than two million titles. At an average of 2.5 centimetres of thickness per book, that many books would require more than 500 kilometres of shelf space — for just one copy per title!

Second, you have your employees. Although you can single-handedly run only the smallest real-world start-up, the Web can handle an awful lot of small virtual start-ups. Factor in the notion that an online store is open 'round the clock, 'round the sun (also known as 24/7 in Geekville). We're sure that many offline sole proprietors would love to keep their stores running all the time but could never afford to staff it.

Should a business start to take off, the "landlocked" company must incur many more expenses than the virtual kind of store. Should you rent another location, hire more employees, invest in more stock, and so on? Or, if you're online, should you just add another dozen pages to your Web site and put more money into marketing? What's interesting is that a number of Net Shop owners have become Web converts after seeing that doing business on the Web can cost 10 times less than the expense of running a mail-order business.

Of course, everything's not a free ride for the Web business. You still face certain costs-of-doing business that are inescapable, such as taxes and licensing fees. But overall, the start-up costs you face are much, much lower than those for a "real-world" business.

Global marketplace

The Internet enables you to shop anywhere and pretty much enables a store owner to sell anywhere as well. Increasingly, markets are opening up across the border and overseas, not because a cadre of diplomats signed some tariff agreements but because of the World Wide Web.

You will see some of the bigger Canadian sites, such as online auctioneer Bid.com, expand into the U.S. — which is a no-brainer, really, considering that Americans have taken to online shopping far more quickly than their Canadian cousins. As good as this situation is for the large corporations, its potential is even better for the small Web storefront. Specialty products online now have the broadest possible market reach and the greatest possible chance for success. Consider the case of Toronto-based Movie Poster Warehouse mentioned earlier in this chapter. Most of the company's business comes from the U.S., but it also regularly fills orders from around the world, including Japan, Saudi Arabia, and European countries. In fact, you will be surprised at the number of successful sites in Canada that actually post their prices in *American* dollars!

And just like many U.S. companies have physically crossed our borders to establish Canadian digs, they're now moving into Canadian cyber territory. Sites like eBay.com (www.ebay.com), for example, offer a special section on their sites for Canadians only, listing auction items catering to Canadian tastes.

Netrepreneurs

Something about a bold, new frontier in any area is sure to attract the risk-takers. And the Internet certainly has that uncharted-territory feel about it. Call it the Technological Revolution or the Information Age — whatever, the rapid growth of the Web has created a new class of net-savvy entrepreneurs or, more correctly, *netrepreneurs*.

The Internet community is very self-supporting. Not only is developing an e-shop relatively less expensive to starting from scratch in the real world, you'll find more and more people or companies who can help you do it. And you find them on the Net, of course.

A real self-starter can, of course, build a Web site store from a knowledge base of zip, nada, no clue. All such a person needs is sufficient time — and the one commodity that most self-respecting entrepreneurs have in abundance is time. After the basic work is under way, the netrepreneurs can find an entire support network (no pun intended, amazingly enough) on the Web for everything from online marketing advice to currency-conversion tools to import/export regulations.

Finding the small shops

The true shopper knows that bringing the off-the-beaten-path discount back home is only part of the fun. The real challenge is finding that one little shop that almost nobody knows about — except for you and maybe a few hundred of your closest friends. Foraging for finds on the Web is a little different than is the same activity in the offline world. For one thing, you don't need to burn up a lot of fossil fuel as you tool around town looking for a "real" find offline; for another, you can indulge your hunting urges at any time of the day or night.

Follow the content

At this stage of the Internet's development, you can pretty safely bet that you can find a lot more information about a particular product than you can places to buy it. A saying's emerged from the flourishing Web: "Content is king." Many Web sites focus on the sharing of experiences and data about specific activities and concerns. Although most of these sites don't engage in commerce directly, you find that many of them connect to ones that do.

"Follow the content" is just another way of saying "follow your nose." If you're looking for an online store that sells a particular item and you can't find any direct references, you can try searching for words associated with your subject by using a search engine. Check out each of the results your browser returned because often a site will include links or references to other related sites that you can check out. Buried within a site may be the widget you're looking for.

The search engine route

Search engines in general are some of the more popular destinations on the Web. As such, they've become centres for the growing trends in e-commerce. And — thankfully — you'll find a shopping area or guide on most U.S. and Canadian search engines. It is the first place we go to when looking for a product online in Canada because it makes the shopping trip so easy. One good example is AltaVista Canada. Aside from being a pretty potent search engine interface, AltaVista Canada has its own Shopping Zone (you can check it out in detail in Chapter 3). While giving direct links to a number of online stores grouped by categories, AltaVista Canada's Shopping Zone also identifies the merchants that not only ship within Canada — thereby involving no duty and extra shipping costs — but bill in Canadian dollars.

As online shopping heats up, you'll see more of these sites trying to expand their popularity by including links to other services.

Following links made easy with Internet Explorer 4.5 or higher

The latest version of Internet Explorer has one of the niftiest features we've seen to help you "follow the content" when you're checking out various links referred to on one Web page. With the browser's "Page Holder," you'll be able to check out what lies behind those links without getting lost and forgetting the Web site from which you started your search. Once you're at a page that lists a handful of sites, click the tab titled Page Holder on the left side of the screen.

IE's home page then splits in two, as shown in the figure below. The links (called *URLs*) on your original Web page — in our example, Canada.com's shopping guide — are transferred and "held" on the left side of the screen. Click on a specific link in the Page Holder, and the Web site appears on the right side of the screen for your viewing. If it doesn't have the gadget you're searching for, click on another link in the Page Holder to view another site.

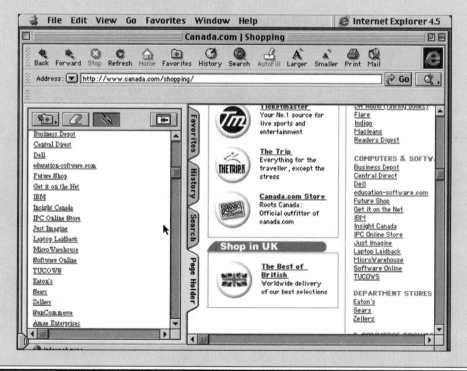

Visiting a portal

Which brings us to *portals*. These types of Web sites act as your gateway to the Net, throwing in everything on their site except the kitchen sink — a search engine, products, news, horoscopes, weather, chat groups, a pink elephant (just checking that you were paying attention) — to create a spot for you that is essentially your home base when venturing into cyberspace. Do they include shopping stuff too? Natch. Like the search engine sites, portals such as Microsoft's Canada's portal MSN Canada (as shown in Figure 4-2), and AOL Canada's portal, include some sort of shopping channel or guide that houses links to a number of Canadian shopping destinations.

Both portals and search engines require that any of their merchants meets a series of security and customer-service criteria prior to putting out their virtual "Open For Business" sign. You'll find them in Chapters 3 and 5.

Impulse shopping

You've probably all experienced that quickening of the pulse as you near the checkout counter and spot that nifty little something on the side. You pick it up, check the price, and, with a little grin and a "why not" shrug, you drop it into the basket. That's impulse buying, and although you find a few parallels in cyberspace, the ads that pop up as you visit a Web site are often more nuisance than enticement and you can easily ignore them.

Figure 4-2:
Portals like MSN Canada take out some of the leg work in your search for online stores by providing a shopping guide with links to virtual merchants.

Selecting your own home page

If you find yourself starting your day by always navigating to one search engine or other mega-site, why not make that site your home page?

The process of changing home pages is slightly different in the two main Web browsers, Netscape Navigator and Microsoft Internet Explorer, but the task is easier in both if you first go the Web page that you want to designate as your new home stop. Then take the following steps in the appropriate browser.

In Netscape Navigator:

1. **Choose Edit⇨Preferences and, if necessary, click the Navigator category.**

   You see the Home Page section in the middle of the Preferences dialog box that appears.

2. **Click the Use Current Page button, or type in the Web page URL you prefer. Then click OK.**

In Internet Explorer:

1. **Choose View⇨Internet Options.**

   When the Internet Options dialog box appears, make sure that you're on the General tab.

2. **From the Home Page section of the General tab, select the Use Current button and then click OK.**

Now, whenever you go online or click the browser's Home button, you're whisked off to your chosen page, where you can start your shopping day.

On the other hand, what the Web makes possible — and really fun — is impulse shopping. The sheer convenience of online ordering coupled with the wide variety of products makes the quick search and the instant gratification a very real possibility.

When may you find yourself impulse shopping? Perhaps if you're thinking of something for someone special — and maybe that someone special is yourself.

Gift giving

We know a number of people swear by the Internet for all their gift giving. In fact, some do all their Christmas shopping on the Web. The constant availability and, especially, the lack of pushing and shoving in the aisles make this form of shopping a pleasure instead of a reason to take a Valium.

Here's a great example of impulse shopping: Say that you're surfing the Web, tracking down some vital bit of information for your work, and you run across a reference to a book that brings to mind your mother or another close relative. Thinking about how such a present would be received makes you smile, so you open your 'Favorites' (or Bookmark) file and scoot on over to your favourite online bookshop. You make a quick search for the title, and soon the book's in your shopping cart. Change the shipping address to your relative's and pick out the wrapping paper — of course, the bookseller gift-wraps — and it's on its way.

Special small shop cautions

Whenever you're ordering from one of the smaller, unique shops on the Web, you should keep a few things in mind. Often, these stores are the online equivalent of a mom-and-pop shop that may not have all the resources of a larger company.

First, make sure that your order is going through a secure server. Most Web pages state their status explicitly, but you can verify it by looking for a closed padlock symbol on the status bar of your browser. You also probably see that the beginning of the URL is changed from `http://` to `https://`.

Second, checking product availability before you order is always a good idea. Some of the larger Web sites have extensive database-tracking capabilities that enable them to tell you whether an item's in stock. Most of the smaller companies don't have this capability, but some do have an e-mail address, usually set up as a Contact us link. You can, therefore, select that link and send an e-mail inquiring about your product's availability. This procedure also gives you an opportunity to check out a company's customer-service response time, which is another important factor in online ordering.

Third, be shipping aware. Most everything you order over the Net is sent by one of the delivery services. Make sure that you know what your delivery options — and costs — are upfront. You don't want to get two surprises when, number one, your package and, number two, its shipping invoice arrives.

Name-Brand Shopping Online

Many national retailers or name brands in Canada have a Web presence in some form or another. Here's a short pop quiz: Match the company name in Column A with the Internet addresses in Column B of the following table.

_____	**First Canadian Flowers**	A.	www.aircanada.ca
_____	**Hudson's Bay Company**	B.	www.thebodyshop.ca
_____	_Flare_ **Magazine**	C.	www.hmv.com
_____	**Air Canada**	D.	www.clubmonaco.com
_____	**HMV**	E.	www.hbc.com
_____	**Roots**	F.	www.1stcanadianflowers.com
_____	**The Body Shop**	G.	www.holtrenfrew.com
_____	**Club Monaco**	H.	www.roots.com
_____	**Holt Renfrew**	I.	www.flare.com

Wouldn't we have made great sixth-grade teachers with easy tests such as this one? For those of you who need to make sure that you got the gold star, here's the answer key, in order: F E I A C H B D G. Just make sure that you don't pass the answers on to next year's class.

As is pretty obvious from the preceding so-called test, a store's name or a product's name brand is just as important online as off, and most companies try to stick as close to them as possible. In fact, some early Net flimflam artists . . . er, we mean enthusiasts bought up many popular-brand domain names and tried to sell them to the companies that owned the brand. Copyright law, however, is coming down heavily on the side of the longtime holders of the trademarked names.

Shopping online for the right info

So why should you care that many major stores and manufacturers have Web sites? Aren't those sites just big advertisement pages? Until recently, that assumption would have been right on the money. As the great Web rush of the '90s was just getting started, a lot of companies merely put up what's derisively known as _brochureware_. Brochureware takes an already-published ad or catalog and posts it to the Web, as is. To be sure, many companies have not progressed much further than that.

Luckily, however, savvy businesses, particularly large retailers, are realizing shopping online is not a passing fad. As competition heats up, the formats of these company Web sites have — and continue — to change. The simple fact that a repositioned ad isn't going to cut it as a viable Web presence is quickly becoming obvious to many — you need something much more on a Web site to hold a customer's attention. Indeed, one thing you will continually come across is Web sites with an "Under Construction" or a "Relaunching" sign, as they try to improve the function and form of their sites to make the buying process more interesting and interactive and a whole lot easier.

These merchants also realize that the Web offers something that major companies never really had access to before: unlimited publication space. What customers demanded — and what companies were all too happy to provide — was more information about the products a company offered. That leads us to one of the great benefits of shopping online: the capability to research virtually anything to death. If you want to know more about the XYZ, Inc., Model 1049-A SuperDuperScooper, just go the company's Web site and look it up. Most company Web sites include an internal search engine that enables you to look up items directly. There you find more product information, spec sheets, and comparison charts than you can shake a virtual stick at.

Comparison shopping

The Web is also a great place to comparison-shop for products, even from different companies. Say you're interested in buying one of those new-fangled digital cameras. You've been checking out the magazine advertisements and you've written down a couple model numbers of types that you're interested in. You go up to the Kodak site (at www.kodak.com) and look for the model under its product categories. Kodak's spec sheet looks good, but what about this other camera you saw in another ad — the one from Nikon? Simply zip on over to the Nikon site (at www.nikon.ca) and see what it has to say. After you actually find the product info, you can do the actual comparisons in any of the several following ways.

- ✔ Use your Back and Forward buttons to shuttle between the two spec sheets online.

- ✔ Print out the information for both by going to the two companies' Web pages and clicking the Print button on your browser.

- ✔ Open a new browser window while you're on one site and surf on over to the competitor's site in the new window. Then you can literally flip back and forth between the two — or even resize the windows so that they're side by side, as we did in Figure 4-3. Now that's comparison shopping!

  - To open a new browser window in Internet Explorer, you simply choose File⇨New⇨Window.

  - To open a new browser window in Communicator, simply choose File⇨New⇨Navigator Window.

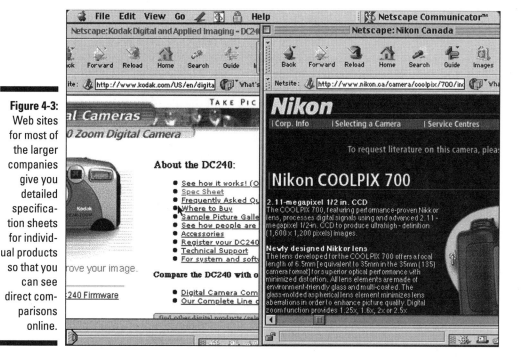

Figure 4-3:
Web sites for most of the larger companies give you detailed specification sheets for individual products so that you can see direct comparisons online.

Technical support and customer service

One of the major advantages that the Web brings to modern life is an escape from voice-mail hell. We're all familiar with the hassle of trying to get through to technical support on that toll-free number to get some help with the computer, the VCR, or even the coffee machine. You listen to all the menus, follow all the prompts, and still end up on hold listening to the Elevator Orchestra's rendition of "Stairway to Heaven."

On the other hand, you can go directly to the source and avoid all that waste of time by accessing a company's Web technical support. Depending on the organization, you may find a mini search engine that enables you to input the symptoms of your problem or access a list of *frequently asked questions* (cleverly known as *FAQs* on the Web). At the very least, you can almost always send off an e-mail query to the company's support staff and wait for someone to contact you.

The International Web-Set

Do you remember when your mother and father would shake their heads at the latest gadget and say, "The world is getting smaller"? Well, guess what? The world just shrunk down to the size of your computer screen. The World Wide Web opens store doors from around the globe for you at anytime, day or night. And Canadians are becoming travelers. Look at any study and you'll find that Canadians who buy online spend most of their money in the U.S.

You can look for your international products in a couple ways: You can search specifically for the product through one of the Web's search engines. Or you can search for the country, together with a keyword such as **shopping**. The method you use depends on whether you're looking for an exact item or just want to browse the country's shopping aisles. What kind of things can you find on the International Internet? Take a look at the following listings.

From the good ol' U.S. of A., for example, you can find the following items:

- The latest creations from world-famous designers like Dolce & Gabbana, DKNY, and Tommy Hilfiger (at www.designerdirect.com).

- The quirkiest of the quirky goods from Hammacher Schlemmer, such as a silent electric violin or a wind-defying umbrella (at www.hammacher.com).

- Toys from F.A.O. Schwarz, the legendary store featured in the movie *Big* with Tom Hanks (at www.faoschwarz.com).

You can access the following products from the United Kingdom:

- Kilts for you and yours from Scottish Tartan Mall (at www.ibmpcug.co.uk/~ecs/mall.html).

- English-speaking books from the Internet Talking Bookshop (at www.orma.co.uk/intabs.htm).

- British-made collectibles decorated with images of Diana, the late Princess of Whales (at www.lady.diana.co.uk).

Africa offers the following goods and services:

- Regional music from Zaire's One World (at www.oneworld.co.za).

- Merchandise from South African craftmakers (at www.safari-iafrica.com).

- Shopping malls in South Africa (at www.samall.co.za).

Australia's good for the following items:

- ✔ The best of fine Australian Chardonnay from Killerby Vineyards (at `www.killerby.com.au`).

- ✔ Australian jewelry, musashi amino acids, raw wool jumpers, Ug boots, fashion leather, and aboriginal art (at `www.aaaustralia.com.au`).

- ✔ Tickets to kickboxing and other sporting events in Australia at The Fight Shop (at `www.thefightshop.com.au`).

And from Japan, check out the following products:

- ✔ Japanese ceramic gifts, including a variety of Happy Cat statues (at `www.bekkoame.or.jp/~ys-trade`).

- ✔ Famous Japanese lacquerware, Aizu-nuri (at `www.meshnet.or.jp/nora /english/shop`).

- ✔ Kimonos designed specifically for those walking down the aisle or walking into a party (at `www.orange.ne.ip/~k-y-m`).

As you start exploring the global Web, don't worry too much about the language barrier. If an online store's interested in shipping worldwide, that store's likely to have set up a multilingual site. Many stores use flags to designate available languages — click the American or British flags, for example, for English.

From the Net to Your Door: Internet Home Delivery of Groceries

We conducted an impromptu survey one night with a bunch of friends and asked them what was *the* one thing they would love to buy on the Net. The answer (albeit, a very unscientific one): food. After all, most of us load up our shopping carts with the same brands of soup, coffee, soaps and pet food time and time again. And do we even need to talk about how busy we are during the week and seem never to have time to get to a grocery store — until filling up the fridge becomes an urgent matter?

Well, our trusty wonderers — home shopping has arrived. Not only can you use the Internet to shop for items around the world and get your packages delivered to your door within a week, you can also shop for groceries and have them at your doorstep — on the same day of your order, depending where you live. The few online grocery sites available now generally service only local or metropolitan areas. But you can order non-perishable groceries over the Web no matter where you live.

How, you ask desperately? Follow these steps to order from The Peach Tree Network, an online group of independent grocers in Canada, and one of the first virtual food stores:

1. **Log on to The PeachTree Network by typing** `http://www.thepeachtree.net` **in your browser's Address box and pressing Enter.**

2. **On the top right of the page, click on the Shop Now button, to register later. (This is for those tired of entering their personal info registering at other sites and just want to shop!)**

   You'll be taken to a page requiring your postal code to determine which grocer in the network will deliver to you.

3. **Enter your postal code and Click Submit.**

   After the site figures out which grocer will take your order, you're sent to the shopping page of the site.

4. **Scroll down the right side of the page and select the Click to Shop button in the area labeled National Delivery of Non-perishable Foods.**

5. **Choose the Food Products link, one of the different product aisles available (others include Health and Beauty and Pet Food).**

   As shown in Figure 4-4, you'll be taken to a page that lists the different product types available in various sections of the virtual aisle you chose.

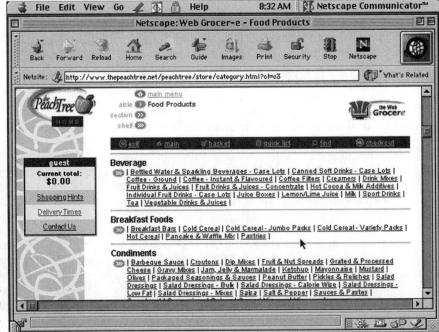

Figure 4-4: Click on any of the non-perishable food items at The PeachTree Network to get items delivered to your home.

6. **Browse through the shelves, choose a product category, like Pizza, Pasta, Rice and Grains, and click on one of the individual product links.**

   Say, you select Pasta. Different types and brands of pasta appear on the main screen.

7. **For each item you'd like to order, enter the quantity you'd like in the "Quant." box.**

   If you plan to use The PeachTree again, you can add each item you buy to a "Quick List," creating a personalized list of your most frequently purchased products. That saves you the trip of searching the aisles for these products the next time you're loading up the shopping cart.

8. **To add a product to your Quick List, simply check the checkbox that sits right next to the Quant. box. To delete the product from your Quick List, simply "uncheck" it.**

9. **When you've finished with this shelf, scroll down to the bottom of the listing and click on the Update Basket/Quick List button.**

10. **If you want to order other types of items, scroll to the top of the page, click on the Main link in the Navigation bar, and repeat Steps 5 through 9.**

11. **When you're done loading up your shopping basket, click on the green-underlined Basket link at the very bottom of the page.**

    This enables you to review your order, update the quantity of items or remove them from your cart. Now you're almost home free.

12. **Click on the red-underlined Check Out link to begin the check-out process.**

    First time buyers will be taken to a membership screen.

13. **Enter your personal and shipping information to register and click on the Register button.**

    You'll be taken to the Check Out Form.

14. **Fill out all the information to complete the checkout process, including your shipping and substitution preferences and payment info and the Press Button.**

15. **Enter your credit card information and press the Submit to Bank button.**

    Once the system gets the thumbs up from your credit card's issuing bank — which takes less than a minute — you'll get a thank you from the grocer. You will then receive an e-mail confirming your order with an electronic receipt of the items you bought for you to review and print for your record.

    Your order is delivered right to your doorstep, according to the delivery arrangements you specified.

To find other online grocery shopping sites, fire up one of your favourite search engines, such as Yahoo! Canada, to help you locate one, or you can check out (oops! it's hard to avoid puns) the links offered within the shopping guides of search engines and portals.

Chapter 5

One-Stop Virtual Shopping

*W*ell, we've had you trotting around the globe pretty good so far, right? One moment, you're in an electronic boutique in Zaire; the next, you're checking out Web sites with designer initials. You must be pooped. Why don't you take a load off, put down those packages, and rest a bit while we talk to you about centralizing our shopping efforts. Surfing around the Net looking for bargains here and there can be fun, but it can also eat up a lot of time.

You can focus your online buying trips on certain types of Web sites without losing the diversity. Hmmm . . . a central location with a lot of variety — that sounds an awful lot like a mall. Imagine it — mall shopping with no parking hassles! We're in heaven!

Making the Most of a Mall

Online malls take their structure from their earthbound cousins — a mixture of well-known stores and those carrying more unique merchandise — and combine it with the convenience of Internet shopping. What benefits does an online mall have over individual virtual stores? The following list describes a few of the key benefits:

> ✔ **A central search engine.** This feature's the equivalent of one of those big, ugly signs that you always find inside malls, often to the left of the fountains, which lists all the stores in itsy-bitsy type with colour-coded maps that no one who's sober can follow. You can search an online mall directory for the company name, category, and even product name you're seeking.

✔ **A shared shopping cart.** Imagine being able to go around to all the shops you want in a mall, carry around all your purchases, and need to stand in only one checkout line. Now imagine that you can add more of any item or, if you overspend (imagine *that*), drop one or more from your shopping cart — without needing to go back to the store to return it. That's exactly what you can do with an online shopping cart at an online mall.

✔ **A community of shoppers.** Whenever you're cybersurfing from individual store to individual store, you're out there all by your lonesome. Some of the biggest online malls, on the other hand, have common areas where like-minded folks (that is, bargain-crazed shopaholics) can gather and chat. Chat rooms, in fact, are great for getting leads to sales events and special promotions as well as for clearing up the odd technical question.

An online mall has one other really cool thing going for it that no real-world mall could match: Its stores can be located anywhere on the planet. The structure of the World Wide Web enables one central controlling Web site to contain links to a vast number of other sites. How vast? One of the largest of the online malls, the U.S.-based Internet Mall (at `www.internetmall.com`) has more than 27,000 stores affiliated with it.

Are Internet malls successful? Well, something must be attractive about them — since hundreds exist on the Web today. In Canada, malls are still just catching on. While some excellent sites are out there, you might also find some that are still under construction and others without the requisite centralized checkout counter (the mall just provides a link to an existing store site which may or may not sell online). But at the speed the Net is developing, you won't have long to wait before being able to choose from a broad range of Canadian online malls.

Hang a left at the @ sign: Finding the malls

Any number of road maps are available to get you to the Canadian cyber-malls. You can use your old, reliable Canadian search engine — type **"shopping malls"** or **"online malls"** into the Search text box, and you get back a bundle of links. Just make sure to limit your search to Canadian sites unless you're prepared for a cross-border shopping experience. (See Chapter 9 for details on buying abroad if you are.)

But another way to search for online malls is by using categories and directories in those search engines. By now, you've probably realized just how big this online shopping thing really is. So you shouldn't be at all surprised to discover that entire search engine categories are devoted to virtual malls. Searching by category is like peeling an onion — just as you think you're done, you find another layer. But don't worry; this type of onion doesn't make you feel like crying because the categories are actually taking you closer to your goal. Take a tour now into the depths of a category search: In Search of Online Malls! You start your journey by following these steps:

1. **Log onto your favourite Canadian search engine.**

   For this example, we're going to use Yahoo! Canada.

2. **On the search engine's main page, find the overall business category.**

   On Yahoo! Canada , it's the Business and Economy category.

3. **If any subcategory that seems relevant to your search appears underneath the main category, select it.**

   This action enables you to bypass one level of information. Yahoo! Canada, for example, has *Companies* listed as a subtopic. That's where we're going.

   Following the Yahoo! Canada trail, the subcategory *Companies* takes us to a screen listing lots of different types of companies.

4. **Select from the list that most closely matches what you're searching for.**

   In the Yahoo! Canada list, we spot *Retailers!* We figure that's a good place to start!

   We're right. The *Retailers* item in Yahoo! Canada is further subdivided into a huge number of subcategories including — drum roll please — *Virtual Malls.* Just the thing we've been looking for!

5. **Peruse the list of virtual malls from the list provided.**

   After selecting *Virtual Malls,* we get to a screen that has a few more subcategories followed by a long list of online mall links. In between, you see a Canada Only button. Click on this, and you'll notice the American mall listings and the subcategories disappear. They've been filtered out because they just don't exist on this side of the border. (If you choose not to filter, the Canadian malls appear first on the list, and have a little Canadian flag beside them, as shown in Figure 5-1.)

6. **Click on the mall you most want to visit.**

   Now you can shop 'til you drop!

   To recap this little journey, here's the path we took: Yahoo! Canada to Business and Economy to Companies to Retailers to Virtual Malls to the exhaustive list of malls (and if we choose, to the filtered list of Canadian malls). Hike!

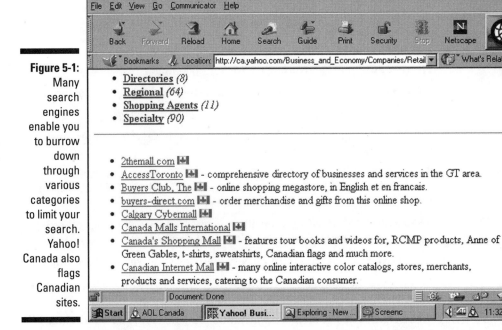

Figure 5-1:
Many
search
engines
enable you
to burrow
down
through
various
categories
to limit your
search.
Yahoo!
Canada also
flags
Canadian
sites.

A mall of malls

Not all malls are created equal — which is a good thing. You'll find as you explore
online malls that they break down into several different types, including:

- **Big Malls.** These malls are the 800-pound gorillas of online shopping.
  Many of these bigger malls include name-brand stores as well as a cornucopia of electronic boutiques.

- **Regional Malls.** This category consists of virtual malls designed to spot-
  light specific geographical areas, most with site-specific shops.

- **Ethnic Country Malls.** Ethnic malls feature centralized shopping arenas
  for online stores from particular countries.

- **Global Malls.** International malls emphasizing stores from different
  countries. A little cyber-trip to Bangkok, anyone? Try the International
  Cyber Mall (at www.959.com).

- **Theme Malls.** Some malls cater to specific tastes, like Multionline (at
  www.multionline.ca), a Quebec-based mall that sells mostly health
  and household products.

- **Virtual Villages.** These online malls are based on a small-town theme.
  Check out Planet411 (www.planet411.com), an online village that brings
  together shopping, services and information about Montreal, Toronto,
  and Vancouver.

Advanced Net surfin': Drop-down lists and frames

After you start checking out online malls, you may encounter a couple different ways of getting around within them. Instead of displaying a list of categories or stores all at once on-screen, for example, some malls feature a drop-down list navigational menu such as the one shown in the accompanying figure. You select the option arrow next to the list box and then highlight in the list the name of the area that you want to visit. Then select the button next to the drop-down list — usually something such as Go or Get It!

Occasionally, you run across a Web site that uses something called *frames*. Frames are Web pages in which one area of the screen is constant while other areas change according to the link that you select. You must have a fairly recent browser (Internet Explorer Version 3.0 or higher and anything from Navigator 2.0 on) to see frames correctly, but the upgrade's worth the effort so that you can view these frames. As you're surfing in a frame, the Back and Forward buttons change only a portion of the Web page.

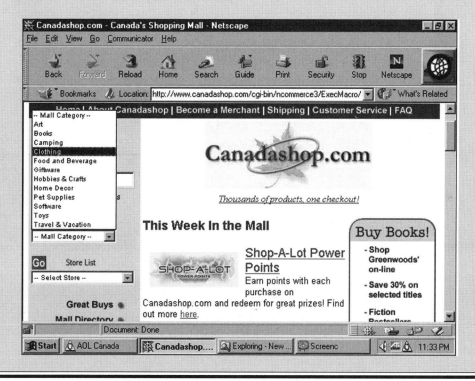

Mall specialties

After you find a mall that you want to explore, you have several routes that you can take. Most online malls include an internal search engine aimed at just their own merchants, which you can use to search for company, category, product, or brand. If you can't remember the name of the store, most malls also maintain an alphabetical index of all their stores, usually presented as a series of links from *A* to *Z*.

Online malls, as do their brick-and-concrete counterparts, sometimes run contests, highlight bargains, feature stores, and offer suggestions on what to buy. Many malls even run advisory services for making gift suggestions. Most often, this feature takes the form of a random, rotating series of advertisements for stores in the mall's fold.

One big Canadian virtual mall we've come across, Canadashop.com (at `www.canadashop.com`) bolsters its offerings with a newsletter to highlight mall specials. Some mega-malls even have *chat areas* so that you can drop in, kick your shoes off, and compare notes with your fellow shoppers. Let's use the example of a U.S.-based mall named Awesome Mall of the Internet (at `www.malls.com/awesome/`). Awesome (yes, we think the name's a bit much too) has a chat area called Café Chat. Here's how you attend these chat sessions:

1. **Connect to the chat area and read over its rules of conduct, or *netiquette,* if you're not familiar with them.**

2. **Scroll down the page until you see a chat window similar to the one shown in Figure 5-2.**

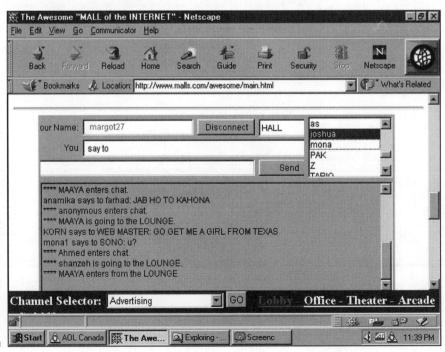

Figure 5-2: Coffee cake, anyone? Some major online malls feature chat areas such as this one, where you can connect with visitors from around the world.

3. **Enter the name you want to use during this chat session in the Your Name (or similarly labeled) text box.**

   You can pick any name or alias that you want to use.

4. **Select the Connect button to jump into the ongoing chat.**

   The main chat window begins filling with messages being passed back and forth among chat attendees.

   Chat areas generally have several rooms through which you can move.

5. **To move from room to room in a chat area, choose the option arrow next to the current location to open a drop-down list and then pick another area from the list.**

6. **To send a message to everyone in the room, first select the Everyone option from the open list of current visitors.**

7. **Type your message in the text box above the main message window and then click the Send button.**

8. **To send a message to only one person, choose a name from the visitors list and repeat Step 7.**

   You can also change how you "speak" to people by choosing among several options, ranging from *say* to *whisper* and *shout.* With the exception of *whisper,* these choices just alter how your message appears on screen, like "John says to Clarice" or "Herman shouts at Ishmael" — however, when you choose to whisper, your message is sent only to one person and doesn't appear in the public chat window.

9. **To change how you speak to others in the chat room, click the option arrow and select a new option from the drop-down list that appears.**

10. **After you finish chatting, click the Disconnect button and surf to another area of the Web.**

Chat areas are a great deal of fun, but you want to exercise a little caution. We recommend that you don't use your real name or give out any personal details, such as a phone number or address, while you're chatting online. Remember that you're in a room with complete strangers — use the same common sense that you'd use in a similar situation offline.

Backorder No More: Catalogues Online

The package you've been waiting for finally arrives, and it's a big one, too. You tear into it, ripping past layer after layer of packing peanuts and shipping stuffing. You extract one teeny-weeny box (instead of the six that you expect) with a shipping invoice attached. The words stab at you: backorder, *backorder,* BACKORDER! Oh, the horror . . . the horror!

At one time, mail-ordering from catalogues offered the perfect shopping experience — it was more convenient for shoppers and cheaper for storeowners. As competition grew the catalogues got more expensive to produce and to distribute. Furthermore, you could never be sure what you were getting or when you were getting your order. Telephone orders were better, but only if the computers weren't down — which seemed to be every time *we* called. Cause and effect?

Well, move over mail order, a new king's in town, known as the Online Catalogue Kid, and he's not taking any backorders. Not only is online catalogue shopping better for customers, it's waaaaaay better for merchants.

Online catalogue advantages: Company side

Why is this category of online shopping one growing fast? The following sections take a look at some of the contributing factors in this cyber phenomenon.

No paper costs

Ever receive one of those notices in the mail that read, "Because of rising paper costs, we can't keep sending you our catalogues unless you buy something from us. So *buy* something, for cryin' out loud!" One of the reasons that prices for catalogue items are no longer as competitive (read *cheap*) as they once were is that, nowadays, printing out the little suckers costs more for the merchants who send out the catalogues.

Not so on the Web. The only paper costs that merchants must bear is for those three-part shipping forms that read, "Thank you for your order." We think that they can handle that much, don't you?

Instant updatability

How many paper catalogues do major companies put out a year? Usually, at least one per season. And still, at various times, a product is available for sale in the stores but no one knows about it.

A company can update its Web page, on the other hand, with very little effort and almost no time delay. Stores are now developing techniques for repurposing their images and copy to make the transition from print to Web effortless.

Got a special sale? Put a blinking, swirling "Hey Buddy, we gotta Sale!" sign on your home page. Better yet, send out an e-mail bulletin to all your online customers and tell them almost simultaneously about the sale — without licking all those stamps.

Order automation

From an owner's perspective, one of the coolest things about having a customer ordering through the computer is that the customer *is* ordering through a computer. The customer's computer talks to the store's computer, which checks to make sure that the merchandise is in stock, adds up the shipping, processes the payment, and sends the order to be fulfilled. The process is all digital, with none of those messy analog-type folks around to muck things up.

Online catalogue advantages: Customer side

Okay, you're sold and you're on your way out the door to start your own online catalogue company. Wait — you haven't yet heard about the benefits that online catalogue shopping offers you, Joe and Jane Consumer.

Straight from our office to you, here are the top ten reasons why you should go online catalogue shopping:

- **Reason Number 10:** You can order anytime that you want without needing to wait for the next available operator. (That's what Marguerite's going to name her kid — Next Available Operator — so that a job's always there waiting.)

- **Reason Number 9:** You can usually search a Web site to look for a particular product easier than you can find most anything in a catalogue's index.

- **Reason Number 8:** You can browse entire departments to see the latest goods at the click of a button.

- **Reason Number 7:** You can order the regular paper catalogue online for poor Aunt Sophie, who's still living without a computer, without needing to listen to "Symphonie Muzak à Telephono," while you wait for the infamous Next Available Operator.

- **Reason Number 6:** You can change your mind about how many chiffon sweaters you want a zillion times without wrecking the order coupon.

- **Reason Number 5:** You don't need to wait for the catalogue to come to you — you can go to it.

- **Reason Number 4:** You don't need to find the most current catalogue in the stack o' catalogues by the fireplace. Whoops — was that one last night's kindling?

- **Reason Number 3:** You can order only those items in stock instead of playing Russian Roulette with the guy who actually pulls the items off the shelf.

> ✔ **Reason Number 2:** You can comparison-shop across competing catalogues at the same time.
>
> ✔ **And the Number 1 Reason why you should go online catalogue shopping:** You can keep handy confirmations of all your orders all in one place — your electronic in-basket — without needing to remember and rewrite all the details.

How 'bout one more to grow on? You never get one of those half-threatening, half-begging letters that start out with "Because of rising paper costs. . . ."

Whose catalogue is online?

In Canada, a lot of catalogue-producing companies have Web sites, but fewer take online orders. You might have to dig around a bit for catalogues that offer the full online experience. Here's a sampling of some that do:

✔ Arbour Recycled Products (www.arbour.on.ca)

✔ The Canadian Heritage Company (www.cdnheritageco.mb.ca)

✔ Cape Breton Catalogue (www.capebretonsmagazine.com)

✔ Prior Snowboards (www.priorsnowboards.com)

✔ Sears Canada (www.sears.ca)

✔ The Shopping Channel (www.tse.ca)

✔ Uniquely Canadian (www.novator.com/UC-Catalog)

✔ Zellers (www.hbc.com/zellers)

Doing the catalogue shuffle

Most of what you discover in your other online shopping sprees you can apply to online catalogues as well. Almost all sites have an internal search engine through which you can track down a specific item — and those sites that don't have a search engine generally contain extensive category listings so that you can quickly zoom in on your target.

A number of sites enable you to choose between a text and a visual display. If you're shopping in a hurry, choose the text option. You don't get as much of the pretty graphic layout — just enough to keep it interesting — but the Web pages load much faster. If you can spend a few more moments, however, the visual (default) mode is worth the ride.

Ready to get your feet wet? Take a stroll through a typical online catalogue shopping session by following these steps:

1. **After you're online, plug your favourite online catalogue Web address into the Address text box of your browser.**

   Both of us love window shopping at Canadian shoe designer John Fluevog's Web site at www.fluevog.com. (The details in the following steps may vary a tad on other sites, but the concepts are similar.)

2. **After you reach the site's home page, choose any of the categories (families of shoes in this case) from the navigation buttons at the left side of the screen.**

   Depending on the site, you can also contact customer service, get help on how to order, search for a gift, read the company brochure, or ask for a paper catalogue by selecting any of the labels across the top of the screen.

   After you arrive at your chosen category, you find links to six or seven items. As shown in Figure 5-3, Fluevog lets you see photos of all the shoe styles within each family of shoes.

3. **Select one of the items.**

   At Fluevog, click on a shoe you like! A more detailed photo will appear as well as a list of colour options. At some catalogue sites, you choose the item you like from a drop-down list, and then click on the Go button or an item link before viewing it.

Figure 5-3: John Fluevog's online catalogue offers secure, convenient shopping for very cool shoes.

4. **Once you've taken a good look at the item you like, and you make up your mind that you just gotta have it, click the Order Now Button.**

   Some sites have a Buy It button instead. Whatever it's called, the button drops the item into your shopping cart. You can now move on to other items, and repeat these steps to add those to your cart.

5. **Click on the Shopping Cart icon to finish the ordering process.**

   Other sites will offer you products related to your purchase before you check out. (If so, there will be a *No Thanks* button or something similar.) You might also be able to increase the quantity of an item by clicking into the Quantity text box and typing in a larger or smaller number.

   Fluevog asks you to choose your shoe size and preferred colour. You can take an item out of your shopping cart by removing the check mark to the left of the shoe photograph and clicking the Redisplay Cart button.

6. **Click on the Check Out button, read through the shipping info and begin your journey through the Valley of Personal Info (where you tell all about your credit card, shipping info, and so on).**

   In the Order Summary, Fluevog displays the total cost of the order *before* taxes and shipping. Once you've submitted your order form online, Fluevog will contact you via e-mail with an order confirmation, including the total cost with taxes and shipping.

Once you get your order confirmation, your delightful new shoes will be on their way. And you thought catalogues were old-fashioned!

Tapping the Portals

Here's an idea: To make sense of the vast reaches of the Web, why not group together a bit of everything people are looking for out there — products, services, a search engine, and so on — and create a spot people can call home? Not a bad plan, eh? Well, turns out a lot of companies think so too because these homey spots, or *portals* (gateways to the Net), are all the rage. A portal is like a home base but better because it brings a lot of the Web's content to you through partnerships. Most portals break that content down into categories, which they call *channels*. The good news for you shoppers is that many portals now have shopping channels among their list of options.

Many portals give you the option of setting the site up as your *home page* — the first site you're computer takes you to when you get online. This is a good option considering the content many have to offer. It's a good option for the site too, since your return visits can mean increased ad revenue. You should see a button labeled Make This Site Your Home Page or Set Default Home Page (or some similar phrase) on the portal's main screen. Just click on the button and follow the steps to change your browser settings.

ISP Portals

Who runs the portals and how can you get to one? That's easy. Just get online! Unless you've changed your settings, you'll automatically start every Web adventure at the Web site operated by your Internet provider (or ISP for you cyber-talkers). This is the company that provides your uplink to the Net. Although there are hundreds of regional ISPs in Canada, only a handful are available nationwide. Happily, many of these have transformed their Web sites into portals. Even more happily, you don't always have to be a subscriber to access their shopping channels. You'll probably recognize some of these Canadian ISPs:

Sympatico

It's not really surprising that Sympatico (at `www.sympatico.ca`) is Canada's most subscribed-to ISP, with over 600,000 member households. After all, the service is owned the company that probably provides your local phone service. Sympatico has a great overall portal, with products and services ranging from news to online Yellow Pages to job postings. You can get to the shopping channel by clicking the *Shop Online* link.

Once inside the Marketplace, you have a range of products and services to choose from, as shown in Figure 5-4, including:

- **Shopping partners**. Just click on the retailer you'd like to visit and you'll be transported to their site.

- **Shopping tools**. Sympatico has links to existing consumer info sites, including a buyer's guide, a comparison shopping guide, a currency converter and more. Keep in mind, some of these sites are U.S.-based — meaning no Canadian dollar listings.

- **Shopping locator**. Under the Canada Toll-Free heading, you can look up toll-free numbers for merchants across the country by choosing a category or entering a keyword in the Search box.

- **Shopping advisories**. Sympatico answers your FAQs on many aspects of e-commerce and online shopping safety.

- **Shopping in-house**. You can buy from Sympatico's own store or use its travel service by clicking on either icon.

Internet Direct

Another excellent ISP portal site is run by Internet Direct (at `www.mydirect.com`). Get to the shopping channel by clicking the Shop tab from the list across the top of the home page. Here too, you'll find a list of Internet Direct's retail partners who get prominent display down the middle of the screen. There are also links to travel car and home sale services. But what we like best is the exhaustive list of links to Canadian online stores on one side of the screen, and U.S. stores on the other. Most of these sites offer the full online buying experience.

Figure 5-4:
Some ISP portals have extensive shopping services, like those offered by Canada's biggest ISP, Sympatico.

Sprint Canada

Starting at the Sprint Canada's portal (at www.sprint.ca), click on Shopping in the Channel Guide. On top of links to some large Canadian shopping sites, including Indigo Books and CD-Plus, you are also given the option of conducting a search for any type of merchandise you're looking for via the Lycos search engine — although you'll find the results will provide mostly U.S. sites.

AOL Canada

America Online is a monolith on the world stage, with more than 17 million members. What makes AOL unique is that you always remain within the AOL service, no matter where you travel on the Web. Using this approach, AOL gives you access to content that you can't find anywhere else on the Web and makes it easy to get back to where you started.

In Canada, consumers who subscribe to the AOL Canada service have access to the members-only AOL Canada content and features (we can't list a URL address because like we said, it's members-only). This easy, convenient and secure portal offers a wide variety of shopping options including an internal search engine, an extensive list of categories with links to Canadian stores, a download store with over 100,000 digital products, and a shoppers chat area much like the mall chat rooms we discussed earlier in the section called "Mall Specialties".

To access AOL Canada's Shopping channel, sign on and choose the Shopping button from the side content bar on the AOL Today welcome screen or the "Channels" button from the top navigation tool bar (in Version 4.0 of AOL Canada).

One unique service that deserves some time here is AOL Canada's Reminder Service. It acts as your personal assistant to help you remember as many dates and events as you want — and then sends you an e-mail reminder two weeks before, complete with a few shopping suggestions. And if you've made it to Absent Minded Professor status, you can even get a second nudge four days before the event.

Here's how the Reminder Service works:

1. **From the Shopping Channel's main menu screen, click the Reminder Service button on the bottom half of the screen.**

2. **Once you click the Free Reminder button, you're given the option to Create Your Reminder or Edit Your Reminder.**

3. **To set up an account, click Create Your Reminder.**

   When you first sign up, you're asked to enter your name and sex. In addition to personal reminders like anniversaries or birthdays, you can also elect to receive reminders about upcoming holidays.

4. **Click the Continue button to begin entering the particular reminder information.**

5. **Type the gift recipient's name, the occasion, and the date in a *mm-dd* format (that is, type 02-10 for February 10) and then mark (or leave blank) the check box that determines whether the occasion's an annual event.**

   You can, if you want, also note whether the reminder's for a child, teen, or adult male or female. This information sets the gift-referral wheels in motion.

6. **Click the Save button after you finish entering this information.**

   AOL Canada's Reminder Service then adds your information to your personal reminder list, as shown in Figure 5-5. As you add more reminders, by selecting either the Add Personal Reminder or Holiday Reminder buttons, the service includes them alphabetically among your reminders.

7. **To change information on any reminder, highlight it in your reminder list and click the Edit button.**

8. **To remove a reminder from your list, highlight that entry and click the Remove button.**

9. **After you're completely done setting or changing reminders, click the Quit button on your reminder list window.**

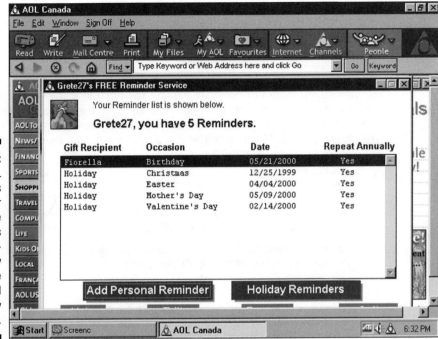

As the reminder comes due, you get a pleasant electronic tap on the shoulder via e-mail, complete with a couple of gift suggestions and direct links to pertinent stores — not all of which are Canadian.

It's worth a visit AOL Canada's non-members portal (at www.aol.ca) as well. Here you can access all of the same Canadian stores that are available to members and many of the same services.

@Home

In Canada, there are several ways to connect to the Internet using an ISP. One relatively new way is through your cable hook-up instead of your phone line. Four of the biggest cable companies, Rogers, Shaw, Cogeco and Videon have signed up together to offer this service using a fully-Canadianized version of an American portal system called @Home. Depending on which of these companies you subscribe to, you'll see a slightly different portal, but the shopping channel is the same for all of them. You'll find it among the channel tabs listed across the top of the portal home page. There's an excellent index of links to shops, including some in the U.S. (but only those that ship to Canada). There are also extensive Canadian listings and some prominently-displayed @Home partners including the Canadian online auction house Bid.com, as shown in Figure 5-6.

Like the members-only AOL Canada service, the @Home portals are specially designed for people who subscribe to the service.

Figure 5-6:
Link to
popular
shopping
sites
through the
@Home
shopping
channel.

Non-ISP portals

Your Internet provider isn't the only game in town when it comes to portals. Remember, we said they were *all* the rage! Many other companies are putting together broad content-based portals in Canada including, prominently:

Canoe

You'll see us refer to Canoe (at www.canoe.ca) often in this book. That's because it's an appealing portal that we Canadians have made very popular! Get to Canoe's shopping channel by clicking Shopping to the left of the title bar, or by selecting it from the drop-down list on the right and clicking on Go! The main screen is called the Canoe Trading Post. Here, you're presented with several shopping options including direct links to featured Canadian stores and merchandise by category (listings appear under the subheadings "Canadian sites" and "U.S. and Foreign Sites"). Canoe even has its own merchandise to sell.

Canada.com

Canada.com (at www.canada.com) is a similar portal to Canoe, offering everything from news to horoscopes to weather to — you guessed it — shopping. Get to Canada.com's featured stores using the direct links on the right side of the portal's home page. But for the site's giant directly of online stores, you should click on More Shopping.

MSN Canada

We're partial to Microsoft's Canadian portal, called MSN Canada (at http://ca.msn.com), because you can personalize the portal home page to include just the info you want to see. You can also store your custom-designed settings you will see them whenever you visit the site. Go to the list of Things To Do on the left side of the page and click on MSN Shopping to view that channel — shown in Figure 5-7. Once you're inside the shopping channel, you add links for your favourite stores to the main portal page by clicking on the blue arrow under Quick Links. You can further customize shopping features by choosing Personalize from the MSN Canada's main navigation bar and selecting Shopping.

Figure 5-7: MSN Canada's shopping channel has links to a number of Canadian online shopping destinations.

Chapter 6

I Found It in the Online Classifieds

. . . .

In This Chapter

▶ Honey, where's the classified section?

▶ Deal Making 101

▶ Clearing out your garage, online

. . . .

*F*OR SALE: One blue dress, women's designer. Worn on just one occasion, but was not dry cleaned. Contact mlewinsky@whitehouseinterns.com.

WANTED: One glove, man's sequined. Willing to pay top dollar for matching unit. Need second glove for comeback. Contact mjackson@thriller.com.

You never know what you may find in the online classifieds — but one thing's for sure: You can find a lot. And Canadians are getting into the act. Although classified advertising has long been a staple in newspapers, it's a relatively new phenomenon electronically speaking. Just as in the papers, classifieds are based on ordinary people buying and selling to other ordinary people, although businesses occasionally get in the act as well. And, just as with the get-your-fingers-all-smudgy variety of classifieds, you need to exercise a little caution — and a fair amount of common sense — in buying anything from a total stranger.

This chapter shows you how to accomplish the following tasks in dealing with online classifieds:

✔ Hunt down the best bargains.

✔ Get in touch with the seller.

✔ Make all the arrangements online.

✔ Protect yourself from scams and not-nice people.

✔ Post your own classified and clear out some of that junk — er, we mean, pre-owned merchandise — from your garage, attic, closet, or what have you.

The Best Classifieds for You

As is the case with so many items on the Internet, finding classifieds isn't a problem; finding the right classifieds . . . ah, now that's a different story. Not only are you looking for a special product, but you're also looking for a good price, and, if at all possible, a Canadian seller who lives in your neck of the woods.

You can begin your exploration in any of several ways: the search engine route, the sites dedicated to classifieds, and the regional classified Web sites. In the following sections, we examine each in turn to help you find the method that's right for you — and, thereby, the product that lights your fire.

One area of the classifieds you find everywhere online, although we don't cover it in this book: the *personals*. Selling yourself and shopping for a mate are topics for about a dozen *other* books.

Searching for classifieds

Looking for something in particular? Something that you just can't find anywhere else? Something that no one in your hometown is selling in the local Penny Pincher? Time to fire up the search engines!

Throughout this chapter, we introduce you to sites specifically designed for classified advertising. Those are great for honing in on category after category — but sometimes just one little thing isn't in any category. There are small Canadian sites on the Web that cater to specialty items. All you need to do is find them.

Here's an easy step-by-step test to run:

1. **Log on to a search engine that searches Canadian Web sites, like AltaVista Canada (**www.altavistacanada.com**).**

2. **Select the Canada option above the Search text box.**

   This limits your search to Web sites based in Canada or sites that have Canadian content.

3. **In the Keyword text box, type the name of whatever off-the-wall item you're looking for, along with the word** classifieds.

   If the name is a phrase, like *beanie babies* — strange, cuddly, stuffed animals people all over the world go nuts for — put quotes around it like this, "beanie babies".

4. **Put a plus sign in front of your word or phrase, and in front of the word** classifieds **so that the results appears as follows:**

   ```
   +"beanie babies" +classifieds
   ```

Remember that the plus signs force a search engine to return links to Web pages that include both keywords. In this case, we're using a phrase, so we type it in quotes and put the plus sign outside the quotes. This forces the search engine to return only the links that contain that particular phrase, as well as the word classifieds.

5. **Select the Search or the Go button — whatever turns your search engine loose on your request.**

We've uncovered some relatively obscure Web sites that house specialized classified sections by using this method. For example, using the preceding search criteria, we found an excellent site (http://www.jam.ca/syrup), where you can buy pure Quebec maple syrup, as shown in Figure 6-1.

Search-engine classifieds

Several of the popular American-based search engines like AOL.COM, Yahoo!, WebCrawler, and HotBot have classified sections. Or they provide links to sites like Classifieds2000, a giant in the world of online buying and selling, open to folks around the world. The problem for Canadians is that most of the people doing business at these sites are south of the border. That means prices are in U.S. dollars, and you will likely get stuck paying special fees,

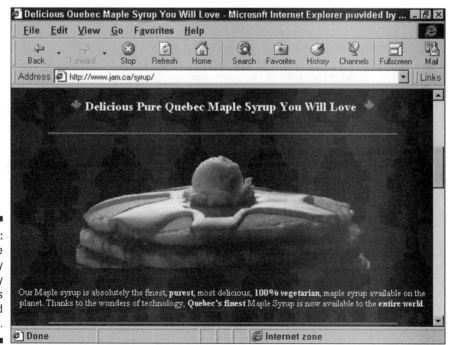

Figure 6-1:
You'll be surprised by how many sweet deals you'll find online.

taxes, and duty when you ship your purchase home. Before you buy from a U.S. site, see Chapter 9 for all the details on shipping and clearing customs. For now, we suggest you start right here at home.

If you live in a border area, it might still be worth your while to check out the classifieds at the U.S. version of Yahoo!, since the listings are organized into specific areas of the country. For example, it could be worth the drive from Windsor to Detroit if you find a once-in-a-lifetime deal there. Keep in mind, duty, GST, and provincial sales taxes will apply when you bring your purchase through customs. To get to Yahoo! Classifieds, start at Yahoo! Canada (www.ca.yahoo.com) and select Today's News⇨Yahoo! Classifieds.

Sites dedicated to classifieds

On the Web, the hotter the issue, the more sites are dedicated to it. So it is with online classifieds. The more Canadians want to buy and sell electronically, the more sites are being built to help find them do so. Still, Canadian classified sites are pretty young in the big scheme of things, so be prepared for a smaller pool of listings, and some homegrown graphics.

CanSell.com

CanSell.com (www.cansell.com) is a site that lists classifieds from across Canada. If you're in the market to buy, you can browse the listings for free. There are several main categories, each containing subcategories. In an interesting twist, you can pinpoint which part of the country you want to buy from using maps. Here's how to look for an item:

1. **Select a general category and subcategory.** For example, select General Merchandise, and then on the next screen, Furniture.

2. **Specify your price range by typing the amount into each of the two text boxes.** Indicate the price to the nearest dollar. Don't use decimal points or the dollar sign.

   Although setting a price range is a nice option, we recommend leaving these boxes blank in order to get the widest range of listings.

3. **Indicate how far from home you're willing to search by using the drop-down list of distances.**

   The default is set to 200km, but you can go up to 2,500km from home, or down to as few as 3km. Ah! Canadian geography! It's a many-kilometred thing!

4. **Enter your postal code or select a province from the map of Canada with your mouse.**

   If you choose the postal code option, enter the code and select search. If you go the map route (pun very much intended!), you'll see a blow-up of the province you've selected, including the names of cities and towns.

5. **Click on a more specific region from the provincial map to hone your search, or, to search the whole province, select the name of the province that appears at the bottom of the map.**

   In Figure 6-2, you can see that we've selected the entire province of Nova Scotia as the place to conduct our search. The arrow and shaded area indicate the province name.

6. **Click on Search.**

   CanSell comes back with a list of likely candidates that match your criteria, including a brief description of the item, a contact number, and the town or city where the seller lives. Some listings even include photos.

7. **Get in touch with whoever's selling, and you're in business!**

Canada Classifieds

Canada Classifieds (`www.canadaclassifieds.com`) has two advantages over your hometown newspaper's classifieds: It's nationwide, and it's free. The home page is divided into main sections. Each section contains a number of categories of goods or services, as shown in Figure 6-3. Here's how to look for that special something:

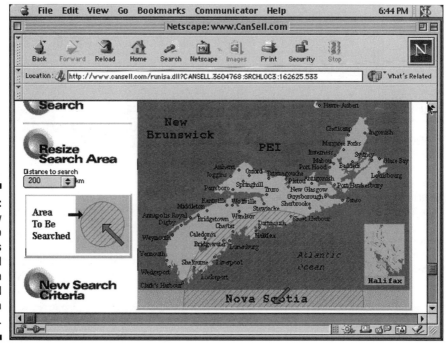

Figure 6-2:
The arrow on this map indicates that CanSell will search for ads in all of Nova Scotia.

1. **Select the icon in the section that most closely resembles what you're looking for, like Sporting Goods.**

2. **Select one category, like Archery, from the list of categories.**

3. **Browse the listings.**

   Notice that each listing has a brief description of the item as well as a contact phone number and/or e-mail address.

4. **Get in touch with the seller and, in the spirit of Monty Hall, make yourself a deal!**

JustCanadian.com

JustCanadian.com (www.justcanadian.com) is a free online classified service available to Canadians from every province. If you're buying, the site gives you two search options.

✔ **Search by province:** To stay local, select your province name from the "street" directory on the JustCanadian home page. On the next screen, select that province name again from the drop-down list called Go Express – Province and click on Go!

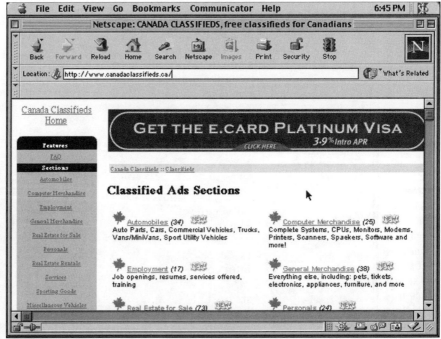

Figure 6-3:
The home page at Canada Classifieds shows you a list of major sections, each including several categories of goods and services.

What you see now might seem a bit confusing. This screen looks the same as the last, but it's not. You can now select any of the categories near the bottom of the page to see classified listings for the province you've specified.

✔ **Search nationally:** If you go to the bottom of the home page, you'll see a drop-down list called Canada-wide search. Pick a category and click on Go! You'll get a list of all the current listings for that category, in all the provinces.

Regional classifieds

We know what you're thinking! Web sites that list classifieds from across Canada and the world are nice, but you just want to be able to pick up an old record player for a few bucks. Can't you look for ads only in your own area without resorting to all these flibberity-gibbets? Well, hold on to your jargon; in the following sections, we take you on a tour of all the regional classified resources available to you.

Regular papers online

A vast number of Canada's metropolitan and community newspapers are now online — and almost every single one has a classifieds section. Some of the biggest online newspapers, such as The Toronto Star (`www.thestar.com`) and The Vancouver Sun (`www.vancouversun.com`), have extensive classified advertisement sections online. But keep in mind, placing an ad at one of these Web sites does not necessarily mean your ad appears in the actual newspaper. Then again, so many people have access to your online ad, it may not matter!

Whenever an online newspaper or other Web site says that it can remember your password, what it's really doing is storing the information on your own computer and calling it up whenever you log onto the site. In browser jargon, the paper's computer has passed your computer a *cookie*. A cookie is a few lines of information that's written onto your hard drive to enable the online service to keep better track of you. All the current browser versions enable you to choose whether to receive cookies all the time or only on a case-by-case basis. Internet Explorer 4.0 users can choose View⇨Internet Options and then click the Advanced tab to see and change cookie preferences. Communicator 4.0 users can choose Edit⇨Preferences and select the Advanced category to alter cookie options.

Most of the larger papers post their classifieds daily. Some, like the Winnipeg Free Press (`www.mbnet.mb.ca/freepress`), give you the option of searching back-issues, as shown in Figure 6-4. All the papers organize their classifieds in familiar categories to keep your search as simple as possible.

Figure 6-4:
The Winnipeg Free Press gives you the option of searching back issues for classified listings, rather than just the new ads.

City networks

Several online services now exist to link up a large number of regional papers. Use them to locate the newspapers in your region that are online, and get access to the broadest possible range of goodies for sale.

Canoe

You can find links to many of Canada's daily newspapers at Canoe (`www.canoe.ca`), one of Canada's most popular Web sites. That's because Sun Media Inc., which owns part of Canoe, also owns newspapers across the country. Here's how to access its online classifieds:

1. **Select the Newstand option from the drop-down window on the top right-hand side of the Canoe home page and click on Go!**

2. **Choose Classifieds from the top menu bar.**

   Canoe takes you to a screen where you can access the classifieds from several Sun newspapers across the country by clicking either one of the cross-referenced bullets in the table provided, or one of the categories listed across the top of the screen, as shown in Figure 6-5.

Canoe's classifieds page also provides direct links to more Sun Media newspapers, like The London Free Press and The Halifax Herald. Click the newspaper's name and that link takes you directly to that newspaper's online classifieds.

Cross-referenced Bullet

Category

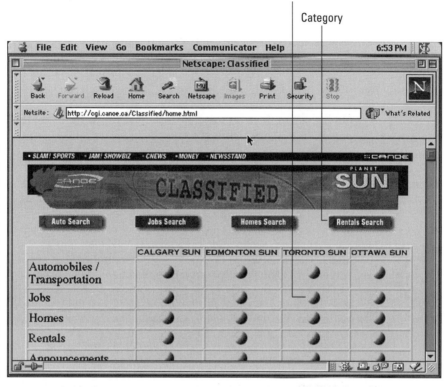

Figure 6-5:
Browse the classifieds in several Sun newspapers at once by selecting one of the categories at the top of Canoe's classified page.

AOL Canada links its online service members to the AOL U.S. service's classifieds, but they do offer thoroughly Canadian job listings through a partnership with The Globe and Mail newspaper. Globecareers.com (www.globecareers.com) is a search engine that helps you find job postings in every province for all sorts of careers. To use it, select "Careers" from the list of *AOL Web Centres* and then click on Search for a job. It is also available at AOL's non-member web portal, AOL.CA.

Canada.com

Canada.com (www.Canada.com), a search engine operated by the Southam Inc. newspaper chain, can also help you access regional newspapers. They're listed at the bottom of the Canada.com home page. Just click onto the newspaper you want, and off you go. To make your life easier, Southam has standardized the online classifieds of many of its papers. They've also consolidated all the car and job listings from newspapers in several cities into two user-friendly sites: Carclick.com (www.carclick.com) and Careerclick.com (www.careerclick.com). You can look in one city or many, for today's listings, or last week's. The search engine scans the classifieds of the newspapers you specify.

Bowes

Another important site for accessing regional classifieds is the Bowes Publishers home page (www.bowesnet.com). Bowes Publishers Ltd. owns a big chunk of Canada's weekly papers, and guess what? They've got them all linked up so you can access all their online classifieds. Here's how to take advantage of their generosity:

1. **Select the Classifieds option from the Bowes homepage.**

2. **Choose a province and specify whether you want to search all of the papers in that area, or just some.**

3. **Enter a key word or phrase like** farm equipment.

4. **Select Search.**

   The search results will show you listings that include a description of the item as well as a contact number.

There are still more online networks linking up regional newspapers and their classifieds. The ones we've discussed so far are national in scope, but others keep it local. Folks in New Brunswick, for example, can use NBClassified (www.nbclassified.com), a site where you can search several of the province's leading newspapers all at once, as shown in Figure 6-6. To find other sites like this one, try using a Canadian search engine and typing a phrase composed of a province name and the word classifieds. For example, Manitoba classifieds.

Figure 6-6:
There are regional networks all over the Web including this site, NBClassifieds.

Answering a Classified Ad

"Okay, we're gonna ask you again. Mr. Hoo saw an online ad from Ms. Watt for a talking alarm clock, the Wenn XL, and now he wants to buy it from her. How does he do it?"

"Who wants what from whom?"

"No, Hoo wants Wenn from Watt."

"Wait, who wants the clock?"

"That's right."

"So who has it?"

"No, Watt has it."

"Has what?"

"Wenn."

"Now. Who has it now?"

"No, Watt has it, but Hoo wants it."

"When?"

"That's right."

Boing! That's the sound of brains exploding while trying to figure out how to transact business between two complete strangers without either of them taking a risk. The seller can't send the buyer the goods until the buyer pays him, and the buyer can't send the money until the goods arrive. Sending your credit-card info to a company with a secure Web site that you trust is one thing, but just how do you handle such person-to-person dealings online?

Canadian classified transactions have been carried out successfully on the Web for quite some time now, but you need to learn some of the steps if you want to join the dance. The exact method that you use and the precautions you take are up to you and the other party involved in the transaction. Ultimately, however, the whole thing comes down to you: You must feel comfortable with your arrangements or, whatever the bargain is, it's not worth it.

Cheque 'em out

Generally, the ball starts rolling for an online classified after the buyer sends an e-mail to the seller reading, in effect: "I want that." The buyer and the seller could be next-door neighbours or a world apart — that's the reality of electronic communication. One of the first bits of information to exchange in such a transaction should be contact info: real names, real addresses, and real phone numbers. The more personal data that's revealed, the more secure both parties feel.

If possible, get — and give — both a home and a work number, especially if you're looking at buying some pricey merchandise. After you have those numbers, use them. Call the buyer at home to confirm the details — and to confirm the number. Most people selling online goods want to feel as good about you as you do about them, and mutual reassurance is a genuinely good thing.

You find a lot of folks on the Net purporting to be the biggest dealers around. If they're claiming to be a business, feel free to check them out as you would any business. Ask, for example, for references from satisfied customers. Legitimate companies have no problem spreading the word about their honest business dealings.

If you're not satisfied with the answers you're getting, move on to the next classified ad. Making a safe choice is far more important than making an immediate choice. Similarly, if the seller you contact doesn't want to work with you so that you're comfortable, just say, "Thanks, but no thanks," and find another deal. As you quickly see, you can find no shortage of sources for online classifieds.

Payment options

When you get down to the nitty-gritty, what form of payment should you use? Credit cards are no good in such deals unless you're ordering from a store or a sizable dealer. Cheques take weeks to clear. Cash is so big a no-no that we can't even begin to tell you about it. What's left?

Many classified sellers and buyers agree on using a *cash-on-delivery,* or *COD,* arrangement. Although the form of payment for CODs can vary — anything from a personal check to cash — the best way to go for all parties is to use the "cash or certified cheque" option available from Canada Post and courier companies like Purolator and UPS. This way, the seller doesn't need to worry about the cheque clearing, and the buyer doesn't need to worry about paying for something and waiting for it to show up.

Who exactly pays the shipping, insurance, and COD fees is up for grabs. Some online classifieds note that the asking price includes shipping as an incentive to get a buyer. (In Chapter 9, we'll walk you through the ins and outs of COD's.)

Trusted third parties

Because of the amount of business handled through the Web in classified dealings, a couple of online services have sprouted to manage these thorny payment issues. Called *transaction* or *escrow services,* these companies act as a trusted third party for a small fee.

All transaction services act as an intermediary between the buyer and the seller. The buyer sends the payment to the service and the service holds on to the money until the goods arrive. Then it sends the payment to the seller. One such transaction service company is *Trade-Direct* (at www.trade-direct.com).

Trade-Direct is a U.S. company, but we Canucks can use it too, particularly when buying something from a stranger in the U.S. It does require payment for its services in U.S. dollars. When you pay by credit card, the currency conversion is automatic. Trade-Direct asks Canadians to prove our existence — move over Descartes! It requires you to fax in a copy of your latest credit card statement, including the part that shows your address and card number. Your other payment options are to buy an international money order for the total amount in Canadian dollars, or have the amount wired from a bank, also in Canadian dollars. (Yep, these services will cost you a fee.)

Trade-Direct has two different services: the *Standard Service* and the *Service For Large Amounts.* For most cross-border classified transactions between Canada and the U.S. valued at less than US$1,500, the Standard Service is the better choice. Here's how it works, step by step:

1. **After both buyer and seller agree to use this service, log on to** www.trade-direct.com.

2. **Click the Start Transaction link.**

3. **After the application opens, specify whether you are a buyer or seller and fill out the on-screen form, as shown in Figure 6-7.**

   Aside from your own information, you need to know the following:

   • The seller's address and phone number.

   • The agreed-on price.

- The agreed-on examination period (time for the buyer to make sure that everything's in working order).

- Description of the merchandise being bought.

4. **After you complete the form, select the Submit button.**

Trade-Direct then sends e-mail confirmations to both parties and asks for payment from the buyer.

5. **Pay Trade-Direct by one of the methods we've discussed, and wait for your goody to arrive.**

Note: Trade-Direct requires you to pay an additional service charge for using plastic.

Canadian buyers beware! Unless you've made other arrangements to have the person you're buying from pay for all the extras, you will be billed for shipping fees, taxes, and applicable duty on whatever you're importing from the U.S.

After payment clears, the seller gets the okay to ship the goods to the buyer. Trade-Direct then tracks the shipment. After the buyer receives the goodies, she has an examination period of two or more days. Unless a problem turns up, Trade-Direct sends the seller a check at the end of the examination

Figure 6-7:
The Trade-Direct Application starts the safe transaction process between buyer and seller once you indicate which one is you.

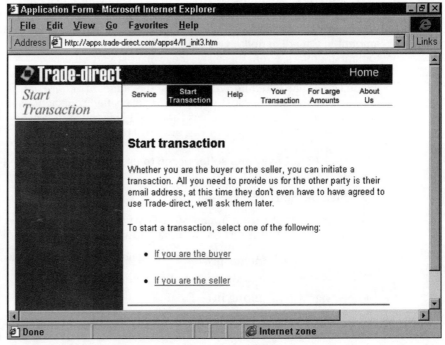

period. If that's you, and you live in Canada, the bad news is that the check arrives in U.S. funds. When you cash it, depending on the exchange rate, you could get a little more — or a little less — than you were expecting!

What's the fee for the Standard Service? Trade-Direct uses a sliding scale based on the item's purchase price, with a US$5 minimum. Up to US$1,000, the company charges 5 percent; from US$1,000 to US$2,000 the fee is 4 percent.

For larger purchases (costing more than US$1,500 for cross-border transactions), you can use Trade-Direct's Service For Large Amounts. The major difference between this service and Express Service is that the seller ships the goods to Trade-Direct, which takes responsibility for inspecting the shipment and then, if everything looks all right, sends both the goods and the money on their way.

Posting Your Own Classified

All the online classifieds have an easy system for sellers to use to post their offerings for sale. Most often, the posting consists of a simple form to fill out and a button to select. Sometimes, for premium services, payment is involved — although many, many services are for free. Some even let you attach a photo to your advertisement.

The posting process

The following steps describe the process of posting an ad on the CanSell classifieds site.

1. **After you're online at www.CanSell.com, select the Place Ad button.**

2. **If you've never posted an ad here before, enter your e-mail address and on the next screen, create a password for yourself; if you're an old hand, just enter your e-mail address and password in the appropriate text boxes and click on New Ad.**

3. **Select one of the major categories for your item by clicking its link, and, in the same way, a sub-topic from the next screen.**

4. **Enter your location, including city, province, and postal code, using the drop-down menus provided and click on Next.**

5. **Fill in an asking price, a short summary of the item, and a description of what you're selling in the text boxes provided, and click on Next.**

6. **Choose how you want to attach a photo to your ad by clicking the bullet beside the one you want, or, if you don't have a photo, click the No Pictures bullet and click on Next.**

CanSell lets you post up to nine photos to your ad. You can send the photo to them by mail, e-mail, or by using your browser.

7. **Enter your contact information including your name, phone number, and e-mail address, and click on Next.**

8. **Indicate when you want your ad to start running and for how many months, then click on Next.**

   CanSell automatically calculates the cost of your ad once you've filled in this information and shows you how much you owe.

9. **Preview your ad (finally).**

   If you want to change something, use the menu bar provided to jump back to the step you'd like to redo. Make your change and use the menu bar again to get back to the Preview Ad screen.

10. **Click on Approve, and you're done!**

CanSell has several different payment options including VISA, check, or money order. Your ad will be posted as soon as payment is received.

Whenever you see online classifieds that include a photo, it means someone has *scanned* the photo using a special machine called a *scanner* that will turn your photo into a file that is *readable* to a computer. Unless you own a scanner, take your photo to a store where they offer the service. The store will save the file, often ending in the suffix .jpg (pronounced j-peg), onto a floppy disk that you can take home. Now, you can either attach that file directly from your disk to an e-mail, or save it to your hard drive where it can be *uploaded* (copied from your computer to another computer).

Chapter 7

Instant Gratification: Buying Software and Information Online

. . . .

In This Chapter

▶ Investigating the wide world of software

▶ Doing the download dance

▶ Info, info who's got the info

. . . .

*W*hat's the biggest problem with buying almost anything online? Waiting. Processing orders, filling those boxes with Styrofoam peanuts and bubble wrap, getting the goods on those trucks, and making the deliveries — all these activities take time. What's an instant-gratification junkie raised on microwave pizza, pay-per-view TV, and instant oatmeal supposed to do?

Download, my friend, download.

A growing world of information awaits you: Raw research information and information shaped into tools — some available for free, some you must pay for, but all available from a computer somewhere else in the world and immediately accessible by the one sitting right in front of you.

Think of the Internet as a vast distribution network. That's what a growing number of software developers and retailers are doing today as more and more folks get plugged-in. Although many ventures are newcomers to the field of online distribution, such as music and video on demand, two areas already have extensive footholds in the Web instant gratification arena: software and research.

Freeware, Shareware, Tryware . . . Everywhere

You go to a towel outlet center to buy towels; if you're in an auto-parts store, you search for booster cables. So where's the best place to get your software? That's right — online with your computer. (Hey, wait — you cheated! So don't tell us that you didn't look at the chapter title.)

You find no end to the wide variety of software that's available directly online. Companies are taking advantage of the open-all-night, no-middlemen-need-apply accessibility of Web-based distribution. In fact, online distribution is one of the leading business categories for the entrepreneur.

Why does online distribution make so much sense for companies? Money. You don't need much to get started, and you can make a lot in the process. With real-world distribution, you need to charge for every little expense you incur. Here's a great demonstration: Next time that you buy a regular software package off the shelf, save every bit of packaging as you unwrap it and spread it all out on your bed — the shrink wrap, the stickers, the box, the manual, the discs, the CD-ROM, the registration cards. Pretty soon, you end up with a completely covered bed. And every one of those elements incurs the manufacturer both a production and a labour cost, because *someone* must put the "New! Improved!" labels on everything, right? Now, guess which of these costs online distribution eliminates? That's right. All of them.

Conduct a search and you'll find yourself up to your ears in U.S.-based sites that let you download software. Canadian-owned sites are few and far between in comparison. But, believe it or not, it doesn't make all that much of a difference to you. That's the beauty about downloading software — there are no borders in cyberspace. About the only thing that may suffer is your wallet once the ticket price is converted to good ol' Canadian dollars. But, hey, at least you have your software program NOW!

The many varieties of software

As more and more people became interested in developing software, alternatives to the "package it like a box of cereal" mindset began to develop. Today, you find more kinds of wares than you can shake a stick at: freeware, shareware, tryware, crippleware, hairware. Oops, that last one is a pet project of ours. We should be shipping it in two weeks.

Each of the categories of software is really a different distribution model, and before you start downloading, you need to know what you're getting into. Or what's getting into your machine.

Freeware

What better way to open a discussion about software in a shopping online book than to start with the freebies? *Freeware* is software that the author (not one of us — the author of the program) is offering at no cost. Why? The software community has a wonderful tradition of giving. Many developers learned their trade by working with free tools and information, and they want to keep the tradition alive. Of course, generosity doesn't mean that the developer is completely selfless. He or she can always hope that the freeware paves the way to payware, either directly through the cultivated audience or through an impressed software publisher who's hiring.

Some freeware goes directly into the public domain, which means that the author is giving up rights to the software and that you may do whatever you like with the program. Other programs are designated as freeware, but the author retains the copyright. Generally, the latter option means that, although the program is free for you to use, you can't distribute it commercially without the author's permission.

Here's another kind of "ware" — BeWare . . . of software viruses in anything that you download. A software virus is a malicious program specifically written to do something unexpected to your system. Some viruses are merely benign practical jokes, but others can wreak havoc in your computer system. Computer viruses get their name from the fact that they're designed to pass from one program (and one computer) to another just as a regular virus does. One of the essential computer programs on any system today is a virus checker, such McAfee's Virus Scan, Norton's Anti-Virus or eSafe.

Sometimes freeware is unconditionally free; at other times, the author asks that you send a postcard from wherever you are or pass the good deed on. Does freeware fall into the "you-get-what-you-pay-for" category? Not necessarily. We've come across some terrific programs that were just what we needed — and absolutely free. You rarely, however, find any support for freeware programs, aside from whatever Help system the program itself includes. If you need more extensive assistance but still want to keep the costs down, you need to take a look at shareware.

Shareware

The term *shareware* comes from the desire of software authors to share the cost of its development directly with the audience that uses it. Shareware is a moral obligation, not a legal one. After you try a software utility or other program for a certain period of time, if you like it and want to continue using it, you should pay the requested shareware fee. The exact fee is completely left up to the author of the program, and as you can imagine, the charge can be all across the map.

Shareware can also vary widely in quality, but make no mistake — some professional-quality programs are available. Most good shareware programs come with a useful built-in Help system, and some even offer a manual — but only after you pay the shareware fee. A few even offer e-mail support — something that's in short supply in the regular commercial realm.

Shareware often includes reminder screens — some more appropriately call them "nag" screens — that appear as soon as you start and/or quit the program. These gentle nudges (hah!) are part guilt trip, part inhibitor. Pay the shareware fee, and the author supplies a software key (or a new version) to make the nag screens disappear. Often the reminders feature a Pay Online button or, at the very least, an address to which you can send the payment.

Demoware

One more class of software's become very popular with the rise of over-the-Web distribution. *Demoware* is commercial software that enables you to try out a program before you buy it. Demoware can differ from the real McCoy in a number of different ways, as the following list describes:

- ✔ **Time-limited.** Many demoware programs are full-featured in every way — for the first 30 days of use, typically. Then the program stops functioning totally. Most programs of this type tell you on the opening screen how many days remain until the program expires.

- ✔ **Use-limited.** Because you don't use all programs day after day, many demoware programs restrict you to starting them only a set number of times, usually 30 to 50 times. After that, if you try to start the program, you get a brief screen directing you to buy the program.

- ✔ **Feature-limited.** Derisively known as *crippleware,* this version of demoware disables some vital — although not program-specific — function, such as printing or saving. Some graphic programs put a watermark on every image that you produce to prohibit the demo version from being as useful as the complete program.

You can find the full-product and registration information for most programs in the Help menu. Depending on the program's design, you may simply plug in a registration number, which you receive on paying for the full program, that unlocks the demo version. Other programs just send you a completely new version.

If you're installing a new version over an older program in a Windows 95/98, you're generally better off uninstalling the old one first. Choose Start➪Settings➪Control Panel and then double-click the Add/Remove Programs icon. In the dialog box that appears, check the scrolling list to find the name of the program that you want to remove, select the name, and then click the Add/Remove button.

Where ware?

If you're looking for a particular software program that you've heard about, you're likely to find a demo available on the company's Web site, just waiting for you to download. Some software developers, such as Corel (at www.corel.com) even offer free downloads of items, as shown in Figure 7-1.

If you don't know the company's URL, a quick-and-dirty method is to just enter www.companyname.ca or www.companyname.com in your browser's Address box, press the Enter key, and see what happens. A good part of the time, you get what you're looking for. The fail-safe method is to plug the company name into your favourite search engine and then select the appropriate link from those that appear as a result.

But say, you want to browse shareware, freeware and demoware from a variety of software developers without having to visit a handful of Web sites. We thought you'd never ask. Ahem. Follow us, please.

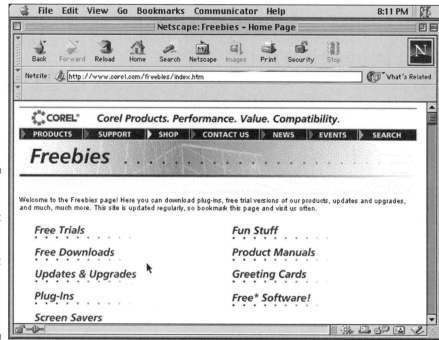

Figure 7-1:
Newbies to Internet shopping can take a shot at downloading freebies at Corel's site.

TUCOWS

For Internet applications and games, start your search at TUCOWS (at
`www.tucows.com`.), based in Toronto, Canada. If ever there was a Canadian
success story on the Internet, it's TUCOWS. It offers one of the largest collections of digital shareware, freeware, and demoware in Canada and the world
and has garnered international recognition.

TUCOWS, as shown in Figure 7-2, makes your downloading life easy no matter
where you live in Canada by using what are called affiliates, or *mirror sites,*
across Canada. Mirror sites got their name because each affiliate's computer
files are the exact duplicate of those on the main Web site. So these sites are
essentially local download sites. TUCOWS' primary sites are ISPs (Internet
Service Providers). That means there's less distance for the software to travel
in cyberspace, which ultimately treats you to downloads with speed!

TUCOWS is more like a software lab than a collection of software free to
download. A great feature offered by TUCOWS is its rating system. All software files are reviewed and recommended by the Web site's reviewers and
editorial staff, and given a rating based on a scale from one to five, er, cows.
(If you're visiting the site long enough, you'll even hear them "Moo!")

You can find a file in TUCOWS' extensive collection in two ways: By operating
system, like Windows 95/98 or Macintosh, or by type of file, such as games
and free themes.

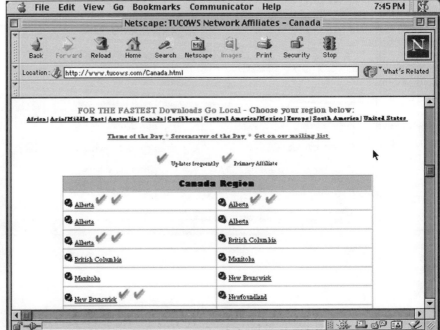

Figure 7-2:
You can
download
quickly by
choosing
one of
TUCOWS'
mirror sites
in Canada.

With each file you'll get helpful and informative capsule reviews. Aside from details about the program itself, there's always a description of the program's license — whether it's freeware, a shareware or a commercial demo, including any time-limitations on it.

The site also has a number of features that may lure you back to the site frequently. Each week, for example, TUCOWS reviewers highlight the Head of the Herd, a specific application they deem outstanding. Or you can find their top 10 top picks when you enter the site's Top Pies area.

If you can't find what you want at TUCOWS, the site includes a link to eBarn (at `www.ebarn.com`), part of the TUCOWS network. The selection at eBarn is bigger — sort of like a barn full of cattle versus two cows — but you actually have to pay for the software.

AOL Canada

AOL Canada gives you access to an online inventory of more than 100,000 digital products in the Download Store, located in the Computing and Games Web Centre on AOL Canada's Web portal, AOL.CA (at `www.aol.ca`). That means you don't have to be an AOL Canada member to access the area. You can get games, utilities, and a wide assortment of other downloads from more than 5,000 vendors — all in Canadian dollars. Check out more of what AOL Canada offers members and non-members alike in Chapter 5.

CompuServe is highly regarded for its extensive software collection and forum support and is one of the founders of the online service industry. In Canada, Compuserve is operated by AOL Canada Inc., which has made it easier for Canadians to tap into its piles of files by launching a Canadian version (at `www.compuserve.ca`).

Download.com and Shareware.com

Download.com (at `www.download.com`) and Shareware.com (at `www.shareware.com`) are very popular U.S. sites. Download.com and Shareware.com are sister sites run by CNet, which airs several computer-related television shows in the U.S. and posts everything it reviews or discusses on one of these two sites.

Both sites are basically dedicated search engines with Shareware.com containing more cross-platform files for the less-pervasive systems, such as DOS, Amiga, and OS2, than Download.com. Not to belabour the obvious, but as you probably can guess, all the files in Shareware.com consist of shareware. You can also select from a number of Canadian mirror sites, from which to download a file. In case you don't initially find what you want on Shareware.com, its creators revised the Shareware.com interface to give you quick access to Download.com. Unlike Shareware.com, Download.com contains several special areas that you may want to check frequently, such as Toolkits and Weekly Picks. There's also a lot of freeware to be had there.

Download.com offers a special program to make your downloading life easier: the **Download Manager.** By using the Download Manager, you can download a file now or schedule your download for later. Download Manager also enables you to pause and resume your download for those times when life insists on intruding. Just type Download Manager in the Quick Search text box and select the Search button to find the program. After you've downloaded and installed Download Manager, you can use its advanced features to get files from both Download.com and Shareware.com.

ZDNet

For a true one-stop shopping affair, visit ZDNet (at `www.zdnet.com/swlib`). It's very similar to TUCOWS in that it provides a host of editorial information including a rating system — this one has good old-fashioned stars. But at ZDNet you can also find a lot of software not related to the Internet.

You find the usual file categories such as Games and Utilities, but the unique thing about ZDNet is that all the categories are further divided into subcategories. It also maintains a Commercial Demos category that's worth visiting as well.

One ZDNet feature that we really like is the Download Basket. On a site as interesting and as diverse as ZDNet's, we can easily spend an hour or more just comparing the various options. The Download Basket helps us shorten our online time by putting all the programs we're considering in one convenient place.

Here's a step-by-step description of how the Download Basket works:

1. **Browse to the description of the ZDNet file you're interested in.**

   Right next to the Download Now button you see the Add to Basket button.

2. **Click the Add to Basket button to put the file in your basket.**

   You see a disk icon appear in your basket, with a Remove from Basket button now added below the basket, as shown in Figure 7-3.

3. **Continue browsing the software aisles, adding the intriguing items to your basket as you go.**

   You can keep up to ten files at any one time in your Download Basket.

4. **Whenever you're ready to leave, either click the Download Basket icon that appears at the top of every page or click the Look in Basket option.**

   Your list of selected files, with a short description of each, appears on-screen.

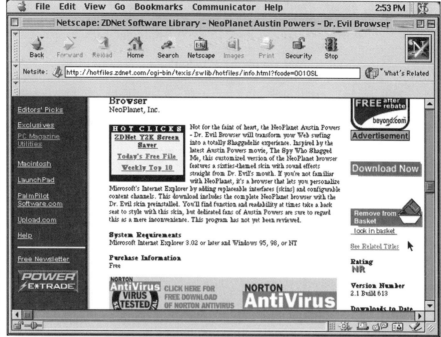

Figure 7-3:
The
Download
Basket on
the ZDNet
site allows
you to store
all your pro-
grams in
one place
as you're
shopping.

5. **To download any of the files in the list, first select the filename and then choose the Download this File button.**

6. **To make room in your basket for more files, highlight the filenames of those files you don't want and then select Remove from Basket button. Select your browser's Back button to go back on the shareware prowl.**

One of the coolest things about the Download Basket is that you can leave the Web site, even go offline, and the next time that you go to ZDNet, your basket — with all your software choices in it — is still there. Try *that* in your local mall!

The Fine Art of Downloading

Now that you've finally located the file of your dreams, what's next? The program doesn't do you much good sitting on that other guy's computer. You need to bring it on over to your place — and the name of the game is down-loading. Downloading just means that you're copying a file from another com-puter to yours. The opposite procedure, copying a file from your computer to someone else's, is known, naturally enough, as uploading.

Downloading and uploading were, at one time, fairly complex matters. You needed to establish a connection at the right modem speed, make sure that the duplexes matched, and choose the right file transfer protocol — Xmodem? Ymodem? Zmodem? You may think that we're making all this stuff up — and, frankly, we're just as glad that you can now regard all these procedures as a joke. Because now, downloading itself is a lot more straightforward than in the past; only after you actually get the file on your computer do the waters become a little murky when it comes to uncompressing and installing the software. But don't worry — we've got a heavy-duty flashlight to lead the way.

Downloading a file

This section takes you through the downloading process step by step. As an example, you're now going to TUCOWS to get the latest version of Netscape Communicator. It's a relatively small file, so it's going to download quickly.

Okay, then — follow these steps:

1. **Get online and go to TUCOWS at** `www.tucows.com`.

   Because you know what you're looking for, you can go right to the source.

2. **In the Quick Search text box, type in** Netscape. **Then to the right of the box, choose the operating system from the pulldown menu.**

3. **Click the Search button.**

   TUCOWS describes the program and gives you its file particulars: file size, number of downloads to date, cost and revision date, Hey, it's free, and at about 15 million *kilobytes,* it's not too massive a beast to fit into your computer. It should take you about 40 minutes to download.

   File size and modem speed are both measured in *kilobytes.* A 38.8K file downloading on a 28.8K modem should take about 2 minutes and 15 seconds, but — as people say in the disclaimers — your mileage may vary. Busy Internet circuits could cause delays and a drop in connection speed.

4. **Select the Download Now button.**

   That will take you to the site's region page.

5. **Pick Canada, then click on Continue.**

6. **Pick the affiliate, or mirror site, closest to you.**

7. **The Save As dialog box now appears with the filename cc32e461.exe in the Name text box. Click Save.**

8. **You can, if you want, change the filename to something more descriptive by entering a new name in the File Name text box.**

In general, keeping all your downloads in one folder is a good idea. That way, you can find them quickly if you ever need to reinstall anything. Keeping them in one folder also keeps a lid on something that we call icon *splatter* — a situation in which you just keep getting file after file on your desktop or in the root directory of your hard drive. If you don't have a folder specifically for downloads, now's a good time to create one. If you're using Windows 95/98, click the Create New Folder icon in the Save As dialog box toolbar; if you're on a Mac, click the New Folder button. In either case, name your folder something pretty obvious, such as **Download.**

9. **Pick a place on your computer to put your new file by browsing to the appropriate folder using the Save As dialog box.**

   If you've got a download folder, use that.

10. **Select the Save button to start the download process.**

    A download progress indicator appears on-screen. After the file completely downloads, the indicator disappears.

11. **Close your browser and your Internet connection — you've got the file!**

Opening your files

Now that the file's in your greedy little hands your next step is to *unpack* it. Yes, as is most any package that you get these days, your file's wrapped up tighter than a sailor on a Saturday night. Although exceptions are out there, files generally come *bundled together* and *compressed* to shorten the download time and also to make the process less complex. The truth is that, if you download a program, you're usually getting a whole bunch of separate files that are necessary to make the program work. The most common form of file compression is *zip* — and the process of unpacking the zipped files is known as *unzipping.*

Zipped files are very widespread in Windows territory, but are not so common in Macintosh land. Mac users more often encounter files compressed by use of a program known as StuffIt; these files have the file extension SIT. A newer form of Mac compression labels files with an HQX extension, but you can unpack both types of files by simply downloading the latest version of the StuffIt Expander program from the Net (you we're paying attention to our directions, weren't you?).

Many computer systems come with an unzipping program already installed. If your system doesn't have one available, get your hands on WinZip, an excellent shareware utility.

To unzip the file that you downloaded in the preceding section, cc32e461.exe (the Netscape browser), follow these steps:

1. **Begin by opening the folder in which you saved the file.**

2. **Double-click the file icon for cc32e461.exe in the folder window.**

   (Because the file has a particular file extension, in this case ZIP, the computer starts your unzipping program. You then see the contents of the zipped file on display in its own window within the unzipping program.)

3. **Click on the Extract File button from your unzipping program.**

4. **Choose a location in which to store the contents of the zipped file by choosing the Browse button and selecting a folder from the Browse dialog box.**

   Keeping all the unzipped files in one unique folder is usually a good idea. This practice keeps similarly named files from overwriting one another. For example, many zipped collections include a file called ReadMe.txt. If you were to unzip two different zipped collections into the same fold, the second ReadMe.txt would overwrite the first.

5. **Once you have a location for the file, click OK to complete the process.**

6. **After the file decompresses, you can close the unzipping program.**

If a download is an especially long one, we have the habit of keeping a copy of the original compressed file. In the event you ever need to reinstall the program — because you need to reinstall your entire system, for example, or you're switching computers — you can avoid repeating the download procedure by keeping the original file.

If you're an AOL Canada user, you can skip the unzipping process because AOL Canada's software does it for you after you get offline. If you didn't designate a special place for the file to go after you first downloaded it, AOL stores all these files in a Download subfolder in its own main folder on your system. You need to locate the unzipped file for the next and final phase: Installing the program.

Once in a while, you run across a file that's already an executable file — or what's known as a *self-extracting archive*. With these files, double-clicking doesn't open your unzipping program — the self-extracting program either begins to install itself or decompresses itself, leaving you ready to execute the executable. Say, that's a snappy title for the next section!

Executing the executables

Our example, NETSCAPE.exe, consists of only one file after you decompress it. This file, Netscape Installer, is what's known as an executable file — meaning that it's a program that the computer can run. All downloads have at least one executable file; sometimes these files are called Setup or Install and sometimes they have unique names, as does our example. No matter what they're called, you can tell that they're executable because, after you double-click its icon, the program starts.

If the installation is even the least bit complex, you're guided through the process. Most often, a completely separate screen appears to take you step by step through the process. The easiest and safest route to take is to accept all the default options with which the file presents you. After you click all the Next and OK buttons, your file is completely installed and ready to run. In our case, the Netscape installation even asks whether you want to run it now. Go ahead — why not? You deserve some reward after all the hard work you went through to get the program. After all, this chapter is about instant gratification, isn't it?

Getting the Info You Need

Before you could shop online, before you could find multimedia extravaganzas on the Web — in fact, before the Web's conception! — the Internet was a thriving centre for information interchange. As the Internet and the World Wide Web reaches mass-media status, that information hasn't disappeared; it's actually expanded.

Although you may think us a tad odd to include a section on obtaining research and data in a book about buying and shopping, such a section's only a recognition of the information age in which everyone lives today. The Net is great as a source for finding things that you want personally or for your business. Especially in business, knowledge is power — and an abundance of power is available on the Web.

We're not the only ones who've figured out this fact. One of the leading growth industries online is information retrieval. Some very large companies are out there that want to help you find the data you need — and they'd like to get paid a small amount for their efforts, too, thank you very much. Happily, a vast amount of information is also available on the Web for free. The main consideration is time — more specifically, your time: How much is your time worth to you? Can you afford the hours that you may need to invest to find the info you're seeking, or should you go to one of the major information clearinghouses and have it do the work for you for a fee? Our advice is to keep your options open. Sometimes, the do-it-yourself method works well, and other times, you must pay the toll.

By now, you can probably guess what we're going to recommend as your first stop on the research trail — your favourite search engine. You can use either the category approach to drill down to your topic, or go right for the keyword search. In any event, you're probably in for some trial-and-error checking of the links to find the right one. Maybe because the whole process is such a needle-in-a-haystack experience, you're almost guaranteed an exultant feeling when you at last find the paper or data you've been looking for.

Naturally, where you start your research search completely depends on your subject, but the overriding concept with which you want to begin is accessibility. Don't rule out any options — know that your "option" is almost certainly online, waiting for you to find it. And information that companies and businesses provide is only the start: You can research material gathered by colleges and universities in Canada and around the world, in technical journals as well as mass-media publications, and by government on the international, national, provincial, and city levels.

Go to the library!

Before the advent of the Internet — and we're pretty such a time did exist — where would you go to research anything? The local library, of course. Today, the library hasn't been replaced by the Web; it's just been made more accessible. The following list names just some of the types of libraries that you can find online:

- Public libraries
- School libraries
- Medical/health libraries
- Provincial libraries
- Biblical libraries
- Arts libraries
- Business libraries
- Law libraries
- International libraries
- Stock footage libraries

By and large, the online libraries don't store the actual material you may be looking for; they supply links to online resources. So instead of going to the stacks to pull a book, you jump to the publisher, author, or resources for the book.

Try the Canadian Library Index (at www.lights.com/canlib), as shown in Figure 7-4. It's a terrific first stop. If a Canadian library is online, it will be listed here. Most are listed with a Home Page link. Some also have an additional link to their catalogue so that you can see what's on their shelves — in all your noisy glory. Since libraries are listed by province, you can hone your search to a library nearest you.

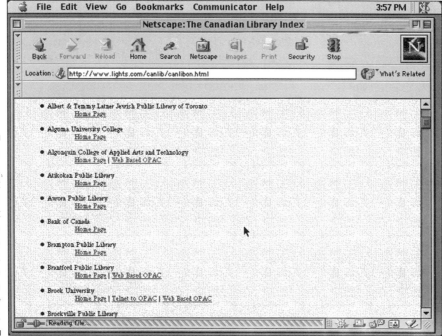

Figure 7-4:
To check out information you don't have to return two weeks later, use the Canadian Library Index.

You may run into sites that charge a fee for retrieving certain documents and the prices can vary depending on what your looking for. So have a credit card handy. Have a look at Chapter 2 to refresh your memory on secure online credit card transactions.

For all the help online libraries offer, you still have to do some hustling — calling, faxing, e-mailing — to get the information you need. That can add up to a real hassle. We know, we know; time is money. So relax, put up your feet — we're about to show you how to retrieve with much more ease.

Pay-for-use research databases

Yeah, we'd say a few people are out there who're willing to do some fetching for you — for compensation, that is. And compared with online software downloads, you won't have a problem finding them in Canada. Inputting the keywords `online information retrieval` on Yahoo! Canada turned up a list of about three dozen companies. With all this choice, it's probably a good idea to do a little hunting before you settle on the service that's best for you.

Electric Library Canada

One service we particularly like is Electric Library Canada (at www.library.ca), recently launched by Rogers New Media. As the name suggests, signing up with Electric Library Canada is like having a reference library on your very own desktop (without anyone telling you to keep the noise down). It's based on the U.S. site, Electric Library, which has been around since 1995.

Electric Library Canada includes access to millions of articles from a wide range of Canadian and American sources.

And like the search engines Yahoo! Canada and AltaVista Canada, Electric Library Canada allows you to limit your search to Canadian sources only, as shown in Figure 7-5. Once you enter your keywords in the search text box, the service scours a database of hundreds of full-text magazines like *Maclean's* and *Canadian Business,* newspapers such as *The Toronto Star,* as well as news wires, books and television and radio transcripts.

When a list of articles that match your search terms appears, you can view it right away — simply click on the citation and read away. What's more, you're charged a flat fee — $89.95 per year or $12.95 per month — unlike some other services that slap an additional charge for each item you view.

Figure 7-5: With Electric Library Canada, you can narrow your search to include only Canadian sources.

Info-Globe Dow Jones Interactive

At the other end of the information retrieval spectrum is Info-Globe Dow Jones Interactive (at www.djinteractive.com). It carries a heftier price tag than Electric Library Canada: It can cost up to $25 for each article retrieved — and that's for a quick search. But if you have heavy duty business needs, you definitely get what you pay for.

And it's no wonder. The service is the result of a combined effort between The Globe and Mail and Dow Jones, the company synonymous with business information. Info-Globe Dow Jones Interactive is essentially a Canadian version of Dow Jones Interactive Service, which provides, among other things, online access to the full text of tens of millions of articles from 6,000 of publications. That's a lot of trees saved! Other goodies include access to current issues of business publications and thousands of in-depth company and industry reports. You can even subscribe to an electronic news clipping service where have other people monitor publications on subjects that you specify.

Saving pages

After you find some information that you'd like to keep handy, how can you get a copy of it? To print a hard copy of the page, just click the Print button on your browser's toolbar. If, however, you need to incorporate the data that you find into a report or other project, you're better off saving the page and bringing the information into your computer, where you can access it quickly.

You can save a Web page in one of two formats: as an HTML source file or as a text file. HTML is the language that you use to build Web pages, and saving it in this format retains the layout and design — although not the graphics — that you see online. Saving the file as a text file converts everything to a series of paragraphs that any word-processing program can read.

 As we note in the preceding paragraph, saving a page doesn't store the images or graphics that you see on the page; this procedure saves only the text portion of the page. To find out how to save an image, see the following section.

To save a Web page, follow these steps:

1. **Go to the Web page you want to save.**

2. **Choose File⇨Save As to open the Save As dialog box.**

3. **From the Files of Type option box, choose either Source (or HTML) or Text.**

4. **Pick a name and location for your file and click the Save button.**

If you are using the more recent versions of Netscape Communicator and Internet Explorer, you can browse Web pages offline at your leisure. After you get to the page you want to peruse later, choose Favorites⇨Add to Favorites and then log off. Then choose File⇨Work Offline, if you're using Explorer, or File⇨Go Offline with Netscape. Finally, choose your page from the Favorites menu. The page appears just as it would look online, with all its graphics, animations, and other content. The only things that don't work the same as they would online are the links — unless, of course, you marked those pages as Favorites, too.

Grabbing pictures

Each Web page consists of text and pictures, and each picture is actually an individual file. You'd be surprised just how many small pictures go into making up an even moderately visually oriented Web page. You can capture any image that you see on the Web and transfer it to your system by the click of a mouse button.

As is true of any work that others produce, graphic images and text are under copyright law protection. Make sure that you check the copyright limitations on the Web site or contact the author before using someone else's words or graphics.

Follow these steps to grab any graphic off a Web page:

1. **Browse online until you find the picture that interests you.**

2. **Position your mouse pointer over the image and open the shortcut menu by right-clicking (in Windows) or holding down the mouse button (on the Macintosh).**

3. **From the shortcut menu, choose Save Picture As or Save Image As.**

4. **Enter a filename in the File Name text box and choose a folder for your image by browsing your system's directories. Click the Save button when you're done.**

You can view your picture in almost any graphics or paint program as well as in most of the latest word-processing programs.

Part III
How Do Ya Wanna Pay?

The 5th Wave   By Rich Tennant

"I don't care if you _do_ have a coalition of kids from 19 countries backing you up; I'm still not buying you an ISDN line."

In this part . . .

*U*sed to be that cash on the barrel-head was your only
option. Now when you belly up to the checkout
counter, your choices have multiplied by 3 or 4 times —
aside from the green stuff, your wallet can also carry
cheques, credit cards and, most recently, debit cards.
When it comes to paying the piper in the virtual empori-
ums, your credit card is the most widely-accepted
payment method — so we take you through the process
step by step.

This part also surveys the entire field of payment possibilities and spells out the best way to use traditional cash
(which we're advising that you keep for offline purchases
as a rule), cheque, or credit card. Because shopping
online mostly means shipping goods from somewhere in
the world to your front door, we explain how shipping
generally works and what it costs. If you're buying from a
site outside of Canada, we also expose the hidden costs of
cross-border shopping.

All in all, Part III should get you ready to spend your
money safely and wisely online.

Chapter 8

Ye Olde Credit Cards — and More — Online

· ·

In This Chapter
▶ Protected plastic
▶ Paying with credit cards on the Web
▶ Using Wallet
▶ Online credit-card services
▶ Alternatives to credit card purchasing

· ·

*C*redit cards are completely intertwined with the modern lifestyle. They're part security blanket, part identification card, part emergency cash card, and part devil in disguise. From your first job or college graduation, the credit-card companies start stamping your name on a piece of plastic.

So it only makes sense that credit-card shopping would take hold on the Web. Most stores that feature online buying offer at least one credit-card option, with many offering a choice of the major ones, including VISA. If you haven't tried credit-card shopping online yet, now is the time to whip out that wallet and start typing account numbers. Not yet convinced or maybe just a little fuzzy on the details? Then the rest of this chapter is for you.

It's Really Okay — Trust the Big Boys

Because we cover the security issue in detail in Chapter 2, why don't we take a moment to review the reasons why using your credit card over the Internet is just as safe as — if not safer than — giving your number to a mail-order desk over the telephone or to a waiter in a restaurant. Check out the following list:

✔ Online merchants use secure Web servers to scramble or encrypt all sensitive information to and from their Web sites.

✔ Merchant-to-bank information uses public-key encryption methods to additionally secure the information and establish the identity of the parties involved.

✔ You're protected with the same rights and privileges using your credit card online as you are when you pull out your plastic in the physical world.

Credit cards are heavily protected under federal and provincial law, although there is no law that specifically covers use of them on the Net. (The government is looking into that very topic as we speak . . . oops, we mean, as you read this.)

If any fraud results from any payments you make by credit card — regardless of whether you place them by phone, mail, fax, or *computer* — you are limited to paying a maximum of $50. (In some provinces, that's written out in provincial consumer legislation.)

That credit card companies will make sure that nothing stands in the way of you and your ability to use plastic money on the Net shouldn't be surprising. Why? Well, it's not out of any sense of philanthropy. Simply put, cyberspace is *the* new frontier for credit companies. Just open any newspaper or magazine these days and you'll read some Net guru predicting an imminent explosion in e-commerce. In Canada, e-commerce put $5.3 billion of revenues in companies' pockets in 1998. In four years, International Data Corporation (Canada) Ltd. predicts that number to climb to $80.4 billion. If you're trying to figure out just how big a jump that is, we've figured it out for you: We're talking about a growth rate of nearly 1,500 percent. So now you can understand why the credit card companies are saying, "Hey we've got something good here."

So, you can dispute any error that you find on your credit-card statement, and you can withhold payment in that amount. That applies both to charges that you make and to charges that you don't make. So if some scurvy hacker hijacks your credit-card info and runs up your bill, the most you're liable for is $50.

To dispute a charge, check the back of your credit statement and call the number provided or the financial institution that issued your credit card as soon as you want to dispute a charge. You must write to the creditor at the address for "billing inquiries" on the billing statement and describe the error.

If you still can't resolve your complaint after following your financial institution's procedures, write to the people in the government who regulate credit cards and banks at:

Director, Communications and Public Affairs

Office of the Superintendent of Financial Institutions

255 Albert Street, 16th Floor

Ottawa, ON, K1A 0H2

Still worried? Check out Chapter 15, where we introduce you to the people who are watching your back.

So now you have big business, the government, and the banking industry telling you that shopping online is not just okay, but safe — so no more excuses. Get to it.

Using Your Credit Card Online: Play-by-Play

Smith drives down the middle of the form, tabbing left and right. Smith spots the credit-card slot, shoots, bounces off the Submit button — and *scores!!!*

Okay, so you really have no way to jazz up typing a bunch of numbers into a computer. And ordering online with a credit card doesn't require any special skill or athletic prowess outside of a steady finger while pounding out digits. In fact, you really must follow only one main rule in ordering anything online. So because it's just that one rule, we're going to raise our voices just this one time in stating it:

USE ONLY SECURE WEB SERVERS!!!

As we discuss in Chapter 2, a secure Web server is one that uses a special type of computer communication known as *SSL* (short for *Secure Socket Layer*, in case the term comes up at your next cocktail party). You can tell that you're hooked into a secure server by the symbols in your browser's status bar: Netscape Communicator uses a glowing locked padlock (also visible in the main toolbar as the Security button); Microsoft Internet Explorer also displays a locked padlock in the status bar and, if you pass your pointer over the symbol, displays the type and level of encryption — for example, `SSL secured (40 bit)`.

Frankly, we believe that sending your credit-card info over the Net even on an unsecured system is far safer than, say, faxing it to some hotel halfway across the country, where it sits on the reservations desk for umpteen hours, available to anyone and everyone. If you really want to steal someone's credit-card number, rooting around some gas-station trash cans or getting a job as a waiter is a far easier way to do so than grabbing numbers off the Internet.

Still, in case you get any crazy ideas:

USE ONLY SECURE WEB SERVERS!!!

Entering the info

If you start buying online frequently, you soon realize that the various order forms have no consistent layout or design. At this stage of the game, each company pretty much creates its Web page independently, and everyone has a different idea of how best to present the form. However, they all require essentially the same kind of information. The key is to stay flexible and follow the instructions on each screen as closely as possible.

After you shop a site and you're ready to buy something, locate and click its checkout button. The name of this button could simply be a variation on the words *check out,* or you may find a fancier button displaying a shopping-cart image. Either way, the actual checkout process usually takes several screens on which you enter personal information, such as name and mailing address, and your order preferences — for example, whether you want gift wrapping or overnight delivery — as well as credit-card data.

Each form along the checkout path contains a series of text boxes in which you type your information and/or drop-down list boxes from which you can choose a selection. Figure 8-1 shows the www.Chapters.ca checkout form, containing both text and drop-down list boxes. To move from one text box to the next after you finish entering that box's info, press the Tab key. If you spot a mistake in an entry, you can press Shift+Tab to return to the previous box.

Here's a good question: In entering your credit-card numbers, can you use spaces to make the number look like it does on your card? It really depends on the site. On some, the shopping-cart system is savvy enough to handle processing your number no matter what you throw at it. On others, the form requires that you use only numbers with no spaces. Some sites eliminate the guessing and simply inform you not to include spaces.

Near the bottom of each form, you find a button that processes the information you entered into the form. Technically, this button is called the *Submit* button, and many sites use that word or a variation of it on the button, such as *Submit Info.* Many shopping sites, however, opt for a friendlier, more informed button message — usually something such as *Continue Checkout* or *Next.* Whatever its name, click that button only once; it's not an icon that you must double-click to start, and clicking twice could actually duplicate your order (although many Web shopping cart programs check for this possibility or allow you to review and remove items in your shopping cart or basket).

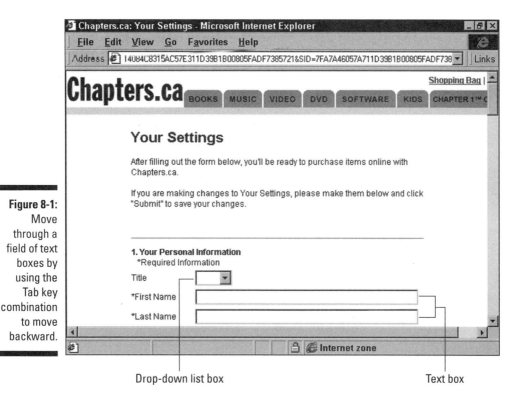

Figure 8-1:
Move
through a
field of text
boxes by
using the
Tab key
combination
to move
backward.

Drop-down list box   Text box

If you left out a required text field, you get a message from the order desk. The better programs tell you which of the fields you left blank that you must fill. If you receive such a message, press the Back button to return to the previous screen and add in the missing info. The checkout program keeps you from going any further in the process until you complete all its required fields.

Don't be concerned if you drop from the secure server to an unsecured server after you get the reminder screen. Just make sure that before you input your credit-card info, you're back in the secure zone.

One of the essential pieces of information that you must provide is your e-mail address. Confirmations of orders are sent via e-mail, usually right after you complete the checkout procedure and the credit-card authorization is approved. If you're using a browser or service that announces your mail, such as AOL Canada, placing an order and then, 30 seconds later, hearing a resounding "You've got mail!" can be quite thrilling. (Don't worry, we're getting a life Real Soon Now — or, as we cybergeeks say, "RSN.")

Setting up accounts at some stores

A number of the more sophisticated stores actually try to make shopping at their stores time and time again easy for you. Imagine that! These enlightened establishments ask first-time visitors to enter all their vital info just once, along with a user name and a password. This practice enables the virtual storefront to keep your information on file and, if you return to shop again, you can access that information via your code name and secret word.

Most of these stores use a protected field for your password — which means that you can't see the info as you type it — it appears only as asterisks or dots. To make sure that you made no mistakes, you're usually asked to confirm your password by typing it again in a second field. Now, instead of needing to enter all the same tedious info repeatedly, all you have to do is remember all your user names and passwords!

Using the same name and password each time may seem a logical choice so that you don't need to remember so many names and passwords, but it's not really the greatest idea. Suppose, for example, that the worst happens and someone does manage to steal your user name and password and posts them online for all the world to see. Then all the online stores would accept any order from "you" and bill your credit card for the goods while shipping them elsewhere. You're much better off keeping different passwords for different online stores.

If you have trouble remembering passwords, Password Pro, a shareware program by CBM Software, does an excellent job of keeping track of these passwords for you. Visit cmbsoftware.com/passpro.htm (note that there is no www in the site's URL) to take a look at its features and download your copy.

Back in Chapter 3 we discussed purchasing a computer modem: "Better, faster, feasier." As shopping takes off on the Net, virtual stores continue to simplify the buying process. One example is the major online bookseller, Indigo Online (www.indigo.ca). As shown in Figure 8-2, you can create an account at this site. Indigo will recognize you each time you return. This will streamline the buying process.

Paying without plastic

If a common complaint exists among those pushing e-commerce, it's this: Online retailers must stop using the same old ways to sell goods that are used in a bricks and mortar store. And so when online shopping began to take off, particularly in the U.S., the thinking was why should people be stuck with the same old way?

Figure 8-2:
Indigo
Online's
virtual store
eliminates
the need for
you to sign
in to the site
in order to
access your
account
each time
buying is on
your mind.

That thinking has now been replaced with, "If it ain't broke, why fix it?" With credit cards becoming increasingly simple to use on the Net, and with security features like SET nearly out of the gate, alternative means of paying for goods on the Net simply haven't become widely used in North America. However, a couple are worth a brief mention because, as with anything on the Net, you never know what the future holds.

Keep Your Cards Handy in a Wallet

After punching in your credit-card number for the umpteen-millionth time, you probably feel like punching something else altogether. Got to be a better way, right? We're happy to report that help is on the way. Microsoft (along with a few other companies in the software biz) has developed a new type of program that enables you to present any credit card that you choose by just pointing and clicking.

Microsoft Wallet works with Internet Explorer and is also available as a plug-in for Netscape Navigator 3.0 and later versions of Netscape's browser. If you use either the standard or full versions of Internet Explorer 4.0, you already have the Wallet program.

Setup and organization

Your Wallet has two main segments: a place to keep your personal info, called the *Address* area, and a place to keep the credit-card info, the *Payment* area. You can set up different profiles in the Address section so that you can use different cards in the Payment area — that way, you can use different cards for business and personal use.

The first step is to set up your Address information. Follow these steps to get that part of your Microsoft Wallet ready for use:

1. **Start Internet Explorer 4.0 and choose View⇨Internet Options.**

2. **In the Options dialog box that appears, select the Contents tab.**

   In the Personal Information area on the bottom half of the dialog box, you see two Wallet-related buttons.

3. **Click the Addresses button.**

4. **After the Address Options dialog box appears, click the Add button to begin inputting your personal info in the New Address dialog box.**

5. **Begin filling out the Add a New Address dialog box by selecting the First: text box in the Name area and entering the appropriate information in that text box.**

6. **Press the Tab key to move to the next empty text box, Last:.**

7. **After you finish entering your name and address info, click either the Home or the Business button in the Display Name area.**

   An icon representing either Home or Business appears next to the various addresses you can enter. These icons allow you to quickly pick which set of information is appropriate for the site from which you are ordering.

8. **Type a name to identify this set of information in the Display Name text box.**

   When you "pull" your Wallet out at a shopping site, you are first presented with a list of your available addresses. The name you choose to enter in the Display Name text box is the name shown in this list. For example, you might label the set of your home address and personal credit-card information as "My Home" and later label the set of business address and business credit card as "My Work."

9. **Click OK after you finish entering this information to return to the Address Options dialog box.**

10. **Repeat Steps 3 through 9 to add more addresses.**

11. **When you're finished adding addresses, click Close to return to the Content tab of the Internet Options dialog box.**

Now that you have your personal data in place, you need to add your credit-card info — for what could be the last time. And that's the beauty of using the Wallet. After you enter your credit-card numbers and the like in a secure Wallet program, the information is passed from the Wallet program to the online store's shopping cart program without you having to retype those blasted numbers.

Continuing from where you left off, adding the addresses, follow these steps:

1. **In the Personal Information area of the Options dialog box, click the Payments button to open the Payment Options dialog box.**

2. **In the Payment Options dialog box, click the Add button to reveal the drop-down list of credit cards.**

3. **From the drop-down menu, select one of the credit cards you want to add.**

   The first time you use the Wallet, the Microsoft Wallet license agreement appears.

4. **Select the I Agree button to continue.**

   The Add a New Credit Wizard should now appear to guide you through the remaining steps.

5. **Click the Next button to continue.**

6. **Enter your card name, expiration date, and number in the appropriate text boxes found on the Credit Card Information screen.**

   You also must enter a display name. Microsoft suggests that you use your first name and the card type — and this combination, like "My Visa," appears in the Display Name text box — but you can change the Display Name to whatever you want to use. Just highlight the suggested name in the Display Name text box, delete it, and enter the name you have chosen.

7. **Enter a display name in the Display Name text box and then click Next to continue.**

   The Credit Card Billing Address dialog box appears next.

8. **Select a billing address for the card from the Billing Address drop-down list box. Click Next when you are finished. Then click the OK button.**

   If you don't see the address listed that you want to use, click the New Address button. This opens the Add a New Address dialog box, where you repeat the process covered in the previous section.

   After you click the Next button, the Credit Card Password dialog box appears. Whenever you present the card online, you must use the password you enter on this screen.

9. **In the Credit Card Password dialog box, enter the password twice — once in the Password text box and then again in the Confirm Password text box. Click the Finish button to complete the process.**

10. **Repeat Steps 2 through 9 to add additional cards.**

11. **Click the Close button to return to the Internet Options dialog box. Click the OK button to close the Internet Options dialog box.**

Pulling out the Wallet

You can use the Microsoft Wallet only at certain sites. For a brief listing of these sites, visit `www.microsoft.com/Wallet/directory.htm`. Once you get there (we'll wait . . .), you'll notice there aren't a huge number of merchants that are Wallet-ready, particularly in Canada — yet. But this, too, is an emerging software (more of which we'll discuss in the next chapter). As more and more retailers take to the Net waves, they'll be doing whatever it takes to make the checkout beeline simpler. So it stands that alternative means of allowing buyers to pull out their credit card will be part of the "whatever."

How do you use Wallet after you get to one of these sites? Glad you asked. Sites that support Microsoft Wallet display an identifying logo that you can click to start the purchasing process. After you click the Wallet logo, your order appears on-screen, along with the first of your Wallet's credit cards. Clicking the drop-down option arrow enables you to choose any other of the cards in your Wallet. To switch to another address, select Payment Options from the drop-down list.

After you choose the card you're going to use, all that remains is for you to click the Pay Now button further down on the merchant's screen. Verify that it's really you who wants to pay with your Wallet by entering your password — and you're done. So instead of rooting around in that nice alligator number of yours, you can just rely on virtual Wallet and a single password. Pretty neat, huh?

Online Credit-Card Services

So now that big business has you running up your credit card online, why don't you turn the tables on 'em? We show you how to use the Net to shop for the best credit-card deals around — and keep some of that interest that's been running away from you.

Shopping for a credit card on the Web

The Web being the hang-out for ne'er-do-wells, computer nerds, and other anti-establishment types, you shouldn't be too surprised to find on it a growing "power to the people" movement on the Net regarding credit cards. While a number of sites help you learn how to control your use of credit cards, you can also shop for the best credit-card deal — with the lowest interest rate and the best combination of features.

A great site for that is i|money (`www.imoney.com`), Canada's only Web site that offers consumers the ability to research a product, compare rates, and then invest in or purchase — at no additional cost — a variety of financial products, from mortgages to . . . credit cards! Fire up your browser and go to `www.imoney.com`. On the left side of the page, click on the drop-down list button called Timely Info, scroll down to credit cards, as shown in Figure 8-3, and click. This takes you directly to the site's credit card page. There you can find a listing of various rates for regular cards, gold cards, no-fee cards, even department store cards. It lists not only cards in terms of their features but also interest rates.

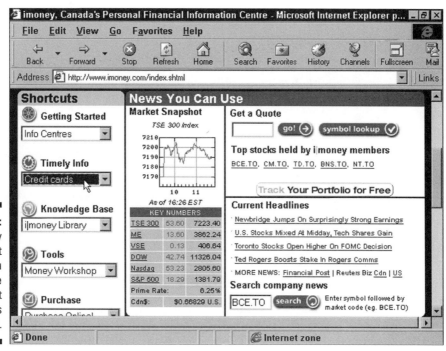

Figure 8-3: i|money aims at getting you some of the best credit card deals around.

A couple of things make this site one of our favourites. First, interest rates are posted and updated daily. And some credit cards (from banks that are i l money members) accept applications online. A limitation is that the site doesn't list every single card available on the market.

To really understand what's out there your best bet is to check out the Consumer Information area at the government Web site of Industry Canada. It's chock full of information for, you guessed it, consumers, (we'll discuss it in detail in Chapter 17), including a Credit Card Costs Calculator. It helps you find the card that will cost you the least in interest and fees over a year, based on how you'll use it.

Here's how it works:

1. **Set your browser to** `strategis.ic.gc.ca/SSG/ca00458e.html` **to take you directly to the Credit Card Calculator.**

   You'll be asked whether you expect to pay your entire monthly credit card bill in full by the due date.

2. **Click on the Yes or No button.**

   If you're answer is No, you'll be taken to a new screen that asks you what is the average balance on your credit card.

3. **Enter the amount you carry on your credit card in the text box.**

4. **Click on the Calculate button.**

   As shown in Figure 8-4, the calculator crunches the information and presents a list of cards that are best suited for you based on your info (you'll get this list if, in Step 2, you clicked the Yes button).

If you find a card you like in this list, go to the Web site of that card's issuer and apply online directly (all of Canada's major banks' Web sites enable you to do that).

So go ahead, rustle up some more plastic. Baby needs new shoes. Unfortunately, Baby is a 300-pound horse, so those are gonna cost ya. Better look for the credit card with the lowest interest rate and the longest grace period.

Credit-card customer services

The banks in Canada have been the real leaders in pushing financial transactions online. Credit card issuers have started offering their customers access to their accounts via the Web. Now, if that offer isn't an endorsement of the Web's security, we don't know what is.

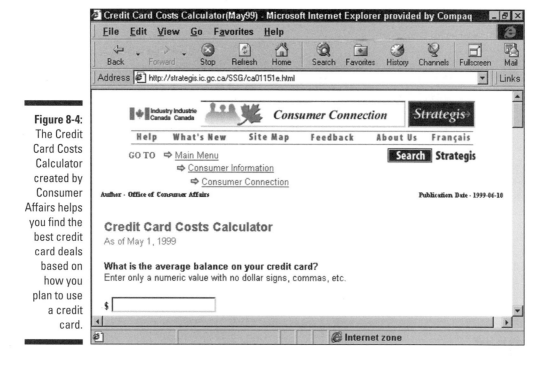

Figure 8-4:
The Credit
Card Costs
Calculator
created by
Consumer
Affairs helps
you find the
best credit
card deals
based on
how you
plan to use
a credit
card.

Royal Bank, for example, has one of the niftiest credit card features in its online banking service. Among the perks of its system, you can check your current charges in this months billing cycle as well as get a summary view of your accounts at Royal Bank, as shown in Figure 8-5.

Perhaps the coolest of cool features many banks offer is the capability to integrate your credit-card info from the bank directly into your money-management software. So you don't need to re-enter the info anymore — you can download it directly into your system.

If you opt to create a download file of your credit account information, the banks' software creates a QIF file type. You can import this file to your favourite money-management software. Intuit pioneered the QIF file type for its Quicken program, and most personal software products also support it, including Microsoft Money.

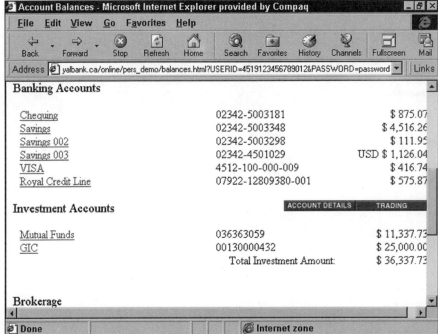

Figure 8-5:
Many banks allow you to check your account information online, such as this demo of services offered at Royal Bank's site.

Chapter 9

Shipping and Receiving

· ·

· ·

*H*ave you ever sat around waiting for a package to arrive? The anticipation can be a killer. But things really start to go downhill if your package arrives with a heftier bill than you'd expected, or worse yet, it doesn't arrive at all.

This chapter is intended as a guide through the logistics of getting both your domestic online buys (from other Canadians) and cross-border acquisitions (Yankee stuff) home. Before you can move it though, you've got to pay for it, right? We figure that's as good a place to start as any.

Billing Options

Okay, you've taken the leap into the wonderful world of online shopping. You're actually going to buy something on the Net. So now comes the yucky part: forking over the dough! When paying online, you should know your options. So sit back while we take you through them one at a time.

Credit card

The easiest and most efficient way to pay for an online purchase is with your credit card. It's got several convincing advantages over other payment methods. With a credit card, you can:

✔ Complete your entire shopping expedition online, from browsing to payment, no hassles, no waiting.

✔ Convert foreign currencies automatically upon purchase; the total amount in Canadian dollars is charged to your bill.

> ✔ Make your online purchase safely; see Chapter 2 for details on Internet security, including encrypted messages, secured phone lines, and digital IDs.
>
> ✔ Access the greatest number of online merchants, since most people who are serious about selling online accept credit cards.

Personal or certified cheque

A personal cheque is a fairly safe bet for you as a buyer unless it's lost (we'd double-confirm that address before popping it into the mail) or stolen. The problem is that many merchants don't accept them, especially for bigger amounts, because cheques can bounce and are relatively easy to forge. Certified cheques get around this because they guarantee the funds are there. You can get a certified cheque from any bank for about $4-$5.

Money order and bank draft

A money order is like sending cash without the risk, and it will only cost you about $3-$5, depending on whether it's going to a Canadian or foreign destination. Just go to a bank or post office, give them the amount in cash that you intend to send plus the fee, and they'll make the order out to the person or company you request. A bank draft is pretty much the same thing, but it's used for larger amounts. It also costs a bit more — about $6.

COD

"COD" used to stand for Cash On Delivery, and it still does in some cases. Nowadays though, the "Cash" is being replaced with "Collect" — which underscores a growing reluctance by shippers to use cash. A COD is a good option for buying from a company or an individual, but they're only available within Canada. Here's how a COD works:

1. **Either the buyer or seller calls up Canada Post or a courier company and asks for a COD.**

2. **The company picks up the package from the seller, who pays the COD cost up front and specifies how much money is to be collected from the buyer and whether payment should be by cash, cheque, or money order.**

3. **The package is shipped to the buyer, but will only be released once the buyer comes up with the amount specified on the COD slip, plus the COD charge.**

4. **The company sends the money to the seller.**

A COD transaction takes about 10-15 days, and costs between $5-$7. If you use Canada Post's COD, the seller will have to pay postage up front, to be reimbursed when the buyer gets the package.

Wire transfer

If you are allergic to all other payment methods, some online merchants will accept a wire transfer. Transferring money from a bank is expensive (about $25) and awkward (for foreign transfers you need to find an affiliated institution and pre-arrange the pick-up on the other end). A better option is a financial service company such as Western Union, which offers fast transfers to locations around the world. Fees vary depending on how much money is being sent and where.

Cash

We're going to go against the better judgment of a certain shoe company here and tell you that in this case, "Just don't do it!" It's not a good idea to send cash in any kind of online transaction. With the exception of times when you can pick up your online purchase in person, we'd advise you to keep your cash in your pocket and choose a safer route.

Paying to Get It Home

Remember the futuristic TV cartoon called *The Jetsons?* We both have fond recollections of watching George Jetson press a button and poof! there was a meal, or whatever else he wanted. (Hey! Didn't they do that in *Star Trek* as well?) Anyway, leaving aside TV history for a moment, the fact is, in the real world, you may be able to complete your online transaction by pressing a button, but you still have to pay for it with real hard-earned dollars and get it home safe and sound. Here, then, are the non-futuristic deal-with-it-today monetary concerns you face when buying online. Don't worry too much though! While it might all sound like a lot to think about, once you get the hang of it, you'll start to feel more and more like a Jetson!

Shipping

Unless your online purchase is a service or a downloadable program, you've got to bring your newest prized possession home. Generally, that means you are responsible for the cost of shipping. Every shipping company does things a little bit differently, but the basic rules are the same. Shipping costs, for example, are universally determined by the following factors:

- ✔ **Weight.** Restrictions on weight vary.

- ✔ **Size.** Takes precedence over weight, so a small object in a big box is usually more expensive to ship.

- ✔ **Distance.** Shipping companies evaluate distance by postal code.

- ✔ **Speed.** Depending how fast you want your parcel to arrive, it will be shipped by land, sea, or air — the shorter the turnaround time, the higher the bill.

- ✔ **Level of Service.** In shipping, as in most things, you get what you pay for; if you want special bells and whistles, like extra guarantees or delivery to very remote locations, you'll have to pay for them.

When you buy something online from a major company, the company usually makes the shipping arrangements for you. On the other hand, if you're buying Frank Sinatra records from a lady in Kansas, it's up to you to pick a company that will do the job right. The good news for you cyber-junkies is that some of the biggest shippers in the world offer a range of services online, including order placements and shipment tracking. (See the section, "Tracking Down a Lost Treasure," later in this chapter, for more details on shipment tracking.) Regular mail is a cheap option for domestic shipments, but if your package is coming from another country, Canada Post has no control over the speed or reliability of the other country's postal system. If you want to get your package home fast from anywhere in the world, and you're willing to pay for their incredible range of services, courier companies are your best bet. You're sure to recognize the following companies:

- ✔ Canada Post (www.canadapost.ca)

- ✔ FedEx (www.fedex.com/ca)

- ✔ Purolator (www.purolator.ca)

- ✔ UPS (www.ups.com/canada/)

All shipping companies have restrictions on the types of objects they will transport. Some objects, like explosives, are obvious no-nos. Others you may not have heard about. Canada Post, for example, will not ship alcoholic beverages. Canada Customs also restricts the entry of some goods on behalf of other government departments. For example, agriculture products (including plants and flower bulbs) may not be allowed into the country because they could carry disease. If you have doubts about something you're buying online, check before you pay.

Handling

How many times have you heard the phrase "plus shipping and *handling*" attached to a late-night infomercial pitch? Handling is what the company charges you to sort through merchandise at their warehouse for the exact item you're ordering, put it in the right box, and get it ready for shipment.

Cross-Border Ouch!

Remember when you were a kid, and you wanted those Sea Monkeys advertised at the back of an American comic book? They were so cute! So weird! Hey, what were those things, anyway? The point is, you were probably as intimidated as we were by the order form that quoted a price in U.S. dollars, asked for a return address including zip code, and explained that you would get your monkeys by something called COD.

Buying online from a foreign (usually American) seller can make you feel a little like a six-year-old buying Sea Monkeys from a comic book. It's possible, but it's confusing. It can also be expensive. On top of the shipping and handling we discussed earlier in the chapter, there are also *destination charges*; a fancy way to describe any charges tacked on when your package crosses the border. So, say goodbye to the 49th parallel, but not before a few words on each of these.

Duty

Duty is a tariff imposed on foreign goods entering the country. Most new manufactured goods are *dutiable,* that is, subject to the border tariff. The exception is goods covered by the North American Free Trade Agreement (NAFTA), which is good news for you, because it allows most American- or Mexican-made items in duty-free.

The rate of duty you are charged varies, depending on the country where the goods are manufactured. For example, if you buy clothes through a British catalogue company, you can expect to pay somewhere between 15-21 percent duty on the total cost of your shipment in Canadian dollars — that ain't chicken feed.

Just because you're buying something from a company in the U.S. doesn't mean that you are buying a U.S.-made product. Many goods — clothes, shoes, and electronics to name a few — are manufactured elsewhere and imported for sale in the U.S. — making them subject to duty.

GST

You're not going to like this, but pretty much everything imported by individuals into Canada is hit with the 7 percent Goods and Services Tax (GST). The

GST is calculated on the value of the item in Canadian funds (and after duty if there is any). So, let's say you buy a silk skirt online from a U.S. retailer for US$100 (it's silk, remember?). The skirt is made in the U.S., so it's duty-free. If you buy it on a day when our dollar is worth 70 cents U.S. (not a bad day considering), the GST will cost you 7 percent of $130 Canadian, or $9, bringing your total to $139.

PST

But wait, there's more! Customs Canada will also collect Provincial Sales Tax (PST) on behalf of some provinces — that's QST for la belle province. Like the GST, it is applied to the total value of the goods after duty, and also like the GST, it applies to nearly all foreign imports destined for an individual like yourself.

Nova Scotians, New Brunswickers, and Newfoundlanders take note: Your province has a Harmonized Sales Tax (HST) that merges the GST and PST. So you get charged a flat 15 percent on most foreign goods crossing into your territory.

Processing and brokerage fees

If you aren't at the border in person to accept a parcel coming from abroad, someone else is going to help process it. Well, wouldn't you know it, both the postal service and courier companies employ specialists called contractors or *brokerage companies* to do just that. Canada Post will pass that charge on to you in the form of a flat $5 processing fee per package. In some cases, courier companies absorb brokerage costs and have them built into their prices. Otherwise, you will be charged directly by the brokerage company on a separate bill. The amount varies depending on the value of the parcel.

Tracking Down a Lost Treasure

Ah, the age of computers. What would we do without them? Well, for one thing, we'd probably have a lot more lost packages. That's because technology now permits postal services and courier companies alike to track their shipments from the moment they're sent to the time they arrive on your doorstep. How does it work? Whenever you submit a shipping order, you are assigned a number, called a pin, destination code, tracking number or reference number. Whatever it's called, it's unique to your shipment. At important stops along the way to its destination (usually whenever it changes hands), that number, which appears on the shipping form, is scanned into a database.

If you want to know where your package is, surf to one of the sites listed earlier in this chapter. Look for the tracking service and enter your pin. You will get up-to-date information telling you the status of your package. Figure 9-1 shows you the tracking service offered by UPS to Canadian customers.

Currency conversion

Buying online gives you a passport to shop around the globe, but it doesn't give you the Mexican Pesos or British Pounds to spend — not yet anyway. That's where an online *currency converter* comes in handy. It's a program that allows you to input an amount in one currency to find out how much it's worth in another. One of the best-known converters on the Web is The Universal Currency Converter at www.xe.net/ucc/. As shown in the following figure, it offers the latest exchange rates for dozens of currencies free of charge. The company that runs the site, Xenon Laboratories, has

also come up with some other very cool services, including the Currency Update Service, which lets you stay up to speed on your favourite type of loot even when you're offline. How? Just register at www.xe.net/cus/, specify which currency you want updates on, and you will get an e-mail once every business day telling you where it stands — for free. Xenon's latest offering, The Personal Currency Assistant at www.xe.net/pca/ is probably its best yet. It travels with you wherever you shop on the net to provide instant conversions.

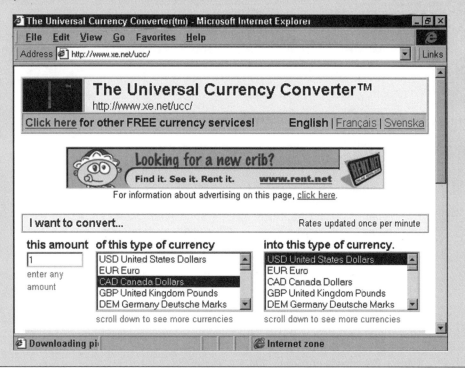

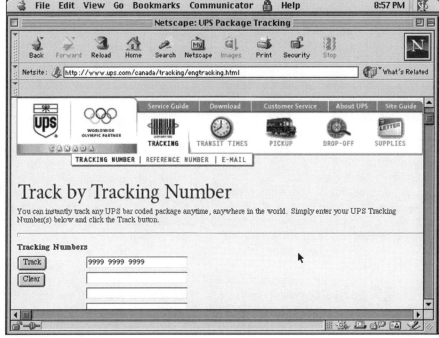

Figure 9-1:
Seek and ye
shall find —
tracking
your pack-
age with
UPS.

If your package is travelling as a regular parcel through the mail, you will not be able to use the tracking service because it won't be assigned a number.

Loopholes Save Loonies

Want to avoid shipping costs altogether? That's tough if, as we mentioned, you're buying online from a company. The norm is for the buyer to foot up. On the other hand, if you're buying from a person, you have a bit more leeway. Two places where you find individuals selling their wares online are the classifieds (see Chapter 6) and person-to-person auctions (more on these in Chapter 12). Usually the seller will specify in the descriptive portion of their classified ad or auction listing whether they're willing to negotiate on shipping costs. If that person lives outside of Canada, ask if they might also be willing to pay destination charges. If so, make sure they make their intent clear on the courier waybill — the postal service doesn't have this option.

What about avoiding destination charges? Well, Canada Customs is a pretty thorough operation with the law on its side. So, you don't want to go messing with the rules. But sometimes, these same rules can work in your favour. Here are some exemptions that will make you smile:

✔ No PST on imported books

✔ No GST on imported certified antiques

✔ No taxes or duty on imports valued at less than $20

✔ No taxes or duty on unsolicited imported gifts worth less than $60 (No, you can't send a gift to yourself.)

Another way to avoid destination charges if you're buying online from the U.S. is to go down and pick it up yourself (yes, we know this is hard if you live in Yellowknife). But for those people who can get there, Canada Customs offers a personal exemption on purchases up to $200 if you're in the U.S. for 48 hours, $750 if you're there for seven days or more.

Part IV
Bargain Hunting on the Web

The 5th Wave   By Rich Tennant

"Ronnie made the body from what he learned in Metal Shop, Sissy and Darlene's Home Ec. class helped them in fixing up the inside, and then all that anti-gravity stuff we picked up off the Web."

In this part . . .

Know how you've gotten your bargain hunting system down pat? How you can tell when a store is going to have a sale by the season or phase of the moon? Well, as some folks like to say, *fuhgettaboutit* — when it comes to getting the most out of the online venues, it's a whole new shopping cart.

Electronic commerce is growing at an astronomical rate and if you don't know your way around search engines, you won't know your way around the best shopping on the Web. Part IV starts by showing you how to find the hottest bargain and the coolest deals anywhere when cybershopping. And when you hit a snag, you can find assistance galore through the chat room, newsgroups, and personalized online shopping services.

If the enormity of the online storefronts poses a problem, you can find some very innovative answers described in this part. Intelligent agents who will bargain for you and side-by-side comparison charts that you can customize to show the features you want to know about are just some of the technologies evolving to meet the challenges that online shopping creates.

In Part IV, we also cover one of the most exhilarating arenas for buying on the Web: online auctions. Whether you're in the market to purchase or peddle, you're in for an exciting — and possibly perilous — adventure at the electronic auction houses. Be sure to investigate it thoroughly in Chapter 12 before you proceed.

Chapter 10

Let Loose the Shopping Hounds!

In This Chapter

▶ Comparison shopping with a vengeance

▶ Getting a nose for newsgroups

▶ Professional gift-giving

*O*kay, quiet now. We might have it cornered. Look! Over there! We're sure we saw a 50-percent-off tag! No, it was just scrap of paper. Wait, that's not just paper — it's a coupon! Grab it!

Okay, so maybe hunting down deals and elusive bargains is not this dramatic, but it can be just as frustrating. That's why, while shopping online, knowing that a super support system's in place to help you get the best values around can be comforting. A number of Web sites have emerged to make comparison shopping, researching your products, and keeping up with all the latest trends easy for you. You can find various degrees of marketing associated with these sites. Some have direct links to their sponsors or partners who just happen to sell the very item you were researching; others carry discreetly placed advertisements on every page. And still others maintain a completely commercial-free Web site to avoid any appearance of prejudice.

You may find that the sense of community that makes the Web such a special place is also extended to those interested in shopping. Various discussion networks, called *newsgroups,* that are devoted to electronic commerce are available on the Internet right alongside the vast number of special-interest newsgroups you find online. If you're too busy to do all the digging yourself, you can use one of the many shopping services that have begun to spring up all across the Net.

All in all, you will find no shortage of folks out there who are willing to help you spend your money. So why not go meet some of them?

Ferreting Out the Info

So you're in the market for a new WhoziWhats? You've found 17 different places on the Web that make them and 145 stores that sell them, but how do you know which is the best WhoziWhats on the market? Better yet, what's the best WhoziWhats for you and your price range?

The Web thrives on filling needs — and advising you and thousands of others like you on the best bargains and products is definitely a need that the Web is ready to fill. The range of helpers out there is really amazing, from well-established organizations such as *Consumer Reports* to Net-only companies such as CompareNet. The beauty about the variety of services offered on the Web is that you can easily sample them all with little or no obligation, which makes getting a second or even a third and fourth opinion very simple as you're shopping around. For Canadians, these consumer tools may not necessarily point you to Canadian online stores, or give you Canadian prices. But because comparable Canadian sites aren't yet up and running, these will at least give you a better understanding of the products you're considering buying — from features to safety to reliability. So venture forth and grab the knowledge that's out there!

Comparison shopping on the Web

In comparing two or more different products for purchasing, you have a couple ways to go. If you're in a grocery store, you can squeeze and smell the grapefruits until you find one that's perfect. If shopping for a television at an electronics store, you can look back and forth between sets, comparing picture quality. On the Web, you can browse manufacturers' Web sites looking for spec sheets and either print them out or view them side by side, as we do in Chapter 4.

You can also get some direct comparison help. CompareNet (at `www.compare.net`) is a terrific resource comparing products before you buy. Although CompareNet is a commercial site with advertisers and partners, the focus is clearly on providing a comparative shopping service. In addition to offering numerous other support services, the main purpose of CompareNet is to enable you to look directly at the features of two or more similar products.

For Canadians, the value of CompareNet is limited by the fact that prices are all in U.S. dollars. You'll also find that any recommendations of where to buy online will point you to U.S. stores. Still, there is universal appeal in finding out how a product stacks up to others in its class. You can also use this site to inform yourself on families of products by reading the reviews and background info.

CompareNet's greatest strength is that it helps you build your own customized comparison charts, focusing only on products in your price range, or offering features that you deem essential. After you access CompareNet's home page, you're greeted with a cover page highlighting the current features, as shown in Figure 10-1.

CompareNet gives you the option of registering with the site, which enables a number of additional features. If, for example, you're a registered member and you're involved in an intense search for a complex item such as a computer system or automobile, CompareNet stores your search criteria for you for future use. You can also get special newsletters via e-mail covering one of CompareNet's main topics.

Running a comparison

Whenever you're ready to begin your product search, click on one of the main categories at the CompareNet home page (including such broad areas as Automotive and Sports and Leisure). Choosing a category takes you to a screen where you can select among subtopics. Follow these steps to generate a custom comparison chart for two or more products:

1. **Select one of the main categories.**

2. **From the following page, select any of the subtopics that appear by clicking its link.**

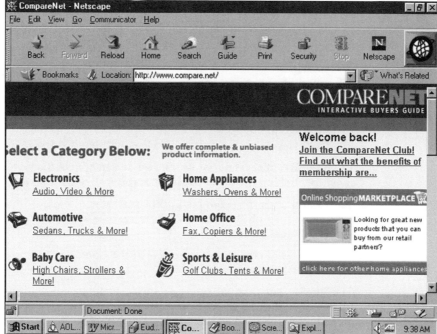

Figure 10-1: Looking for the skinny on cars, computers, or most anything else? Drop by Compare-Net for customized comparison charts.

For the purposes of this demo, we choose Electronics as our main category and Digital Video Cameras as our subtopic. Gotta love that picture quality!

You are now given the option of reading up on this type of merchandise by clicking an option under the heading Educate Yourself. Or, if you want to get started on your comparison, you can choose among several types of searches under Start Your Search.

We want to create a custom chart to compare several brands of digital video cameras, so we're going to click on the Search by Price and Features option.

3. **To direct your search, enter a price range in U.S. dollars and then select which features you're looking for and how you want your search results sorted.**

CompareNet helps you choose a price range by showing you the minimum, maximum and average price range for this type of product in U.S. dollars.

Below the price range text boxes, you can also narrow your search to products available for sale online by putting a check mark beside that option.

Specify the features you want in the product by using the drop-down option lists. Features under Digital Video Cameras, for example, include Format, Color Viewing Screen and Editing Deck Available, among others. For the widest selection, leave the option set at No Preference.

Finally, choose whether you want to sort products by Manufacturer, Model Year and Price, or just Model Year and Price.

4. **After you finish setting all your criteria, choose the Search button at the bottom of the screen.**

Your search results will appear as a list of models that match your criteria with a brief description and price. If a model has previously been reviewed, CompareNet gives you the option of reading it by clicking the Read a Review icon that appears on the right-hand side.

5. **From the list of search results, choose the products that interest you most by clicking the right-pointing arrow called Save Item To List.**

This action adds the products to the area called *Compare Tool* — located on the right-hand side of the screen — where they will be compared in detail.

6. **After you create the list of products in the Compare Tool area, click on Compare These.**

The Side-By-Side Comparison page appears and provides a complete feature-by-feature breakdown of your chosen models. Check marks indicate that the product includes that feature. You can see part of the customized comparison chart we created for digital video cameras in Figure 10-2.

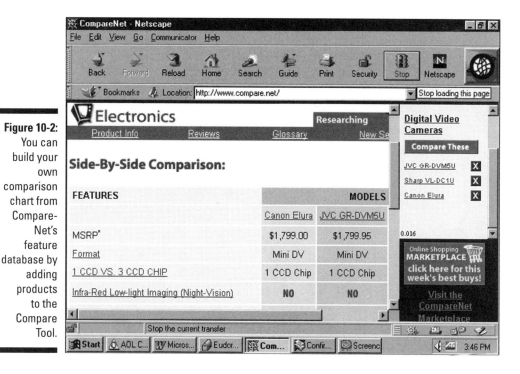

Figure 10-2:
You can
build your
own
comparison
chart from
Compare-
Net's
feature
database by
adding
products
to the
Compare
Tool.

You can also use the Compare Tool to print individual comparison charts for offline perusal, or you can e-mail them to yourself or someone else — someone else, say, who can't decide what to get you for your birthday. All in all, it's a pretty cool tool.

If you know exactly which brand and model you're interested in, you can choose Search By Model Number from the list of search options. Pick from the list of brands and models and you'll be taken straight to a detailed list of features.

Other CompareNet services

Although its capability for creating the customized comparison charts is CompareNet's crowning glory, this feature isn't the only bargain-friendly service offered on the site. So often, if you're investigating an item that's new on the market — or new to you — you could really use additional assistance. CompareNet offers the following helpful guides to steer your research:

Reading Up

As we mentioned, you'll find the heading *Educate Yourself* on each "Start Your Search" page. The tips you'll get by clicking the links here are prepared by CompareNet's staff and go a long way toward explaining new technologies (such as convergence units that combine computers and television), offering a glossary of new terms noted in the product charts, or pointing out super-cool, not-to-be-missed features.

Recommendations

Whichever subtopic you choose, you'll be given the option of viewing CompareNet's in-house recommendations. These are broken down into ratings like Best Value, Best Mid-Price, and Top-of-the-Line. Each rating comes with the model name, price, and a brief description of what makes the product so special.

All the CompareNet charts and pages offer Where to Buy links. Keep in mind that these sites are CompareNet partners and not all may offer the best prices available (especially since they're American). The ones that we checked out, however, were certainly in the ballpark and worth investigating.

Just the facts, Ma'am: Consumer Reports Online

Although CompareNet limits its advertising, Consumer Reports Online, as is its parent magazine, is totally commercial free. Consumer Reports Online (at www.consumerreports.org) is full of valuable, unbiased reports that can point you to the best value for your money; it's also the best single source online to check out if you're concerned about product safety.

As is the magazine, Consumer Reports Online is completely dependent on subscription revenue to stay active. The site offers numerous free areas (such as the sections on recalls and safety alerts), but to get all the recommendations and ratings, you need to subscribe to the site. To sign up, click the Join button at the top of the Consumer Reports Online home page, as shown in Figure 10-3.

You can find much to check out on this site even if you don't join. All the feature reports are accessible — current ones include articles on kitchen appliances, frequent flyer programs, and, surprise surprise, a guide to online shopping — with lots of overviews of the market and things to look out for. Select any of the nine topic areas at the left of the screen to see what feature reports are available.

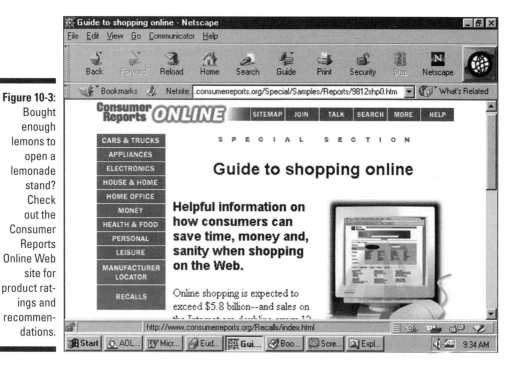

Figure 10-3:
Bought
enough
lemons to
open a
lemonade
stand?
Check
out the
Consumer
Reports
Online Web
site for
product rat-
ings and
recommen-
dations.

After you reach a specific category, you can also take a look at two of the other free areas: Manufacturer Locator and Recalls. The Manufacturer Locator is a very useful resource, especially in an online world, because it gives all the real-world contacts, such as toll-free telephone numbers and Web addresses. The Recalls section lists all product recalls for the last five years. If you got stuck with a defective product, check out this section to see whether you're eligible for a replacement.

Although the free sections are helpful in a general sense, if you want the meat, you must fork over the bread. *Consumer Reports* is world-renowned for the thoroughness of its ratings and recommendations. Not only does it tell you what features actually work (and which ones don't), but *Consumer Reports* also rates your best buy and tells you which product offers the loud-est bang for the smallest buck. Consumer Reports Online features the same attention to detail as the magazine. A site subscription also entitles you to access to Consumer Reports Online Message Boards, where you can swap tales of products that set your moustache on fire or other key info. You can also engage in scheduled expert forums hosted by *Consumer Reports* techni-cal experts and other subscribers.

Consumer Reports Online even has Canadian content! Whenever a product report includes Canadian details (including pricing and availability) a red maple leaf appears beside the article's heading on the Current Issue's content page. The site also maintains a separate database for Canadian recalls. To find it, at the home page choose a category of interest, then click on Recalls. Look for the Canadian Recalls link under the heading "Other."

Birds of a Feather Shop Together: Using the Newsgroups

Remember that old slogan, "It's like having a friend in the business"? Well, with the Internet, you've got millions and millions of friends in the business. No matter how unusual or arcane your interests, you're almost certain to find somebody else on the Internet who's interested in that subject as well. In fact, you can usually find a lot of somebody else's — and they talk to one another. Well, talk is not really the right term. They advise, harangue, help, vent, discuss, support (and so much more) each other. An enormous community of communicators is alive and well on the Internet, and it's known as the *newsgroups*.

Newsgroup is the generic term for the free-wheeling discussion forums in the *Usenet* area of the Internet. Newsgroups center around particular topics, and that includes more topics than you can shake a proverbial stick. And because an unlimited number of people can participate in any one newsgroup, literally millions of folks are sharing ideas and information at any one time.

Why should you care about newsgroups? So far, you've investigated the Web and seen its wide variety of manufacturers and merchants, right? Well, newsgroups are your link to the third leg of this transactional triangle — consumers like you. What better way to get the real story, scoop, and skinny — the truth — about a product or service than to get it from the people who actually use it? Aside from the advice aspect of newsgroups, they're also a great place to hear about bargains or make owner-to-owner sales.

Newsgroup basics

Just as Web pages come to your computer via a Web server, newsgroups are handled through *news servers*. You use a special type of software program, known as a *newsreader*, to communicate with these news servers. Both Netscape and Microsoft browser suites include newsreaders; the latest Netscape version is called *Collabra*, while Microsoft uses *Outlook News*. Older browser versions can access newsgroups as well. Separate newsreaders also are available: *Free Agent*, from Forté, Inc. (at www.forteinc.com), is a terrific shareware newsreader.

At the time that you first set up your newsreader, you need to know the address of your news server. Most ISPs either have their own news server or are affiliated with one. Keep in mind that not all news servers are created equally. Some maintain only a limited number of groups. Newsreaders enable you to switch to different news servers through the Preferences feature of the program.

Newsgroups are organized similarly to the categories and subcategories found in a search engine such as Yahoo! Newsgroup categories are known as *hierarchies* — major hierarchies include *comp* (computers), *rec* (recreation), *news* (newsgroup-related topics) and the granddaddy of all hierarchies, *alt* (alternative). A period in a newsgroup's name separates each level of the hierarchy. If you're looking for a good deal on a used goldfish, for example, you may want to check out the `rec.aquaria.marketplace` newsgroup; whereas if you want to ask for some advice on Goldie's latest escapade, you can drop in to `rec.aquaria.freshwater.goldfish`. To keep a constant tab on a newsgroup, you use your newsreader to *subscribe* to it.

After you first open your newsreader and click the Subscribe button, your system goes online to get the latest list of newsgroups and their associated messages. Depending on the speed of your Internet connection, this process may take anywhere from two to ten minutes. Figure 10-4 shows the very tip of the newsgroup list in its Subscribe dialog box. To see what subgroups exist, double-click any folder with a plus sign next to it. After you find a newsgroup in which you're interested, highlight it and click the Subscribe button — and you see a check mark appear next to its name.

Just starting out with newsgroups? Subscribe to `news.newusers.questions` and `news.announce.newusers` to get your feet wet. These newsgroups are composed of "newbies" such as yourself and others who are there to help answer questions and calm fears.

Searching for a group

Newsgroups are like Web sites — so dang many of them are out there that you can't find the right one without some work. Just as you do with Web sites, you need to search for the newsgroup that's the best fit. You have two basic ways to search for a newsgroup — through the newsreader and through a regular search engine.

To search for a newsgroup in your newsreader, click the Subscribe button and, after all the groups appear, switch to the Search tab. Next, type the keyword in the search text box that best describes the topic in which you're interested and then click the Search button. This search only compares your criteria against the actual newsgroup name. You can Subscribe to any of the groups that show up from your search by highlighting it and clicking the Subscribe button.

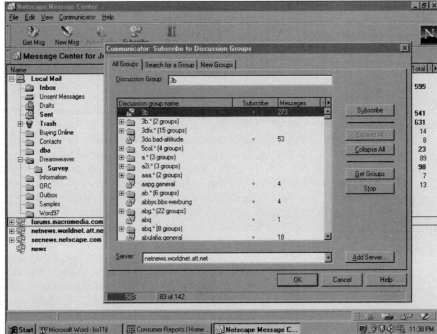

Figure 10-4:
Newsgroups appear alphabetically in hierarchies; double-click any folder with a plus sign to see the available subgroups.

You can enter more complex search criteria by using a regular search engine. Most of the major search engines enable you to limit your quest to Usenet (as opposed to the entire Internet). To do so in Yahoo! Canada, click the Advanced Search link next to the Search text box and then select the Usenet radio button. Instead of matching your keywords to a newsgroup name, Yahoo! Canada shows you links to matching messages from different newsgroups. Click any link to read the message — if you find a number of appropriate responses in any one group, consider subscribing to that group. And you'll see a link to the newsgroup that allows you to do just that — with a single click.

Following the threads

Think of a newsgroup as a really big bulletin board where anyone can come up, read any or all of the messages posted on the board, and then, if so moved, post a reply to any of them. All the other participants in the newsgroups can read the replies. A particular message and its replies are known as a *thread*. After you use your newsreader to select a newsgroup to which you've subscribed, you see a long list of message subjects, or *headers*. Double-click any header to read the message. After you have the message on-screen, you can take a number of actions, as the following list describes:

- ✔ Read replies to the message by clicking the Next button.

- ✔ Save the message to your hard disk by choosing File⇨Save As from the menu bar. Saving those messages in which you're really interested is a good idea because most newsgroups can hold only a limited number of messages. Older messages expire and are deleted automatically to make room for new ones.

✔ Get a hard copy of the message by clicking the Print button.

✔ Send a posted message to someone else via e-mail by clicking the Forward button.

✔ Reply to the message yourself. You can either post your reply to the newsgroup or e-mail it to the author — or do both. Generally, the "both" option is the most helpful choice — that way, other members of the newsgroup can benefit from your knowledge, and the author gets a speedy response to the original message.

Emily Post-ing, or following proper netiquette

How do tens of thousands of people from all around the world get along? Surprisingly well, thank you very much. That's partly because, over the years, certain rules of behavior have evolved — rules generally known as *net etiquette,* or *netiquette.* Don't get the wrong idea — no one person or entity enforces these guidelines; in fact, not one codified set of specifications exists. Instead, the rules are generally understood and maintained by peer pressure from newsgroup participants.

If you're posting original questions or replies to any newsgroup, keep the following rules of netiquette in mind:

✔ Use uppercase words rarely, if ever. In the context of a message, IT LOOKS AS IF YOU'RE SHOUTING!

✔ Post the query only to the most appropriate newsgroup — avoid putting your question on multiple newsgroups. This practice is known as *cross-posting* and can be very annoying to folks encountering your message over and over again, especially in inappropriate newsgroups.

✔ Try to make your subject header as informative as possible. "Best Photocopier Under $400?," for example, gets many more responses than does something as general as "Copy Question."

✔ In replying to a post, remember to include the essential parts of the original message. Most newsreaders have a Quote button or Paste as Quotation menu command to help you with this task.

✔ Many newsgroups maintain a *FAQ* (*Frequently Asked Questions*) file to handle those inevitable problems that everyone seems to encounter. After you first subscribe to a newsgroup, read the FAQ file to see whether someone's already answered your question before you post it.

✔ Remember that you're communicating with a worldwide audience. Do your best to avoid posting personal attacks (or *flames*), commercials, political advertising, or chain letters on any newsgroup.

To shorten typing and hasten comprehension, a whole new category of abbreviations has emerged on the Net. *FWIW* (for what it's worth), these abbreviations are, *IMHO* (in my humble opinion), generally useful and some, occasionally, may have you *ROFL* (rolling on the floor, laughing).

It's Deja all over again

Deja (at www.deja.com) is a very cool site that has grabbed the ball and run with it when it comes to newsgroups. On top of a massive archive of messages from the majority of newsgroups available — with links to discussions on over 60,000 subjects — the site also lets visitors take part in a very cool ongoing ratings game that covers just about every topic under the sun. It even has entire "communities" of its own — in-house discussion groups on all sorts of issues. We think it's probably worth your while to check out all of the following features:

Searching

The top half of Deja's home page, as shown in Figure 10-5, looks pretty similar to your classic search engine. You've got your text box, your Find button, and your Power Search options. You can use all the standard tricks of the trade — such as putting a plus sign in front of words that you want to make sure that the results include or group a phrase in quotation marks. The regular keyword search turns up messages as a result.

If you're searching for the answer for a particularly daunting question — and you can't get through to technical support or your computer buddy down the road, you may try searching Deja. Enter your keyword search criteria as you would in any search engine and then click the Find button. Deja responds to your query with header links to all the matching messages. Scan the headers to find a promising message and then select it. After you read the message, you can click See Thread to check out any responses or earlier discussions on the topic. Clicking the Next Message button displays the succeeding header in your search results.

Just as you can with any other newsgroup message, you can reply to those you find in Deja or send an e-mail to the author. Deja also enables you to check up on the author to a limited degree. Clicking Posting History gives you a statistical picture of the posts made from that e-mail address: How many over what period of time and so forth.

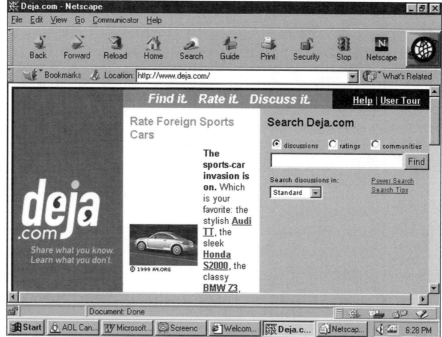

Browsing

As Deja has grown, so has its ability to help you find the newsgroup topics you're looking for. Probably the site's greatest strength is its categories, which are very extensive and will be familiar if you've ever used a site like Yahoo!. Whereas Searching led you to specific messages containing key words, Browsing through categories will lead you groups who are discussing your subject. To browse, follow these simple steps:

1. **Click on a category that interests you from the list on the Deja home page.**

   We're interested in fashion, so we're betting that's probably in the Arts and Entertainment category.

2. **From the next screen, click on a subcategory that interests you.**

   We're right. Under the Visual Arts subhead, we click on the fashion link.

3. **Click on the title of the newsgroup that most closely matches your interest.**

   Deja has found 12 *Forums* — another way of saying *discussion groups* — related to fashion, as shown in Figure 10-6. We think the group called Designer Fashions (at alt.clothes.designer) sounds just about right, so we're going to see what people in this group have to say.

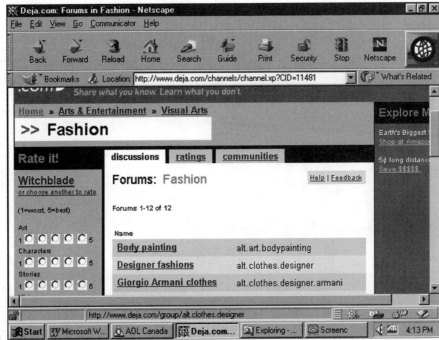

Figure 10-6:
Designer
clothes
anyone?
Some of the
newsgroups
you can find
by browsing
Deja's
categories
for fashion-
related
discussions.

4. **Read the latest messages that have been posted to this group, post
your own, or if you really like what you see, subscribe to the group.**

   We couldn't resist posting our opinion about the fact that haute-
   couture fashions are just a tad over-the-top these days! On a more
   serious note, we could also send out a message asking where to buy
   new fashions online in Canada. You never know who might be out
   there with the answer.

Deja has some other nifty features that you can access by using the navigation tabs after you pick a main category. Here are some of the coolest:

✔ **Daily Highlights:** Want to check out the results of the latest ratings on
subjects in your category? What about linking directly to a thought-
provoking message from a related newsgroup? Deja lets you do both and
provides other fresh info in its daily highlights.

✔ **Ratings Polls:** For each main category of subjects, Deja conducts hundreds of polls on related topics — we've seen poll results on everything
from action movies to running shoe brands. Click the Ratings navigation
tab to see the topic areas, and the specific topic's link to see how other
people rated it. To add your two cents, fill out the simple ratings chart
for a subject and submit it to the overall poll.

✔ **Communities:** The communities tab takes you to in-house discussion groups related to your category selection. You can either join an existing community and add your message, or create your own.

Deja also offers its own free, customizable Web-based newsreader, *My Deja*. You can use it to subscribe and unsubscribe to any of the newsgroups you so desire and stay within the Web browser interface you've come to know and love. Or know and tolerate. If you find yourself perplexed by your browser's built-in newsreader, by all means, make sure that you check out My Deja.

Shopping Services: Call in the Pros

Hey, you shop; we shop; everyone shops, right? So why would you — or anyone, for that matter — ever need gift-buying advice? Try on the following scenarios for size and see whether any of them fit:

✔ You need to buy a birthday gift for Little Suzie's Sweet-16 gathering, but you're clueless as to what the modern teenager wants out of life. Well, there's a shocker.

✔ Your life has gotten so busy that you can't even remember whether you put underwear on this morning, and your loving spouse has bets placed all across town that you don't remember your anniversary, much less come up with an appropriate present.

✔ You're in a beautiful, although desolate (not a shopping mall in sight), land, and you'd give your left-handed nutcracker for a taste of something from back home.

✔ You've been designated by the office to pick up "a little something" for the boss, and you don't want to admit that you're the poster child for the Stylishly Challenged.

Although the Web makes shopping more convenient than ever, times do crop up when you just can't do it all, whether because of a lack of time, resources, or desire on your part. Gift-buying services exist to fill your needs at such times.

Personal shopping assistance anyone?

Personal shopping services have sprung up here and there on the Web, catering to the busy shopper who's got the money but not the time to buy. Usually, you're required to fill out a form describing the person you are buying for and their tastes. Then, through the magic of computers — or just common sense — the site can make buying recommendations. Sites offering this service usually have it well marked on the home page.

Here's an example to illustrate. If we say "shopping" and you think "5th Avenue," New York First Personal Shopper is made for you. Here's how to use the service:

1. **At New York First's home page (at** www.newyorkfirst.com**) click on Personal Shopper on the main navigation bar.**

2. **Fill out the form, as shown in Figure 10-7, to give the Personal Shopper a better idea of what you're looking for, including the name of the "giftee," the occasion, and their interests.**

3. **Click on Submit and the Personal Shopper will contact you via e-mail with a list of gift suggestions.**

   Keep in mind that all the gifts at New York First are priced in U.S. dollars, and that you will be responsible for shipping as well as applicable duty and taxes (see Chapter 9 for more details on cross-border shopping).

Figure 10-7:
So what if you live in Edmonton! Let New York First's personal shopper help you pick out something from the Big Apple.

Do we hear wedding bells?

One of Canada's biggest department store chains, The Bay, offers online versions of its traditional gift registry which can really make your life easier when buying a gift for special events like weddings, anniversaries, or birthdays. Search the store's cross-Canada databases for friends and family who are already registered, pick out a gift, or fill out your own registration form. The Bay's site, as shown in Figure 10-8, even offers to send you the list of gift possibilities for a registered customer via e-mail, so you can take your time choosing after you're offline.

Reminder services are all the rage on the Web these days. Fill out a form with all the birthdays, anniversaries, and special events you want to remember, and you get a reminder notice via e-mail about two weeks prior to the affair. And the service even makes a few gift suggestions in the deal, too. AOL Canada offers an excellent reminder service.

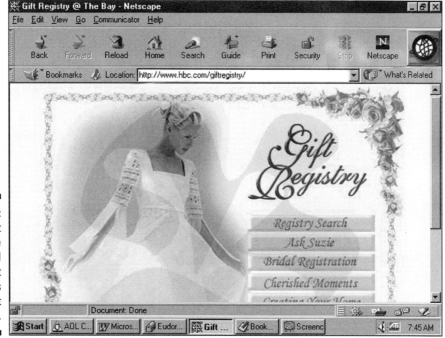

Figure 10-8:
Picking out a gift for the bride and groom at The Bay's online gift registry.

Chapter 11

Letting Your Computer Shop for You

· ·

In This Chapter

▶ Agents with a license to shop

▶ The future of smart shopping

▶ Your passport to intelligent shopping

· ·

*I*ndulge us as we offer the following opening:

[Cue spooky music]

"Meet Johnny Public. He's a man, like many men, who is trying to get a little more out of life."

[Flash lightning]

"Johnny's trying to buy himself a little something. But Johnny will soon find that he is getting more than he bargained for. Because Johnny is going shopping in . . . the Internet Zone."

[Fade out]

Wasn't there a *Twilight Zone* or a *Hitchcock* episode where the lead character rubbed a magic pie plate or something and wished for all the gold in the world — and then all the gold in the world started filling up the room, until our hero was drowning in his riches? Shopping the Web is a little like that sometimes (without the smug narrator). You start looking for a particular item and there it is! And there, and there, and there — in fact, it's all over the Net. You have what is known in the trade as an embarrassment of riches.

There's just too much choice, and these are just the deals you've found. What about all the Web sites you haven't uncovered? How do you know where the best price is, and when are you going to have time to shop all of these sites? You sure could use a little help.

What would be really great is a helper who knows the Web, knows where to start searching, knows how best to handle those search results and, most of all, knows what you want. What you need is someone who can do your shopping for you. What you need is an *intelligent agent.*

Using Intelligent Agents

Intelligent agents can be thought of as software robots that you can program to do your bidding. In this case, the "programming" involved is similar to giving your kids a shopping list and asking them to pick up a few things at the store. Like your kids, intelligent agents learn from experience; if you pitch a hissy fit when the tykes come back with Sugar Coated Cigarette Butts, chances are, they'll know not to buy that ever again. Especially if you make them eat a whole bowl.

Although it scours the Web looking for the best deal for you, don't get the idea that an intelligent agent is simply a glorified search engine. We're pretty impressed with what search engines are capable of, but they do have some shortcomings. Here are some of the key differences between search engines and intelligent agents:

- ✔ Search engines depend on the keywords or phrases that you provide. If a search engine doesn't find an exact match on the Web page, that page is not included in the search results. Intelligent agents, on the other hand, use the keywords you give them in combination with other tools, like a thesaurus, to broaden the parameters of your search while keeping the intent focused.

- ✔ Ever log on to a search engine, type in your keywords, hit the Find button, and then watch the cobwebs grow on your screen? Search engines are among the most accessed Web sites on the planet. Even the biggest, most powerful ones are going to run into bottlenecks with so many people needing their services. However, the intelligent agent lives on your computer and starts its hunt under your command — which can be the least trafficked times on the Net.

- ✔ Weeding through irrelevant search engine results has to be one of the most tedious tasks of the 20th century. Looking for information on the home of the Greek gods will give you lots of references to Olympus cameras that you don't need to see. Search engines pick up on words in any context whatsoever, whereas an intelligent agent selects results on a context-sensitive basis.

✔ One aspect of using a search engine that drives us bananas is the number of dead ends that are presented. The Web is a huge, dynamically growing organism, and Web pages move, accounts expire, and companies close their doors — but not as far as the search engines are concerned. If it's been discovered and indexed once, it's in the database for all eternity. Intelligent agents learn from their mistakes. After uncovering the dreaded "Error 404 - Page Not Found" error, the agent knows never to reference that page again.

Intelligent agents aren't going to replace search engines anytime soon. It's more likely that as both agents and search engines become more sophisticated, they will begin to take on each other's characteristics.

Come to the Market Maker!

Intelligent agents are a bit of a Holy Grail in computing. No one has developed the ultimate agent yet, and there are many different approaches under way. Not surprisingly, the electronic commerce field is one area where agents are potentially very important and successful. One of the leading institutions in the world in cutting-edge technology, the Massachusetts Institute of Technology's Media Lab, has an ongoing intelligent agent experience that you can participate in.

What better way to understand the complex world of intelligent agents than to use one to buy or sell goods. The Market Maker project at MIT's Media Lab does just that. Once you've logged into the Market Maker, you can create your own agent to attempt to purchase or peddle any one item — your agent can even haggle for you! Here's how it works:

1. **Browse to the Market Maker site (**www.maker.media.mit.edu**) and select the Become a member link below the log-in boxes.**

   An online form appears.

2. **Enter a user name, avoiding spaces and special characters. Next enter your e-mail address (in the form of** yourname@yourmail.com**). Further down on the page, switch the location option to Not at MIT (unless you're a student there, of course).**

   You can leave the remaining text boxes empty if you choose or enter your name and phone number.

3. **Click the Submit button when you're ready.**

   A temporary password is immediately mailed to you at the address you just gave. You need it to log in to Market Maker.

   The next screen displays the legalese that must accompany everything these days, as well as the log in to Market Maker link.

4. **After you've retrieved your temporary password from your e-mail, click the log in link.**

   You're now back to the main screen.

5. **Insert your user name and your password in the appropriate text boxes and click the Login button.**

   Once you're in Market Maker, you have several options, all selectable from the menu on the left side of the screen:

   - **Home:** Returns you to the current page.

   - **Create an Agent:** Begins the process of customizing an agent to buy or sell your goods.

   - **Browse:** Looks through the available categories and subcategories of items for sale.

   - **Search:** Searches for an item currently for sale by keyword.

   - **Market Info:** Shows the number of agents buying and selling various items currently in the marketplace.

   - **Log Out:** Your exit from the Market Maker.

6. **For the purpose of this example, select the Create an Agent option to demonstrate the potential of Market Maker.**

   Another screen opens with available product offerings. You can also choose whether to buy or sell.

7. **Choose your options from the current screen and click the Submit button.**

   We're going to see if our agent can buy a book we've been looking for.

   Depending on whether you choose to buy or sell, you have a more detailed form to fill out. Because we're hunting for a book, we're asked whether the book is in paperback or hardcover, its title, the author's name, its condition and if there are any keywords that will help our agent to find the item.

8. **Click Enter when you finished filling out your form.**

   Next, you get to opt for either a simple or a customizable agent. A simple agent will only offer one fixed price, whereas a customizable agent will haggle with other agents. Naturally, we're choosing the fun-loving customizable agent.

9. **After you've made your choice, click the Submit button.**

   Another screen appears, as shown in Figure 11-1. Here, you have control over a number of factors that influence how a customizable agent works for you.

10. **Name your agent, decide the deadline for when the item should be bought or sold, and then set its lowest and highest price.**

11. **Determine just how your agent is going to haggle. There are three scenarios depicted by three graphs:**

    - The first shows a straight slope; here, the closer your deadline is, the lower your agent goes from start to finish.

    - The second allows you to gradually drop the asking (or increase the selling) price as the deadline approaches.

    - The final scenario lets the agent hold onto its highest price until the deadline has almost arrived and then rapidly change the price.

Figure 11-1:
You can control your intelligent agent's buying and selling parameters through the Market Maker setup screen.

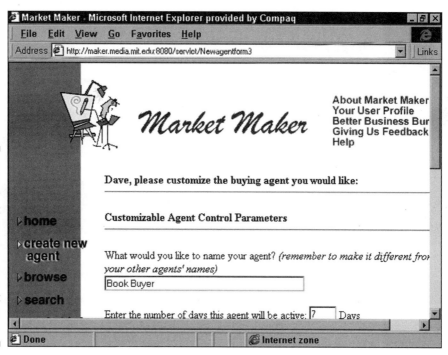

12. **On the same form, answer the queries about how you want to be contacted by your agent and how often.**

   The final options of the form allow you to determine which other agents yours can bargain with — those within MIT or all agents and those of what reputation (from Horrible to Great). The Horrible ones never give an inch and the Great ones are where you get your best deals. We had good experiences when we just left the option at the default, Average.

13. **When you're ready to finish, click the Create Your Agent button.**

After you've created your agent (in your own image, of course) you can log off and just let your agent do its thing, or you can go back and make another agent to sell or buy another item. A good experiment is to make an agent that is selling the item you're looking for — at a different price point, naturally — and let the haggling begin! And may the best agent win.

Keep in mind that the Market Maker is a prototype built to explore the future of intelligent agents. Before long, the real virtual marketplace will open without limitations to either the type or quantity of product. Ah, we can hear the call of the Market Maker even now.

This Way Please

Market Maker is a university experiment that lets you glimpse the future. But there are businesses out there trying to turn a profit *today* by making intelligent shopping agents a reality. We can't resist telling you about one Canadian innovation, called *Net People*. Developed by Inago (www.inago.com), Net People takes intelligent agents out of the realm of text boxes and gives them a human form, including a voice and a name (Mona, to be exact). The idea is that Inago will sell Mona to companies who want to do business on the Internet. When you get to a site that uses Net People, Mona will act as an online greeter and salesperson rolled into one. She will say hello to you and help you find exactly what you're looking for, learning your preferences over time, answering questions, and even making recommendations. Inago just recently launched Mona, and it remains to be seen whether companies will go for the idea of a virtual salesperson, but at the very least, we think Mona, whom you can see in Figure 11-2, looks like a pretty cool chick.

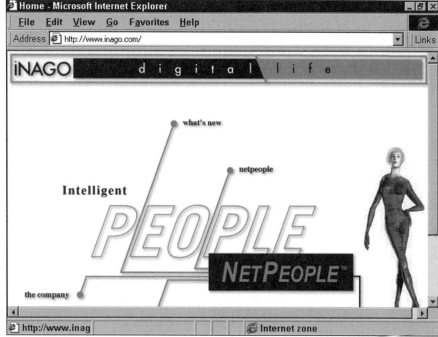

Figure 11-2:
Mona, an intelligent salesperson, can guide you through your online purchase.

Passport Please

A while back, a U.S. company called Firefly Network developed technology that was both intelligent (like Mona) and very secure (nearly impossible to break into), to make online shopping smarter, safer, and easier. The system was so good that in 1998, Microsoft bought it outright. Thus, MSN Passport was born. After you register all your personal information into the central Passport database (like your name, e-mail address, and credit card number) you become a passport-holder. You use this passport to buy from any enabled online merchant without having to go through the annoying process of filling out personal information again and again. The site recognizes you automatically, and knows your profile. Not only that, Passport's technology permits merchants to "remember" your previous purchases, and make recommendations on similar things you might like. Once you have your passport, your buying history travels with you, eliminating the need for you to repeat yourself! As we write, Microsoft is on the verge of launching MSN Passport on the World Wide Web. So, look for it at your favourite Canadian shopping sites.

Chapter 12

Going . . . Going . . . Gone!
(Online-Style)

*A*h! Attending an auction! The thrill of it! The fast-talking auctioneer! The cool customers in the front row, waiting to go in for the kill! The ticking clock! The gavel falling as the crowd hears, "Sold to the highest bidder!" The ride home during which you pout and feel sorry for yourself for losing. . . . Uh, maybe that's just us.

Well, here's the thing about online auctions: They don't exactly conform to the traditional image of an auction that most of us carry around in our collective imagination. They're invisible. They can involve any number of people around the world. Some take place over weeks. Glad you're not sitting in one of those uncomfortable front row chairs now, eh?

But here's the other thing — and this probably explains why so many people are bidding online — the thrill of the auction is intact! The fact is, auctions of any type, whether held in a barn in rural Alberta, or in cyberspace, are pretty darn exciting. You can get great deals and feel like a winner.

Online auctions are one of the hottest growth areas on the Web. Estimates are that this one segment of the online buying market could be worth more than $1,000,000,000 within the next five years. This growth isn't too surprising when you consider that Bid.com, an giant Internet auction house available to Canadians, is reporting 100,000 North American visitors a day, with some people returning as many as 10 times in a single day. They're that compelling.

This chapter takes you through the ins and outs of online auctions, shows you who's got what where, and points out some pitfalls to avoid. Online auctions are kind of the Wild West of Web buying — full of action, adventure, and the occasional shoot-out. So saddle up, pardner, and see whether you can rustle up some bargains.

What's Up for Auction?

The short answer to the question in this heading is, "One thin hair shy of everything." Drop by any search engine and plug in "online auction" if you want an eye-opening surprise. The list starts somewhere around A&A Auction, where you can find antiques, glassware, art, coins, Oriental rugs, jewelry, and unclaimed property, and continues all the way to Z Auction, for computer equipment, cameras, consumer electronics, recreational equipment, and more. You find a fair amount of overlap in the major areas, such as collectibles, memorabilia, and fine art, but because you're dealing with the wild and woolly Internet, you can also find online auction houses specializing in computer software, medieval manuscripts, sporting equipment, and seafood. (Yes, seafood.)

The long answer to the question in this heading (we warned you, didn't we?), is that if you want to buy from a Canadian online auction house, you might find the scope of merchandise for sale *slightly* more limited. We stress *slightly* because even as we speak, the number of Canadian sites and their listings are growing. That's the beauty of the Net. It's constantly evolving.

As an example of what's available, Table 12-1 takes a look at what's on the boards at Bargoon.com, one of Canada's largest auction sites, as shown in Figure 12-1.

Table 12-1	Items Available at Bargoon.com	
Category	*Items for Sale*	*Some of What's Included*
Collectibles	2,261	Antique dolls, Beanie Babies, hockey cards, porcelain, movie posters, paintings
Computers	2,076	CPUs, CD-ROM drives, games, joy sticks, laptops, software, video cards
Entertainment	725	Comic books, musical instruments, Star Wars memorabilia, slot machines, videos
Fashion	74	Bags, brooches, sunglasses, jackets, jewelry
Home and Garden	561	Candle sticks, chests, faucets, flags, tables, vases
Sports and Leisure	1,762	Bicycles, diving masks, golf clubs, sleeping bags, vacation packages

Figure 12-1:
Bargoon.com
is one of the
largest
Canadian
auction
sites on
the Web.

How an Online Auction Works

So just how do you get your hands on some of this fabulous stuff? Even better, how do you keep your online neighbour from beating you to 'em? Although exceptions do exist, most of the online auctions work in a very similar fashion. We hate to admit it (because that means that more people are going to be bidding against us!), but participating in an online auction's as easy as 1-2-3 — just follow these simple steps:

1. **Register (or log in if you're already registered).**

2. **Locate the item of your heart's desire.**

3. **Place a bid.**

What makes the whole process so simple is that the majority of auction sites use some form of *bidding agent*. A bidding agent is a little bit of software that looks at the current bid, the preset increment of bidding increase (how much more each bid must be), and what you're offering. The bid that you put into play is actually the maximum you're willing to spend for the item. The bidding agent doesn't jump to your final offer but rather ups the ante only by the increase increment — provided yours is higher.

Say that you and a few other intrepid souls are bidding on a two-seat, gold-patterned beanbag chair. (We swear to have seen this up for auction very recently!) The opening bid is set at $1 — it's not unusual for online bids to start ridiculously low to lure more bidders in — with a $10 increment. The current bid is already at $350, so the next possible bid is $360. You could put in a bid for $360, but unless the auction is almost over, someone else is almost certainly going to top your bid. So you decide to go for the proverbial gold (as in, the same colour as the chair), and put in a bid of $500 — you must *really* want that unique bean bag comfort. The bidding progresses and gets up to $400, with one minute and one fingernail on your left pinky left to go before the bidding closes. Your bidding agent puts in another bid for you, bringing the cost up to $410, and the bidding closes. You've won! Doesn't it feel good? And you did it without blowing your complete wad.

The auction monster that is eBay

No chapter about online auctions would be complete without at least a mention of the grandmommy of them all, eBay (www.ebay.com). Started in 1995, the company now boasts a staggering 250,000 new items for auction every day in 1,600 categories! Whoa! Figure 12-2 shows you some of those categories, including their subcategories.

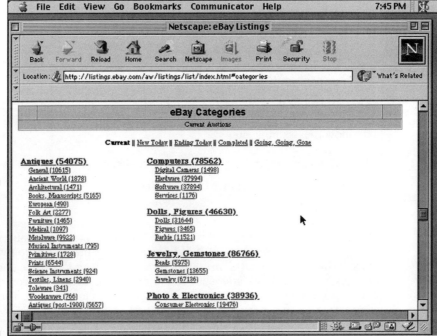

Figure 12-2: eBay has created a giant list of subcategories to deal with the volume of listings.

eBay is what's known as a *person-to-person* auction site. Unlike the famous auction houses with which you may be familiar (the kind we imagined at the beginning of the chapter) such as Sotheby's or Christie's, a person-to-person auction site merely hosts the transactions — it doesn't get directly involved.

Don't worry about the site too much, however, as it gets a small listing fee from the seller for all items (somewhere between 25 cents to US$2, depending on the opening value) as well as a percentage of the closing value for those that sell. Hmmm, if eBay is selling all 250,000 items that it lists every day — and at the low end of 25 cents an item — it will pull in US$62,500 by the time you hit the sack tonight for just listing the goodies! Not a bad biz to be in, eh?

eBay is an American company that likes to think of itself as a global operation. And with registered members in 50 countries, it's probably right. But Canadians should keep in mind that prices are still listed in American dollars, and most sellers, if they're American, expect payment in American funds. Remember that whenever you're buying from another country, taxes and duty may apply. See Chapter 9 for all the details. And don't forget, when you're browsing upcoming auctions at eBay, times are based on Pacific Standard Time (we can hear you British Columbians cheering!).

If you're going to buy through a foreign auction house such as eBay, you'll probably need a *currency converter,* a program that will help you calculate how many loonies and toonies to put away for that special something priced in American dollars. Two online currency converters are The Universal Currency Converter (www.xe.net/ucc) and the OANDA Currency Converter (www.oanda.com/site/cc_index.html).

The Canadians

As the popularity of online auction houses grows, you can expect more and more to pop up here in Canada. A few big sites merit some description here.

Bargoon

Bargoon.com (www.bargoon.com), resembles eBay in that it is a person-to-person auction house. But unlike eBay, there's no listing fee. Bargoon makes its money by charging 3 percent of the final selling price for each item.

What makes Bargoon unique is that it's designed to guide you to items being sold in your home city. So, if you live in Halifax (where Bargoon happens to be based), you'll see only the antique dolls, talking watches, and power saws posted by other Haligonians. This is especially handy when it comes time to pick up your treasure; forget shipping, just get into your car and drive there!

Bid.com

Bid.com (`www.bid.com`) is one of the biggest auction houses on the Net. It attracts more than 100,000 visitors a day and lists new brand-name items all the time. What puts it ahead of a lot of auction sites though, is its excellent Canadian division; you get all the same services as the American side, but with prices listed in Canadian dollars and shipping done entirely within Canada's borders. That's progress!

Unlike the person-to-person sites like Bargoon and eBay, Bid.com sells merchandise directly to you. (More and more companies are using auctions to move products that may not be selling as briskly otherwise.) In other words, go to Bid.com to buy, but take your autographed Guy Lafleur hockey stick to sell elsewhere!

Bid.com also holds a special type of auction in which you can bid on multiple items during one bidding session. This is called *dutch bidding,* and we cover the details about it in the section, "Going Dutch," later in this chapter.

Edeal

Edeal, (`www.edeal.com`) was started out of Toronto in November 1998, and is growing by about 50 percent a month, based on the number of registered members. Prices are generally posted in American dollars, and only fifteen percent of the listings are Canadian, but what's interesting about Edeal is the scope of its services. It offers:

- ✔ **A currency converter.** Edeal has its own currency calculator, as shown in Figure 12-3. It also allows people to list in their own currency if they want to attract buyers from their home country.

- ✔ **An *escrow* service.** Edeal can act as an intermediary between a buyer and a seller to make sure everything is on the up-and-up. For details on escrow services, go to Chapter 6.

- ✔ **A chat area.** This is like an electronic bulletin board where you can post messages about auctions and exchange comments with other users.

- ✔ **A *computer evaluator*.** The evaluator is a program that calculates how much you should expect to get at auction for your used PC.

At Yahoo! Canada you'll find a link just under the search box for *Auctions.* While most of the listings here are placed by U.S. sellers, you have the option of filtering subcategories for listings that are available to Canadians (still in U.S. dollars) or those originating in Canada. (There are few of these, but they're listed by other Canucks in our very own currency!)

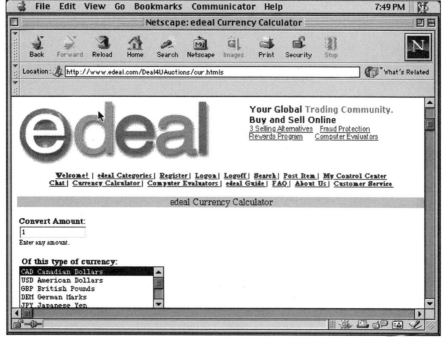

Figure 12-3:
Edeal has its
own cur-
rency con-
verter — a
big help for
Canadians
bidding on
American
listings.

Getting Into the Game

Okay, you've got the basics. Now, let's get down to the nitty-gritty. You wanna sell? You wanna buy? You gotta read on!

The bidding war

To illustrate the art of bidding, we use the example of Bid.com. With all online auctions, both bidders and sellers must register. Although we're not talking about a tremendous amount of personal information, most sites require a phone number and a regular mailing address in addition to the essential e-mail address. This requirement is made to raise the comfort level of all parties involved — selling something to a stranger is easier if you can raise the person on the phone.

Make sure that you check the auction site's privacy policy before you register to make sure that the auction house doesn't divulge your name and address to outside companies. Privacy is a pretty big deal in the industry now, as well it should be, and you can usually find an auction site offering both the goods you want and the privacy you need.

Although the practice isn't universal, we've seen a number of sites that don't permit you to register unless you're making a bid. The important consideration to keep in mind is that, if you place a bid, you're putting your money on the table. Any bid put into play is an intent to purchase and can't be withdrawn. In other words, don't make a bid unless you're ready and willing to fork over the dough. If you default on multiple bids, the site reserves the right to suspend your participation.

Part of the registration process involves picking a user name and a password. You need these phrases to log in each time you start the bidding process. After you're in, you can start hunting. As with many search engines and larger online stores, you can look for your goods on an auction site by browsing through categories or entering some keywords into the search engine. Make sure that you put aside some time for your search — so much is offered out there that you need to read a lot of descriptions to find exactly what you want. Perhaps that explains the 10 visits a day some folks are making to online auction houses.

After you get down to the product level, you start to see lists of items offered for auction. These lists include a brief description of the item, the current winning bid, and a time that the auction is going to close. Some sites have a very limited bidding window, such as one hour, and show you items that are coming on the block at a scheduled time. Others give you plenty of time — days and even weeks — to bid. Click any of the item links to read a more detailed description of the article.

The auction-item description, at the very least, includes the beginning and ending times for the auction, the opening and current bid, and the increase increment. Most descriptions also include a brief paragraph about the item and its condition; some descriptions, such as the one shown in Figure 12-4, even include a picture.

After you find something you want, click the Bid or Bid Now button. Then enter your highest bid — the most money you'd be willing to pay for the item — in the Bid text box (in whole dollar amounts only, with no commas or dollar signs). The bidding agent recognizes your entry as your bidding ceiling and enters the lowest possible bid in your name first. Finally, you enter your user name and password so that the bid is credited correctly.

Timing is as critical in online bidding as is in real-life auctions. If you submit your bid before another bidder offers an equivalent amount, you take the lead. Bid.com puts about a minute-long delay between each increase that the bidding agent makes for you. You could give your agent the go-ahead only to find that someone else came in with the same bid earlier than yours. Your only option then is to raise your own bid.

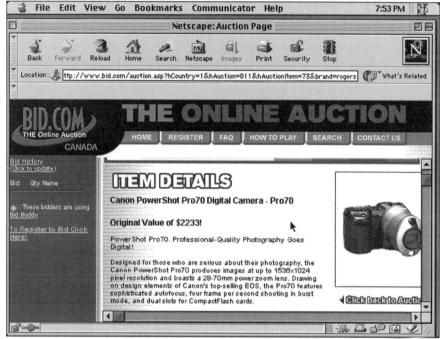

Figure 12-4:
Many auc-
tion sellers
include a
picture in
their
description,
but even
without one,
you're sure
to be
tempted by
some of the
awesome
bargains on
the block.

As the auction draws to a close, the action tends to get pretty fast and furi-
ous. Bid.com uses what we'd call a *five-minute rule* to govern when the final
gavel comes down. If no one enters bids within the five minutes prior to the
posted closing time of the auction, the item goes to the highest bidder at that
point. If a bid comes in within the last five minutes, however, the auction goes
into overtime to enable people to make any last-minute bids. The item may
be going, but it's not gone until a full five minutes pass with no additional
bids. At Bid.com, that window could be stretched up to about ten minutes,
depending on the volume of bids.

After the dust settles, the seller and the owner of the winning bid receive
notification via e-mail. In the case of Bid.com, all the merchandise on the
block comes from a central source, so the auction company debits your
credit card and ships out the merchandise to you. In person-to-person auctions, the buyer gets a limited time — around three days — to contact the
seller and make arrangements. The buyer is obligated to follow through with
the bid made; otherwise, the seller can file a complaint with the auction
house and have the buyer banned from the site.

The selling side

Putting an item up for auction isn't much different from placing a classified ad. You try to cover the essentials — a brief description, the condition of the item, and contact information — and cross your fingers. With all auctions, you can specify the lowest amount you're willing to take for an item. Generally, this amount becomes the opening value, and the auction system determines the increments.

One type of auction enables you to set a low opening bid and a separate figure for the lowest offer you're willing to take. This type of auction is known as a *reserve bid* and is clearly noted as such online.

To sell your goods at the highest price consistently, you need to keep in mind a few key factors, as the following list describes:

- ✔ **Enter the most accurate description that you can.** A good technique is to try to anticipate all the questions a potential buyer may have and answer them as best you can.

- ✔ **Specify the shipping rules.** As the seller, you have the power to include the cost of shipping in the bid or lay it on the buyer as an extra expense. If you do decide to pick up the shipping, make sure that you spell out the type (second-day air, ground, and so on) and the acceptable destinations ('within Canada only,' 'no overseas,' or whatever).

- ✔ **Give 'em time**. You set the length of time that your item is on the block. Not everyone is online all the time, so if you establish too short a time frame, you don't get as many nibbles as you may if you open it up a little. Again, the average auction time varies from site to site. Bargoon keeps its listings open for a month, but some Bid.com auctions take place over a few hours.

- ✔ **Let the auction run its course.** Most auction houses enable you, as the seller, to end the auction at any point. If, however, you've gotten even one bid, you're honour bound to sell to that buyer. The more experienced players wait until the last hours of an auction to begin placing bids. Don't miss the good stuff.

- ✔ **Reach out and touch someone — the buyer.** After the bidding closes, the transaction's just begun. Generally, your best course is to go beyond e-mailed notes by speaking to your buyer on the phone. The minor amount that you spend in long-distance charges are more than compensated for by the warm and fuzzy feelings you get knowing that you're talking to a real, live human being.

Going Dutch

So you say that you're in dutch with your dutch uncle, and you want to go out, but you must go dutch? Well, we're going to add one more term to the pile of phrases that have nothing whatsoever to do with the land of windmills and tulips: dutch bidding. Dutch auctions are designed to handle situations where the seller puts a number of the same item on the block.

The basics of dutch bidding

The seller starts by specifying the starting bid and number of items available. Bidders bid a particular amount at or above the minimum for a particular quantity. By the close of the auction, the highest bidders earn the right to purchase the items at the lowest successful bid. That's right, "the lowest successful bid." A successful bid in a dutch auction pairs the price with the quantity. If you bid the most, you have a successful bid. However, if you didn't want all the product on the block, the next bid under yours is also a successful bid — and a lower successful bid, to boot. A dutch auction guarantees that all the merchandise is going to be moved, no matter what the bid.

Here's an example: Say that you've got ten steam cabinets just clogging up the garage, and it's spring cleaning time. You put them all up for a dutch auction with a minimum bid of $100 per unit. The bidding is less than stellar (who wants a steam cabinet if summer's coming?), and you get only two offers. One is from Sam's Fine Steam Emporium, which is looking to pick up all your cabinets for spare parts; Sam offers $100 per cabinet for all ten. The other bidder is Elvis Pelvis, famous Olympic roller skater, who just needs one to help his aching back; Elvis bids $150 for just one unit.

So who wins? Actually they both do — Sam gets nine of those fabulous cabinets and Elvis gets one because his bid was the highest. Now, here's where we go dutch: Elvis is the real winner because he has to pay only $100, the lowest successful bid. For the price to get above the minimum in a dutch auction, you must have an equal or higher level of demand for the quantity available. If another bidder came in and wanted all ten machines for $175, the lowest successful bid raises to that level.

Before you get involved in such an auction, a good idea is to check out the bidding history of an earlier one. After all, we'd hate to lose our shirts at a dutch auction, wooden shoe? (If the last line doesn't make sense, read it out loud.)

Live dutch auctions at Bid.com

At the beginning of this chapter, we described the differences between an online auction and a traditional auction. Bid.com would like to narrow the gap between the two. It's developed a video component for its live Dutch Auctions that lets you watch the action. Bid.com has an *event host;* a person who provides information about the items being auctioned off, and responds to bids as they come in. To watch, you will need a special software program like RealVideo, which you can download from their Web site at www.realvideo.com.

Bad Bid-ness

The vast majority of auction transactions are as smooth as silk; the winner wins, and the seller ships the merchandise. Everybody is pleased as punch. Normally. But sometimes, the dealings go awry.

Play it safe

As with online classifieds, you have one basic rule in buying anything from a total stranger: *Never send cash.* Too many opportunities abound for temptation to rear its ugly head. Use money orders, certified checks, or cash-only C.O.D.s instead.

The dark side

Well, just one look at the volume of online auctions and the amount of dollars changing hands and you know it's bound to happen: Some bad apples roll into the barrel and try to take advantage of everyone's good nature. Luckily, the scams are pretty well defined by now, and most auction sites take action against the perpetrators.

Keep an eye out, however, for the following schemes:

✔ **Bid shilling.** The auction is getting toward the end, and all of a sudden, the bids start pouring in, each one raising the price to an astronomical level. What was a bargain two minutes ago is now costing more than retail — but you're in the heat of a bidding war, and the urge is to buy, buy, buy! But wait! All the up-the-ante bids are coming from the same buyer, one I.M.N. Honestman of Truthtown, P.E.I. Could Mr. Honestman tell a lie? You bet he could. He's probably working with the seller — or could even *be* the seller under another fake, registered name — to artificially raise the price of the bid.

✔ **Bid shielding.** In looking over the bidding history of the last auction you lost out on, you notice that the high bidders, whose offers had skyrocketed the price, dropped out right before the end. The winner was a distant third. This buyer's bid was being shielded by the other high, pseudo-offers. For example, you might be bidding at the $100 level along with one or two others; your bid has just been topped at $110. Suddenly someone else bids $1,000. Another bid comes in at $1,500. Way outta your league, you take off. Later, it turns out that the first- and second-place winners are fake and the merchandise goes to the $110 bid — who was in cahoots with the fakers.

✔ **Bid siphoning.** You're in the auction of your life, bidding for a super-cool lava lamp kit, when you get an e-mail offering you the same item for less than the current bid. Suddenly, everyone's dropping out of the auction because they all received the same e-mail. After detecting the interest in an item, an unscrupulous party siphoned off the bidders one by one. Because there are fewer bidders, the merchandise didn't bring as much as it could have — and the aforementioned unscrupulous one really shouldn't be offering merchandise under the table.

✔ **Bid retraction manipulation.** Suppose that you entered your maximum bid in the bidding agent. Another bidder comes in very high but not over your limit, pulling your bid up to its maximum. One more counter-bid from the other party and your bid doesn't move — it's at its limit. The second bidder then retracts the initial bid and rebids a little bit higher than your highest bid. By using this technique, the bad guy can discover your maximum bid and top it by just a hair — but enough to take home the bacon. (The bigger question is why you're bidding on bacon.)

If you detect any of these types of actions, alert the online auction house staff. By and large, the auctions are very diligent about such abuses and want to stop this bad bid-ness from continuing.

Chapter 13

The Push Is On

*T*ired of seeking out those bargains on the Web? Ready for a virtual sample salesperson to come knocking on your door? Well, search no more. The companies of the world are ready to deliver as much content as your desktop can handle. And that info can come in all formats — everything from the relatively low-tech newsletters by e-mail to the sexy, high-end multimedia channels.

The general technology that accomplishes all this is called *push*. Push is the opposite of the regular method of browsing the Internet where you, the user, must actively seek out a specific company's address and ask (through the click on a Internet link) for specific information. You can imagine how an industrial society raised on billboards, radio, and television would react to such a scenario. Why must they come to us? Can't we go to them? Well, indeed they can — all you have to do is know where to put the welcome mat.

Signing Up Online for Offline Browsing

So, after virtually years of searching, you've finally found the Web site of your dreams. You add it to your list of Favorites (also known as bookmarking) and vow to visit it daily, if not more often. But soon, other Web sites are demanding your attention and your former heartthrob is a distant memory. "What was that URL again? I remember bookmarking it, I've bookmarked so many — which one was it?"

For those services that really matter, a gentle reminder in your e-mail box from time to time is really ideal. Luckily, some of the more sophisticated Web sites recognize the value of this type of service and have begun implementing a variety of event-driven alerts, monthly newsletters and ongoing discussion lists.

Be alert

Sometimes the simplest ideas are the best. A store wants to sell what a customer wants, right? How about letting the customer know when the product
is in? Hey, there's a revolutionary thought! Customer service! A number of
online stores have implemented an e-mail alert system. If you can't find what
you're looking for on the first pass, you can ask to be alerted when your item
does come in. Consider the example of Air Canada, which has created a
direct e-mail system called Websaver, as shown in Figure 13-1. With this service, you get an e-mail every week telling you about everything from special
fares for the upcoming weekend, to seat sales to frequent flyer promotions.
Here's how it works:

1. **Surf to the Air Canada Web site (**www.aircanada.ca**).**

2. **Select Schedules, Reservations and Fares from the list of options on
   the home page.**

3. **Select Direct e-mail and Websaver.**

4. **Enter your e-mail address and click on Submit. That's all!**

If you want to get off Air Canada's e-mail list, just repeat these steps, but
before clicking on Submit, select the bullet beside the "Please remove my
address from Air Canada's direct email list" option.

Figure 13-1:
Sign up for an
e-mail alert
from your
favourite Web
site.

All the news that fits in your e-mail

There are probably ten times as many Web sites offering e-mail newsletters as there are those with personalized notification services. It figures because the monthly (or sometimes weekly) newsletters are marketing vehicles aimed at a much broader market — much broader than one person, that is. Still, if you can find a Web site catering to a special interest of yours that offers a newsletter, grab it. While you won't find every item of interest, every now and then, it'll have an article or a note that makes it worthwhile.

Not that there's much in the way of cost or effort. Occasionally, you'll run across an e-mailed newsletter that is available on a subscription basis, but those are few and far between. Almost all of the ones offered by an online store or merchant are free for the asking.

And the "asking" — signing up for the newsletter — is a very straightforward procedure. As an example, the following steps walk you through the sign-up procedure Comet, the e-mail newsletter for a superb travel site, Lonely Planet.

1. **Browse on over to the Lonely Planet Web site at** `www.lonelyplanet.com`.

2. **Scroll down to the bottom of its home page and select the Subscribe to Comet link shown in Figure 13-2.**

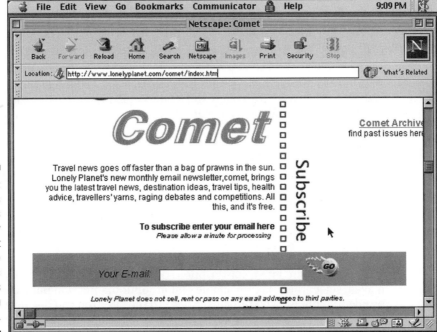

Figure 13-2: Web sites such as Lonely Planet offer free electronic newsletters to keep you up to date.

3. **On the subscription form page, just enter your full e-mail address (such as** `jsbach@classymusic.com`**) and click the Go button.**

   Your information is processed, and a "thanks for subscribing" message comes on screen. You have a second opportunity to double-check your e-mail address and correct it if necessary.

That's all there is to it. In just a nonce — maybe two nonces — you'll get an e-mailed verification regarding your newsletter subscription service. Usually, there's an e-mail address in the message that tells you how to unsubscribe to the service.

Actually, it's probably a bit harder to get off a list than to get on it. You probably noticed the "Unsubscribe" button on the Comet subscription form. You'll keep getting any monthly newsletter you subscribe to until you directly take your name off the list. Some Web sites offer a button like this one to unsubscribe, others require that you send an e-mail to a specific address, often with a special subject heading or message. The details are almost always contained in the newsletter itself.

We find monthly e-mail newsletters to be very refreshing. Unlike dead-tree magazines that we subscribe to in hopes of getting the Prize Patrol to stop by, there's no clutter, and if we don't have time to read them when they're delivered, we can always select the message later.

The Magic of Offline Subscriptions

E-mail notices and newsletter are convenient, but they tend to be a little on the dry side. In order to reach the broadest market, most e-mail is kept in a straight-text format. Kind of miss the color, design, and fun of the modern Web site, don't you? With Microsoft's Internet Explorer 5.0, there is a way to combine the convenience of e-mail alerts with the multimedia nature of a Web page: *subscriptions.*

Using a subscription, you can view up-to-date content from your favourite Web site even when you're offline. Let's say you want to wake up to the news from CBC Newsworld (`www.newsworld.cbc.ca`). With a subscription, you can get your computer to go to that site at 6 a.m. to download the latest headlines. When you roll out of bed at 7 a.m., just turn on your computer — no need to connect to the Net — fire up your browser, choose CBC Newsworld from your list of Favorites, and there you are!

To turn a Favorite into a subscription, right-click on it. From the menu displayed, select the "Make available offline" option. After you put a check mark beside that option, you're "subscribed" to the site. You can decide when and how often to retrieve information from it by selecting the Customize option from menu. Subscriptions are particularly convenient for people travel a lot with their laptops. A quick overnight download, and you can browse the latest from your favourite sites during the day — offline.

The PointCast Network

Any discussion about the power of push technology would be lacking if it didn't mention the outfit that got it all started: PointCast. The folks behind PointCast took a look at how computers are actually used and saw a tremendous amount of downtime where the most the computer was doing was running a screen saver. Wouldn't it be better if that idle time was put to use? And how about that screen saver — couldn't that be put to better use as well?

PointCast uses its own network of content partners and news sources to provide a user-configurable screen saver that always has the latest info. You can get the Canadian version by visiting its Web site (www.pointcast.com). Just click on Download Now and specify that you want the Canadian edition, then choose the region where you live. PointCast will automatically provide you with all the Canadian content available through its network.

After you've installed the system, you can further customize your screen by choosing exactly which features you want. You do this by selecting the Personalize⇨Personalize Channels option from PointCast main interface. This opens up a multitab dialog box, where you can pick and choose from dozens of different categories. Among those categories are several Canadian features including:

- ✔ **The Globe and Mail:** Choose the types of stories you want to follow.

- ✔ **Top News Stories:** All the latest news from Reuters Canada.

- ✔ **Companies:** Playing the market? Keep the latest info in a ticker tape on your desktop. You can follow the performance of Canadian companies on the Toronto, Alberta, or Montreal Stock Exchange. PointCast even has a function that helps you find the correct stock market symbol.

- ✔ **Industries:** Want to keep track of the mining sector or looking for the latest on Conrad Black's progress in the media biz? PointCast lets you track events in up to ten different industries.

- ✔ **Weather:** Keep an eye on the scene in your neck of the Canadian woods as well as some far-off locale you're saving your pennies for with weather updates and maps. Choose up to 50 international cities to monitor.

After you personalize your choices, all you need to do is go online. PointCast will automatically update the information you've selected and a typical screen will look like the one shown in Figure 13-3. If you're connected to a network (that's online all the time), PointCast will update the information throughout the day. Otherwise, you can go online to explicitly update the data or give PointCast a set schedule by choosing the Update All button.

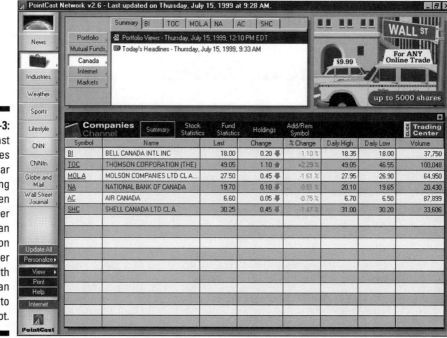

Figure 13-3:
PointCast
changes
your regular
boring
screen
saver
into an
information
power
center, with
Canadian
content to
boot.

Part V

When Bad Shopping Happens to Good People

The 5th Wave   By Rich Tennant

"Awww jeez-I was afraid of this. Some poor kid, bored with the usual chat lines, starts looking for bigger kicks, pretty soon they're surfin' the seedy back alleys of cyberspace, and before you know it they're into a file they can't 'undo'. I guess that's why they call it the Web. Somebody open a window!"

In this part . . .

*I*n a perfect world, there would be no need for Part V —
but who lives in a perfect world? Just given the everyday transactions that occur over the Web — orders
placed, misshipments made, credits requested — sooner
or later, a mistake is bound to happen, and you need to
know how to take care of yourself when it does.

When a problem surfaces, you need to be able to
communicate effectively, and most Internet-related communication happens through e-mail. This part shows you
all you need to know about e-mail correspondence, including mail forwarding and attaching files. Once you get the
hang of it, you'll see why e-mail is known as the "killer
app" of the Internet.

This part lays it all out for you: your rights, your resources,
your courses of action. From the simplest tracking of packages to strategies for handling e-mailed correspondence to
outright fraud complaints, this part explains how it all
works. Just as the Web has spawned a few unscrupulous
individuals who'd rather have your money in their pocket,
a new breed of civic organizations — from both government and grass-roots origins — have emerged. You can find
them listed throughout these chapters.

Chapter 14

Tracking 'Em Down

. . . .

. . . .

*I*t's a perfect world. The sun is shining, the birds are singing, and your order from WebShops.com was just handed over — three days early! — by the friendliest delivery person ever to walk the planet. Wait, what's that up in the sky? A blue moon? Then this must be. . . .

Actually, the odds are that your online order is going to proceed smoothly. But keep in mind that the industry is young and very spry. The number of online orders is relatively low compared to traditional mail and telephone orders. Undoubtedly, as Web shopping expands, the fulfillment side is going to suffer some growing pains. Turn to this chapter for answers when your shipment begins to go awry — or arrives and turns out to be a case of rye when you ordered whole wheat!

Checking Your Order Status

When do you have time to call up customer service and check on your order? Nights and weekends, right? When is customer service open? Business hours, weekdays. What's wrong with this picture?

One of the most wonderful advantages that online shopping has to offer is that it's always available to you, 24 hours a day, 7 days a week, and that applies to online customer service as well. Most major online stores allow you to check the status of your order any time, day or night. Not only can you check the progress within the store — finding out if it has been shipped or not — but once it's on the proverbial big brown truck, you can track it as well, thanks to modern Web site technology. The only item you have to keep track of is your order information, and some sites will even provide that for you.

A question of status

Every Web storefront — like every real-world storefront — handles customer support in its own way. We're very appreciative when the signs pointing the way to checking on an order are very clear, but frankly, it's not always the case. You have to be a little loose when you start looking for the Customer Service page. If you don't see a clearly labeled option, try the Help or the Info buttons on the Web page.

One very good example of customer support is maintained by Chapters.ca, the online bookstore. Let's take a tour to see how it's done:

1. **Having placed a book order earlier today (technology is great, isn't it?), we log on to Chapters (www.chapters.ca) to see if the book has shipped yet.**

2. **On the left side of the home page, we see a list of options under the heading Your Information. We select the only likely candidate: a button labeled Your Order History. We notice, to our delight, that we are now working within the site's secure server (the little lock at the bottom of our browser is closed).**

3. **Before Chapters lets us see our order status, it wants to be sure we are who we say we are, so we are taken to the main Sign-in screen, where we are asked to enter our e-mail address and password. That done, we click on Submit.**

5. **Now, we're taken to the Your Order History page. Here, we can see the date of our order, the order number and the order status.**

6. **Clicking on the order number brings us to a page where we can view Marguerite's complete order information, including her shipping address and a breakdown of the total cost of her order.**

All the details of our order are right there, as shown in Figure 14-1. We can see while everything is in place, the order hasn't shipped yet, so there's no need for us to be on the lookout for the delivery truck just yet.

Filing your own backup

Okay, a show of hands: How many people out there have placed telephone orders from a catalogue? Oh, quite a few. Okay, now how many write down the details of the order that you're placing? Ah, not so many. Now how many note the day you placed the order? Yeah, we always forget that part, too. Which means that our calls to customer service usually end up sounding like, "Well, we think it was last Tuesday, or maybe Monday. No, We're sure it was a week ago Wednesday." And order confirmation numbers? We usually find ourselves *pretending* that we're writing them down because we can't find a pencil or pen when the service reps start rattling off those impossibly long numbers.

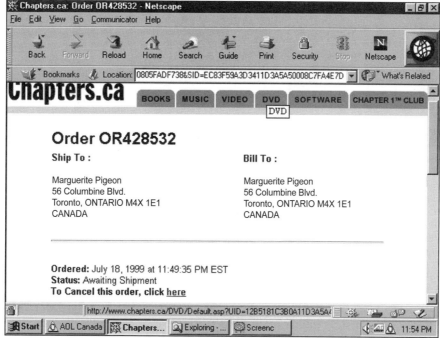

Figure 14-1:
Has
it shipped
yet? Has it
shipped yet?
Now, you
can bug the
computer
all you want
without
fear of any
reprisals
from over-
burdened
Customer
Service
reps.

Happily, there's one feature we've seen implemented consistently in all the major online stores: an e-mailed confirmation of your order. The confirmation contains all the pertinent info such as an order number (yeah!), the date, the shipping information (where it's going and how), the charge, and all the order details, item by item. We can't tell you what a boon it is to have all this information delivered to you, in a format that's easy to hang onto.

So what do you do with the order info? There are a great number of options to choose from — it all depends on how you organize your life:

✔ **File a hard copy:** Print out your confirmation and file it wherever you'd like. It's probably easiest just to keep a folder with all your order confirmations in reverse chronological order; that is, put the latest one on top.

✔ **File the electronic copy:** You'll notice that your mail program (probably Microsoft's Outlook Express, Netscape's Messenger, or maybe Eudora Pro) is organized in folders. The Inbox is one folder, Sent Mail is another and so on. You can make your own folders by selecting File⇨New Folder or File⇨Folder⇨New Folder. Make a new folder just for your orders and place all your confirmation in there. No muss, no fuss.

✔ **Search for 'em when you need 'em:** If you haven't figured it out by now, we're pretty lazy. We tend just to keep all the confirmations in our general Inbox and, if there is a problem, track it down from there. We use our mail program's Search in File feature, which allows us to specify any part of the message or who it's from as a search criteria. We can usually remember who we ordered the goods from — and we can take it from there.

And the Waybill Number Is . . .

After your order has, like Elvis, left the building, how do you keep tabs on it? Most online stores ship their packages via one of the commercial carriers, such as FedEx, UPS, or Purolator. With the exception of packages shipped via UPS ground service and those shipped by Parcel Post, this allows all shipments to be tracked. Until recently, you had to call the shipping company, park yourself on the phone, and wait for those very busy people on the other end of the line to get the info from their computers. Now, you can cut out the middleman (or middlewoman) and use the wonders of the World Wide Web to handle the trace yourself. Not only is it faster, but you can also get a hard copy of the tracking details. It's a snap. We'll show you the ropes in the following section. We'll even show you how to tackle up to 20 packages in one fell swoop. Let's go!

If you want more details on tracking and shipping in general, see Chapter 9, called "Shipping and Receiving".

Doing the FedEx, UPS, and Purolator Rhumba

There's only one essential element necessary for tracking your order from your store's doors to yours: the number. FedEx calls it the airbill number, as shown in Figure 14-2; to UPS, it's the tracking number (although the company also has a reference number service); and to Purolator, it's the PIN. Each package has a number, and you need it before you can trace shipments over the Web. The number should be part of your order record, after the item has shipped. If not, you can get it by e-mailing customer service.

All the major shipping companies have massive (in terms of data) Web sites that are tied into their own internal routing computers. When you go through their Web sites, you're pulling from the same information database that the telephone operators are using. You're just getting it directly.

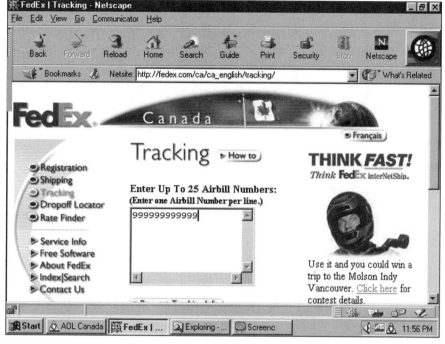

Figure 14-2:
Want the
inside scoop
on where
your
package
is? Try the
FedEx online
tracking
service.

Once you reach each of the companies' sites, you have to find the tracking page to start the procedure. To give you a bit of a boost, here's the direct address for the services we'll discuss here:

- **FedEx:** www.fedex.com/ca/ca_english/tracking/
- **UPS:** www.ups.com/canada/tracking/engtracking.html
- **Purolator:** www.purolator.com/cgi-bin/pt1005e.pl

Keeping a copy

What do you do after you've tracked down your elusive package on the computer? If you're really having problems finding your package — and not just excited and/or idly curious — we'd recommend two approaches. First, print out a hard copy of the information screen that details your tracking info. Second, use your browser's Save feature to keep an electronic copy of the same data. Choose File⇨Save when the data is on the screen to start the process.

If you're starting to have long, drawn-out discussions with customer service about a missing package, you can't have too much backup. And having it in multiple forms means that you can reply in various ways. The hard copy is great for faxing, and the electronic copy works well when e-mailing your customer service reps.

Ordering a bunch? Track it in bulk!

We promised to show you how to check up on multiple packages at one time via e-mail, and we always keep our word. FedEx, UPS, and Purolator all have this service within the tracking area. You don't have to enter a subject, but the body of the message needs to be in a particular format.

For example, with Purolator, you can send your message to track@purolator.com. The company asks that you list each PIN on a separate line in the body of the message. For UPS, the process is slightly different. You have to send a separate e-mail for each package, including the tracking number in the body of your e-mail. Address the message to totaltrack@ups.com.

You can send your FedEx each package to track@fedex.com. For each package, enter

the word "airbill," the airbill number (without spaces or separators), the two-character code for the destination country, and the shipment date in MMDDYY (month-day-year) format. For example, here's an e-mail message for three FedEx packages:

```
airbill 42123456789 us 061799
airbill 40012345678 ca 050399
airbill 42301254689 jp 022499
```

The two-character country codes are known as the IATA (International Air Transport Association) codes, and FedEx has a chart of them on its site at www.fedex.com/ca/ca_english/ tracking/countrycodes.html.

In the next section, we'll tell you all you need to know about communicating with customer service via e-mail, including how to attach an electronic copy of your shipping info.

Corresponding with Your E-Reps

The Internet has ushered in a major new era of interaction and its name is e-mail. Electronic mail has revolutionized the world's communication in the 1990s, just as fax machines altered it in the 1970s. Most online stores offer an e-mail address as their first option of contact, and there are some good reasons why:

- ✔ **It's asynchronous:** You can send anyone a message at any time. You don't have to wake up West Coast service centres early to handle East Coast calls.

- ✔ **It's cheap:** Internet access is just a local phone call away. No more hanging on a long-distance help line, listening to bad Muzak while watching your phone bill add up.

- ✔ **It's manageable:** You've got an instant record of every communication you ever sent or received. You can even organize your electronic mailbox to show the thread of the conversation.

> ✔ **It's flexible:** While plain text messages are the most common, they're not the only way to communicate. You can attach additional files, be they other e-mail messages or from another program entirely. You can even include photographs in your e-mail.

For many people, e-mail is the best reason to get on the Internet. In the next few sections, we look at some of the ways you can use e-mail to correct any problems that arise with your online shopping.

And you can quote us!

The basic method of sending a message to a store's customer service department is, as they said in the old days, simple as dirt. Almost all virtual shops have a Contact Us or similar link that leads to one of two communication options. Sometimes, selecting the Write us link takes you to a form, very similar to the ones you're used to filling out when ordering anything online. There is generally a text box for your name, your e-mail address, a topic, and then a large text area for your message. Fill out all of the form — especially your e-mail address — and then click the Submit or Send button.

The second type of communication link opens a blank message form from your browser's e-mail component, such as the one shown in Figure 14-3. You'll find that the electronic letter is already addressed — and in some cases already has the subject filled out. If not, all you have to do is enter a heading in the subject line and then complain your heart out in the message area. When you're done, just click the Send button and your e-epistle is on its way. Your return address is already attached to the letter for their swift reply. Pretty zippy, eh?

When you get a message from the customer service reps, you can reply with the click of a button. Amazingly enough, that button is labeled Reply. Because electronic mail has become so pervasive, it's best to refer to their message when responding and the easiest way to do it is by *quoting* their entire message, which allows both parties to have an easy reference to their ongoing discussion. Both Netscape and Microsoft allow you to automatically include the original message in a reply; you can set the option through each program's preferences.

To make Netscape quote original messages, choose Edit⇨Preferences, and from the Messages tab of the Mail & Groups category, enable the Automatically quote original message when replying option. For Outlook Express, choose Tools⇨Options, and from the Send tab, select the Include message in reply option.

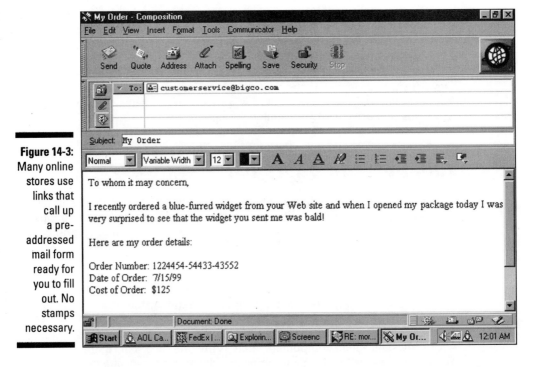

Figure 14-3:
Many online
stores use
links that
call up
a pre-
addressed
mail form
ready for
you to fill
out. No
stamps
necessary.

Depending on your other mail settings, the quoted message may just be separated by a line that says "Original Message." Or each line of the message may begin with an angle bracket like this:

```
>Dear Ms. Grossi:
>Thank you for your letter of July 10th. We apologize for
>the mix-up with your order.
```

The angle bracket serves to differentiate your current message from the older, quoted one. In fact, because you can quote a quoted message, it's not uncommon for the angle brackets to get several layers thick.

We cc you, you bcc us

Any temp will tell you, cc's on a letter are a headache, and bcc's are a nightmare. Adding a 'cc' to your business correspondence indicates that you are sending a carbon copy (or the equivalent thereof) to each of the listed parties. The letters 'bcc' stands for blind carbon copy and indicates that only you and the person receiving bcc know about it — neither the original recipient or any of the cc'd folks are notified. You can send both cc's and bcc's electronically.

When should you use a cc or a bcc? If you're not getting any satisfaction through your dealings with your customer service rep, you might want to start letting others know. Often a cc of a complaint letter sent to president@bigco.com will have the desired effect.

Outlook Express has individual lines for both the cc and the bcc designation, but Netscape's Messenger is a little harder to find. Select the To: button to drop down a list of available address options, including Cc: and Bcc:.

Be a little forward

Sometimes you need to send along an e-mail that you received from one person to another. All mail programs allow you to *forward* a copy of your mail. When the e-mail in question is highlighted, just click the Forward button and fill in the address field.

You don't have to send the message by its lonesome, either; you can add any comments you'd like to the forwarded page. Simply click into the message area and type away. The recipient will see your notes and the complete forwarded message.

When dealing with customer service, a good candidate for forwarded e-mail is the order confirmation you received electronically. We told you that would come in handy.

Netscape adds a [Fwd:] designation to the front of the forwarded e-mail's subject line, so you can easily track which e-mails are originals and which are forwarded.

We all have our attachments

Every so often, you'll need to send an additional file with your e-mail, just like you'd send a fax cover letter with attachments. In fact, the very clever e-mail program designers refer to these added-on files as *attachments*. To attach a file to an e-mail that you're composing, click the Attach button in the main toolbar. This brings up an Open File dialog box, which allows you to select any accessible file. There's no limitation to the type or number of files that you can attach to any one e-mail.

Netscape's Messenger uses the word "Attach" with a paper clip icon, as shown in Figure 14-4, and Outlook Express just has the paper clip symbol for its Attach button.

Attached files   Attach Button

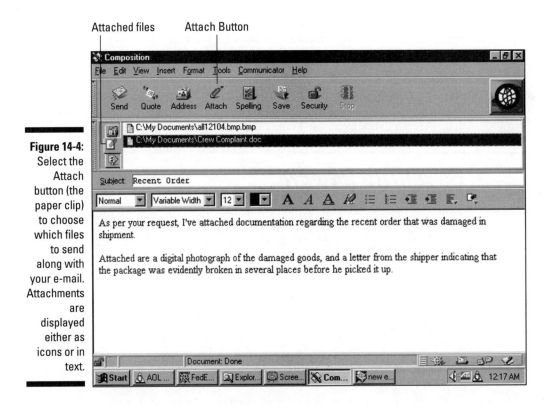

Figure 14-4:
Select the
Attach
button (the
paper clip)
to choose
which files
to send
along with
your e-mail.
Attachments
are
displayed
either as
icons or in
text.

When you're attaching a file to send to someone, you need to be sure of just one thing: The person reading the file has the right tools to read it. Not everyone has the same software that you do — and if they have the same software, they may not have the same version as you. If you've never sent a particular type of file to an individual before, it's worth an e-mail or a call to make sure that everyone is speaking the same language.

Chapter 15

Protecting Your Online Rights

· ·

In This Chapter

▶ Finding online consumer-rights info

▶ Watching out for cyberfelons

▶ Making your complaint heard

· ·

*T*he following preview is rated G for general audiences:

"They were all alone."

[Spotlights sweep the empty night sky.]

"At the mercy of greedy online merchants."

[Unshaven men squint through cigarette smoke.]

"Overcharges, delayed shipping, unfulfilled backorders."

[Packs of hundred-dollar bills slapped down on a card table.]

"When no one else could help."

[Unshaven men squinting and laughing.]

"They were all alone. Until he came to town."

[Man walks through smoke with spotlights sweeping sky behind him.]

"CyberShop Cop"

[Begin montage of explosions, car chase, glass breaking, vicious dogs barking, rapid typing, computer graphics of spinning logos, more glass breaking, cars chasing, vicious dogs, computers exploding, and so on.]

Starring John-Clod van Darne. Coming this summer.

Face it — the more successful any commercial venture is, the more likely are some folks to try to take advantage of it. Selling on the Web has been called a "gold rush" — and as was true any frontier town, the good citizens of the Internet could use a little law and order every so often. But because of the global nature of the Web, traditional legal structures can go only so far. Luckily, some civic-minded Netizens have come forward and temporarily slapped on a deputy badge to help out.

In this chapter, you discover who's out there watching your back while you surf the wild 'n' woolly Web shops. You also find out how you can protect yourself and others from the less-than-scrupulous.

Walking the Cyber Watchdogs

You're going to be amazed to hear this tragic fact, but people are out there on the Web who'd like to separate you from your money without giving you much in return. "No!" we hear you say. Well, it's true — sad, but true.

The amazing part is that you're not alone — a lot of powerful people are out there who want to stop them. What's surprising about the array of organizations that are bent on protecting you is that they're not federal government authorities — those guys are still figuring out how to change the laws to actually recognize the existence of e-commerce — but organizations and companies from within the Internet itself. Also keep in mind that there isn't much in terms of Canadian-based organizations. That isn't surprising, though, since Canadian retailers are only now trying to establish an online shopping presence. Rather, consumer groups protecting you are primarily in the United States. The good news is that their reach does extend, albeit in a very limited way, to Canada.

Because we are paying for their services, we're going to examine what the government is up to first.

What's up on the Hill

Industry Canada's Office of Consumer Affairs aims for a fair and efficient marketplace that supports and advances the interests of Canadians as consumers. One way to achieve that is through education. To that end, Industry Canada's Web site called Strategis (strategis.ic.gc.ca) is an incredible resource for all sorts of business guidance and consumer information.

The Web site is fairly large, so knowing your way around to the various-consumer-oriented areas is helpful. Your best bet is to start by selecting the Consumer Information link from the Strategis' home page. The Consumer Information page highlights Hot Stuff Information — recently it was telephone fraud and financial services charges — as well as consumer awareness information.

But you'll find Web-oriented info by clicking the Consumer Connection link, as shown in Figure 15-1.

After you reach the Consumer Connection page, you can find most of the information by clicking the Consumer Quarterly link under the section titled Our Work. Here you can access online editions of the publication put out by the Office of Consumer Affairs. If you have any questions or concerns about your finances and making major purchases, online or offline, you can find information here.

Follow this link to some great information with some of the most pun-laden headlines you've ever encountered, including the following:

- Holes in the Net
- Cavenet emptor!!
- Mending the Net

One of the most informative volumes of Consumer Quarterly is simply titled Consumers and the Internet. It's a very concise source of information to give you a general overview of cybershopping, from explaining potential consumer hazards on the Internet to outlining security solutions.

Figure 15-1:
You've got a highly placed friend who's there to safeguard your rights as a consumer: the Consumer Connection page on Industry Canada's site.

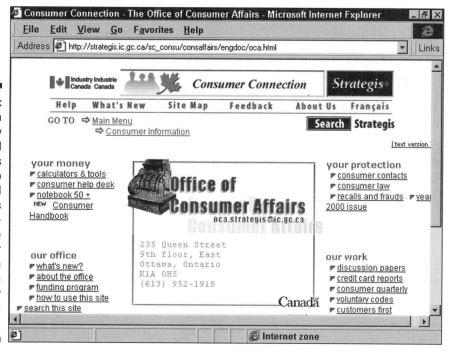

If you have questions regarding e-commerce, write to: Office of Consumer Affairs, Industry Canada, 235 Queen St., C.D. Howe Building, 9th Floor, East Tower, Ottawa, ON K1A 0H5.

In The Public Eye

Industry Canada's site is great for warnings about ongoing scams and trends to look out for, but sometimes, you need a reality check for a specific online store or service. And a once-a-decade kind of rating wouldn't do either, because Web sites change so frequently. You really need an organization that facilitates 24-hour monitoring of the full range of shopping experiences. You really need the Public Eye.

The Public Eye (`www.thepubliceye.com`) is a private organization with a public sensibility. WebWeek magazine has likened the site to the Good Housekeeping Seal of Approval, but the Public Eye provides much more detail than Good Housekeeping ever did. Its home page accesses a tremendous variety of certified merchants by category and through its "A" list, as shown in Figure 15-2 — and yes, there are some smart Canadian sites included.

Figure 15-2: Read up on a merchant to see how the company rates as scrutinized by the Public Eye.

The Public Eye offers the following two classes of certification for virtual merchants:

- **Gold Certification.** After its army of "undercover shoppers" visits a site, transacting business left and right, the shoppers evaluate the shop according to real-world tests of reliability. The stores aren't notified before or during this audit process.

- **Platinum Certification.** Merchants can apply to the Public Eye for certification by providing a link to the Public Eye's Customer Satisfaction Database. This link enables 24-hour monitoring of the company's shopping services and gives consumers easy access to a database of comments — both good and bad — filed by actual customers.

The Gold Certification program calls for evaluation of each merchant in the following five different areas:

- **Accessibility.** What happens if something goes wrong in Shopping Land? Are we talking to a live customer rep or some canned entity?

- **References.** The Public Eye requests a list of current customers who it then contacts and surveys.

- **Service.** How quickly does the staff respond to questions and problems? The Public Eye rates each site's staffers according to their helpfulness and how informed they are.

- **Stability.** Are we talking a fly-by-night or solid-as-a-rock company? The Public Eye also looks for any reported trend of customer dissatisfaction.

- **Warranties/Returns.** Does the company stand behind its products and services? The Public Eye also takes a hard look at return policies and follow-through.

After an undercover shopper visits a site under consideration for Gold Certification, the site is rated from 1 to 5. To qualify for a Gold Certification, a Web store must receive a rating of at least 14 out of a possible 20 points. The final category — References — is rated independently. Any significant legal action against the company or discovered trend of customer dissatisfaction immediately disqualifies the company from certification.

Anyone can enter comments for a company participating in the Public Eye's Platinum program. A customer can click the link to the Public Eye's report form, where the customer can give the site a rating ranging from an "Excellent" to a "Very Bad." Shoppers visiting the Public Eye can then search or browse for the company's report or merchant record, as shown in Figure 15-3. Many of the Canadian sites we checked up on didn't have customer comments. But the fact that they were willing to put themselves up to the glare of scrutiny speaks volumes.

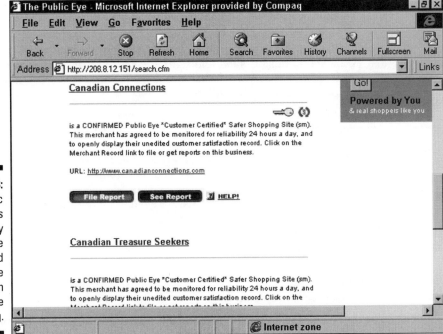

Figure 15-3:
The Public Eye offers an easy way to spot the gems and avoid the dreck in online shopping.

The Public Eye hasn't forgotten that you and millions of others may still be leery of using your credit card when online shopping — no matter how many stars a site may tout. The Public Eye has a nifty program to further calm any shopping jitters. All Public Eye "Platinum" certified merchants are covered by the site's Credit Card Fraud Protection Program. If you experience unauthorized use of your credit card as a result of shopping at any one of these sites, Public Eye will cover your losses that you're stuck with.

Doing business the BizRate way

You can find another excellent customer service organization at the BizRate Guide's Web site (www.bizrate.com). BizRate enables you to browse by category and subcategory or search directly for a company. It lists 18 headings with which you can start out, as shown in Figure 15-4.

BizRate grades Web shops and the products they carry on an astounding array of criteria, including price, product selection, product information, Web-site aesthetics, Web-site navigation, on-time delivery, ease of returns, customer support, and customer report. You can also find succinct information about each merchant's capabilities and site features, such as the security protocol employed, the languages supported, its return procedures, the payment methods accepted, and its available delivery options.

Figure 15-4:
When you
want to see
how an
online com-
pany really
rates, go to
BizRate,
where you
can get a
complete
report card
on 'em.

What's truly amazing is that BizRate makes all these ratings and explanations comprehensible by compiling them into company report cards. Furthermore, you can search the merchant database by these features. Here's how the process to search for a merchant works:

1. **Log on to the BizRate site at** www.bizrate.com.

2. **Click on Merchant Guide, which takes you to a listing of categories.**

3. **Enter the name of a merchant in the search text box, or choose the category that interests you and click on any subtopic to take you to a listing of all the merchants in that subtopic.**

   The listings that appear from your selection are separated into Gold (customer certified) and Blue (staff reviewed) groups, with those merchants receiving the highest rating, measured in stars, listed first.

4. **Click the Edit button inside the box titled Your Shopping Filters, on the right side of the page.**

   The Filters page appears, as shown in Figure 15-5.

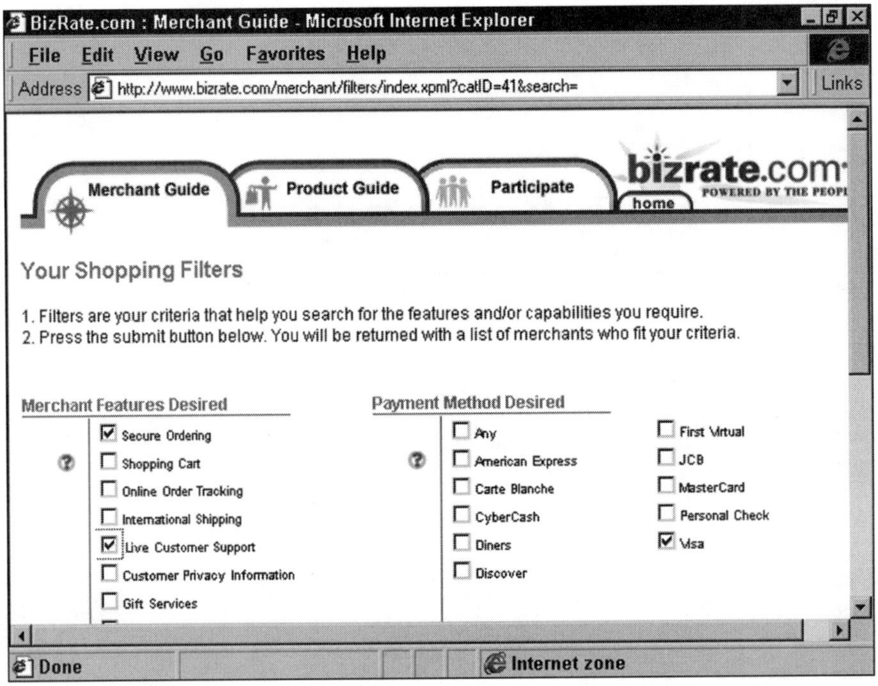

Figure 15-5:
Looking for
online mer-
chants who
let you buy
with your
Visa card,
offer live
customer
support,
offer secure
ordering,
and speak
Chinese?
Select your
filters from
the BizRate
site and
track 'em
down.

5. **Select those options that you require for online shopping by checking their radio buttons and checkboxes.**

   If, for example, you have only a Visa card and, therefore, want to deal only with those merchants who accept it, select that checkbox among the Payment Method Desired choices. Or choose the merchant services that are important to you, such as Order Tracking and Gift Wrapping and select those checkboxes.

6. **After you make your selections, click the Submit button.**

   Your category or subcategory options are then filtered through the options you select, and the Web sites matching your criteria appear as before, sorted with the highest rated first.

7. **Click on the View Report section next to a company's name in the list to obtain a detailed report card on the site.**

8. **You can jump directly to the chosen company's Web site by selecting its linked name from the Report Card screen.**

You can also use BizRate to search for a product offered by the merchants that BizRate grades. Here's how:

1. **Log on to the BizRate site at** `www.bizrate.com` **and click on Product Guide.**

2. **Select the product category that interests you by clicking on its icon.**

3. **Enter the name of the product in the text box, or click on the product's link if it's made it to the Top 10 Searches list, as shown in Figure 15-6.**

   (A listing of the companies from which the product will be searched is located at the bottom of the page.)

   You'll be taken to a results page that provides a listing of companies that offer the product you want. As shown in Figure 15-7, you get a short description of the product the merchant sells, its price, and whether it's in stock. The merchant is also rated based on how prompt it is getting your product delivered to you. Of course, you can check out the company's report card.

4. **Click the Buy Info button once you've decided which merchant to buy from.**

   You'll be taken directly to the company's Web site to make your purchase.

The BizRate Guide is a tremendous service both for the valuable information that it provides consumers and the opportunity that it gives shoppers to rate the shops themselves. Had a bad shopping day and you need to vent yourself? Read on, dear shopper.

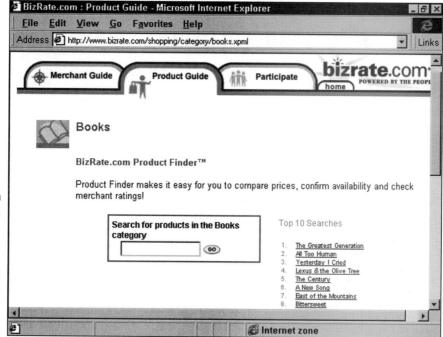

Figure 15-6:
BizRate lets you search for a specific product from the site's merchants.

Figure 15-7:
BizRate will
show you
which of
its rated
merchants
offers the
widget you
want to buy.

Expressing Your Customer Dissatisfaction

BizRate and other services like it enable customers to rate the site after they finish shopping there. But what about those complaints and concerns that go far beyond a mild rebuke of "slow service" or a judgment call on the Web site's design? Who's going to take your serious complaints seriously?

If you have a problem with an order placed on a Web site, you should always go through the store's customer-service representatives initially. Using the techniques that we describe in Chapter 14, make sure that you e-mail the company all the pertinent details and keep records of all its replies. Such a paper trail (or, in the worst cases, a lack of one) can prove essential to making your case.

Just look at what the top three current problems Web shoppers experience, as compiled by National Fraud Watch (www.fraud.org) for its Internet Fraud Watch program that also includes Canadian content:

✔ **Web Auctions.** Items bid for were never delivered by the sellers; the value of items was inflated; or shills were suspected of driving up bids.

✔ **General Merchandise.** Goods were never delivered or weren't as advertised.

▐ ✓ **Computer Equipment/Software.** Computer products were never delivered or were misrepresented.

Despite — or maybe because of — the Internet's rep as a rollickin' frontier
town, a great number of organizations are interested in making it a safer,
better place to shop. Chief among them, as in the offline world, is the Better
Business Bureau.

Better Business Bureau

The Better Business Bureau (BBB) is an American way of life that Canada has
wholeheartedly embraced. Currently more than 150 branches across the
United States and Canada provide information on local, regional, and national
businesses.

The Better Business Bureau's online presence (www.bbb.org) enables you to
quickly search for pertinent consumer alerts, browse its buying-guide library,
and — most important to our discussion — file a business complaint or check
on a company's reliability based on complaints (or lack of them) online. Hey, if
you're buying online, why shouldn't you be able to gripe online too!

Visit this site, whether the company you're checking up on is American or
Canadian. But if it's a Canadian company you're after, why not go directly to
the BBB offices in Canada, as shown in Figure 15-8.

There are a few BBB Web sites servicing specific regions, including Nova
Scotia, Southern Alberta, Vancouver Island, Western Ontario, Metropolitan
Toronto and Windsor and Southwestern Ontario. Simply search for "Better
Business Bureau" to find their URLs. (Note that each BBB site has access to
files on companies only in the site's service area.)

The complaint form is intended for most commercial activities, both online
and offline. The list of offenses includes but isn't limited to misleading advertising, improper selling practices, nondelivery of goods or services, misrepre-
sentation, guarantees or warranties not honoured, unsatisfactory service,
credit/billing problems, contracts not fulfilled, and so on.

This form is a slightly more complex version of the order form you've probably seen dozens of times by now. It simply asks for your personal information, information about the company and then details about your complaint,
including how you'd like to resolve this complaint.

Filing a complaint with the Better Business Bureau is not a revenge tactic —
it's a way of trying to resolve the issue without going to court. After you file
your complaint online, the BBB sends it to the company itself and, if applicable, to a local Bureau if one has jurisdiction over the particular area where
the company is located.

Figure 15-8:
If you got trouble at your online mall, who ya gonna call? One of the Better Business Bureau online Canadian sites, of course.

Generally, whenever the BBB comes calling with a complaint in hand, companies sit up and notice, and the dispute often gets resolved. If the BBB gets multiple unresolved complaints about an organization, it includes these issues in the BBB's records and makes them available to the public. In extreme cases, the Better Business Bureau talks to another type of bureau — one working in the law-enforcement field — to determine whether the situation calls for further action.

When you go online to make your accusation, make sure that you have all your information ready. You may even consider printing out the empty form in one preliminary visit and then returning after you're sure that you're ready to file the complaint. Also, the BBB can't process your request if the issue is already the subject of a lawsuit.

Part VI
The Online Shopping Directory

The 5th Wave   By Rich Tennant

C/S COMPUTING

WAN

JUST KEEP FOLLOWING THE SIGNS.

In this part . . .

All right, you've made it through the rest of the book — or maybe you just skipped ahead to get here. No matter what your strategy, "The Online Shopping Directory" contains the fun stuff — where you really get to stretch your online shopping wings and soar.

Looking to lay down some serious bread and you want to make sure you're getting the best deal around? Be sure to check out the sections on car (and boat and even plane) buying as well as the really big investment of a house or apartment. We'll even show you sites where you can learn how to shop for a mortgage.

Taking a trip? Online travel is extremely hot these days. Travel Web sites are among some of the fancier multi-media-enhanced offerings, and deservedly so. After all, when you want to check out a sample dive in the Great Barrier Reef, you'd like something more than a static brochure, wouldn't you?

You can find plenty of down-home pleasures in this part, as well. Fantastic book bargains, exotic music, and much more are yours for the purveying, online. And if you're looking to take care of those around you, be it family or friends, look no further than the "Great Pastimes" section.

Let us offer you a couple of words of caution that should accompany any Web directory before you jump in. The Web is a very dynamic organism — which is a super-fancy way of saying that things change online. Existing Web sites change addresses and close down while new ones are coming on all the time. If a Web site listed in the directory is at the given URL — and if the page doesn't automatically forward you to their new address — don't let it bother you. Move on to the next site where you'll find an equal or better experience waiting for you. Finally, as in the rest of the book, we've tried our best to make this directory as Canadian as possible. But if there's an unbeatable non-Canadian site (check out some of those global travel research sites) we're going to let you know about it. So surf away! We know you'll have a good time.

Shopping Online For Canadians For Dummies Internet Directory

The Web is full of sites where you can buy, sell, and trade products and services. This wonderful yellow directory lists our favourites — some run by and for Canadians, others that appeal to people around the world.

As you read through this directory, the following little icons indicate the various features of each Web site:

The site allows you to buy stuff.

$ The site requires a fee for its services.

The site requires you to sign in before you can access its features.

The site offers files for downloading.

The site allows you to upload files.

The site requires that your browser have certain plug-ins.

The site offers sound clips or music.

The site offers video clips for your viewing pleasure.

The site features lots of graphics.

The site offers a chat room.

The site has a message board.

Aloha, Bonjour, Howdy: Traveling on the Web

If Microsoft hadn't co-opted the slogan "Where do you want to go today?" it could easily be the banner for an array of Web sites devoted to travel. From the travelogues of the large destination-planning Web sites to the nitty-gritty details of a trip across Canada, the Web has it all. This time, then, a journey of a thousand miles starts with but a single click.

Where to, Buddy?

Destination research must be one of the best chores ever handed down. Today's Web sites give you a rich flavour of the most exotic locales with enough specifics so that you can maximize your journeys. Because the destination planners attempt to convey the sights, sounds, and sensations of distant lands, their Web sites tend to be fairly graphic- and multimedia-intensive. They become, in fact, destinations worth visiting all by themselves — even if you aren't booking that trip around the world just yet.

Arthur Frommer's Budget Travel Online

www.frommers.com

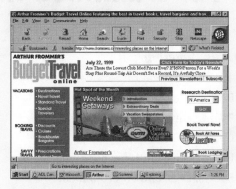

Insight into two hundred destinations worldwide, in great depth: Frommer's, publisher of the famous travel guide, has assembled an online resource filled with first-rate travel writing to help you make plans for a simple weekend getaway or the grand adventure. A little more refined (read: *less hip*) than some of its avant-garde competition, Frommer's Web site is nonetheless a great pleasure to peruse. If you're an avid reader or travelogue fan, the knowledgeable essays on the world's most visited places that you find in this site are certain to have you dreaming of Chinese junks at sunset in the fragrant harbour of Hong Kong.

Aside from the extensive destination entries, check out these features:

- *Novel Travel:* A compendium of "alternative" travel options that threaten to "stretch your mind and change your life," with suggestions for Cerebral Travel, Political Travel, Volunteer Travel, Vacations for Health, and New Modes of Travel (such as trekking and sailing on the tall ships).

- *Standard Travel:* Divided into 17 distinct categories from Beach Vacations on Tropical Islands to Wilderness Trips and Theme Park Vacations.
- *Special Travelers:* Options for seniors, young singles, students, the physically challenged, honeymooners, religious pilgrims, and intellectuals, to name but a few.

Make sure that you check out the Archives for the previous week's travel specials, which, although time-sensitive, are likely to still be in effect if you move fast. You also find a varied collection of Travel Boards online and ready for your input. Arthur suggests a Java- and frames-capable browser, operating under Windows 95 or Mac OS 7.5 or later, to fully enjoy his offerings. Pleasant graphics, legible typeface, and easy to get around — in short, a classic gem.

Attractions Canada

www.attractionscanada.com

From sea to shining sea: Probably the best thing about living in a country as big as ours is that a devoted traveler could spend years exploring without ever leaving Canadian territory. Attractions Canada is a site designed to encourage exactly that. Aside from links to all the online

provincial tourism associations and a list of useful toll-free numbers for Canadian travelers, the site has a bunch of nifty add-ons, including a time zone page, weather updates, games, electronic postcards, and even an archive of memorable attractions from the past.

If you're visiting the Attractions Canada site, be sure to check out its central feature: a search engine that lets you seek out attractions across the country in categories including cultural events, sporting events, interior sites, and exterior sites. Searching through the Cultural Events listings for the province of Ontario, we found info on tulip, blues, and wine festivals including dates and contact numbers/e-mail addresses. Some of the larger listings also have Web links so that you can go directly to the source to plan your next Canadian vacation.

Canada Tourism

www.canadatourism.com

You got your searches, your planning guide, and your helpful hints: The Canadian Tourism Commission has put together another nicely designed and thorough travel site for Canadians who want to explore their homeland. For the armchair traveler, we suggest the *Virtual Tour,* a photo gallery of many Canadian tourism hot-spots. If you're ready to actually pack up and go somewhere, use the *Travel Planner* to search for events, link to outfitting companies for everything from ski to canoe trips, or just get acquainted with a particular province. Canadians may want to skip *Before you travel,* which offers basic info for people travelling here from abroad. But don't leave before trying out the advanced search functions that let you look for travel publications, associations, and tourism news across the country.

Use Canada Tourism as well for its link to Live The Legacy (at www.live-legacy.com), a beautifully designed Web site also run by the Canadian Tourism Commission to promote travel to aboriginal tourism destinations across the country. It's got very thorough listings of native art galleries, pow-wows, parks, and conferences.

Fielding Worldwide, Inc.

www.fieldingtravel.com

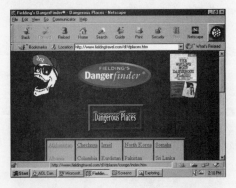

Far out travel guide of faraway places: How we could have lived as long as we have and traveled as far as we have without ever hearing of these wackos is beyond us. The gang at Fielding's has "A Passion for Travel." That's not all those folks have — they also possess an irreverent mondo-gonzo-bizarro sensibility that's sure to keep you alternately intrigued, appalled, befuddled, and, ultimately, laughing out loud.

Here you can find featured categories like the following:

- *CRUISEfinder:* Among other things, this category compares all cruise lines to hotel chains in terms of character. Windjammer Barefoot Cruises, therefore, is Club Med; Carnival Cruise Line is the MGM Grand, and so on — with World Explorer Cruises coming in last (or perhaps first) as the rough equivalent of "summer camp." These ratings are a lot of fun, even if a cruise is the last thing you had in mind.

- *DANGERfinder, BLACKflag,* and the wondrous *LINKfinder:* Fielding is most notorious for these elements, all a far cry from the Love Boat. DANGERfinder informs us that it is a guide to "The World's Most Dangerous Places." Among the subjects discussed at length are such categories as *Dangerous Places* — for example, Tajikistan, where "For now the only tourist attractions are a ring of armed border forts manned by 25,000 Russian soldiers, weekly firefights with Afghan smugglers and Tajik rebels," and Albania where "It's OK to be paranoid..."

We think you're going to agree that Fielding's Worldwide offers you a flipped-out, rollicking good adventure without so much as leaving your (mouse) pad.

Fodor's Travel Service

www.fodors.com

Top-quality ratings of top-quality destinations: Fodor's pretty much says it all with its disclaimer that precedes the restaurant and hotel guides: "You won't find every restaurant/hotel in town . . . but, you will find expert reviews of those establishments that meet Fodor's standards for quality, service and value." Raatherrrrr!

That being said, in the areas Fodor's deems worthy of appraisal, it does a most admirable job. The *Restaurant Finder* is particularly useful (especially in the absence of a comprehensive online Zagat Survey at this point). The *Hotel Finder,* although abbreviated, is of unmistakably good breeding. Other notable features include the following:

- *Focus On Photography:* An entire, beautifully presented short course on the art of photography.

- *Cruise News:* A roundup of the "big-boat" scene (along with links to all the major cruise lines).

- *Hosted Forums:* Where you go to get advice on travel from well-known travel writers.

Additional highlights include the *Create Your Own Miniguide* service, which permits you to construct "your own travel guide to 99 destinations worldwide," and the Resource Center, an amalgam of useful links. The graphics site-wide are clean, crisp, and lovely, and the illustrations are often whimsically reminiscent of Saint-Exupéry's *The Little Prince.*

Lonely Planet Online

www.lonelyplanet.com

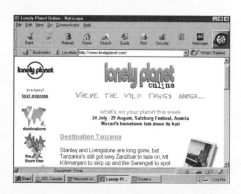

Excellent travelogue stories and pictures: The planet wouldn't seem all that lonely with these folks traveling by your side. Warm, friendly, with a good sense of humor throughout, this site has many glowing features. Self-described as a good place for "Web monkeys and travel junkies," roaming *this* lonely planet seems more like an invigorating evening stroll with an old friend — a very well-traveled old friend. Destinations begin with hot interactive maps that zap you around the globe and enable you to zoom in and out with great ease. Zoom in and the fun begins — simple, colourfully written articles with anecdotes, maps, and slide shows galore.

Unlike on some other travel sites, the destination pages are only a small part of the planetary info that you find here. Here are some of the others:

- *Optic Nerve* features hundreds of striking high-definition photos from pretty much everywhere, as well as savvy and helpful tips for the amateur photojournalist in us all.

- *On The Road* is a pretty hip collection of travel writings that lives up to its name.

- *The Thorn Tree* is filled with interesting topics and postings, especially for those who are less-well-to-do vagabond . . . er, intrepid voyagers.

- *Postcards* contains traveler updates and other material that's worth keeping.

- *Propaganda* is the online ordering facility for all Lonely Planet guidebooks.

- *Health* is part traveler's medical dictionary, part important links to alert you to local health conditions where you're headed.

- *The Scoop* offers daily news updates of international, national, regional, and local events crises, revolutionary uprisings, and so on — in short, anything that may increase your sense of security (and possibly your personal longevity).

- Finally, the *Subwwway* is a comprehensive listing of travel-related Web sites that's truly mind-boggling in scope — a fascinating grab bag of online destinations.

Lonely Planet has laid down one fantastic, romantic Web site.

Outpost Magazine

www.outpostmagazine.com

Outward bound: It may be based in Toronto, but Outpost Magazine is a window onto the world. And the seasoned travelers who bring you the online edition have made the site so fun and interactive, you'll be hard-pressed not to catch the travel bug yourself. First, you can read the current *Feature* article (recently, a probing piece on the pains of modernity in Kazakhstan). Then, in *Expedition,* follow brave (read "crazy") Canadian travelers on journeys to some pretty out-there destinations. You can check out package tours in the *Travel Bazaar,* sample the music of other cultures at the *Outpost Listening Port* (PC users will need a RealAudio G2 Player plug-in for this) or add your two cents to a number of ongoing discussions on subjects like Great Travelers of the 20th Century. Beautiful site. Great content. We're sold.

Parks Canada

www.parkscanada.pch.gc.ca

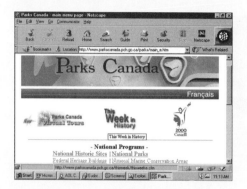

Information on all of Canada's best green spaces: Parks Canada, run by the Federal government, oversees all of Canada's federally-sanctioned parks, historic sites, heritage buildings, conservation areas, and those ever-popular historic railway stations. (Hunh?) The Parks Canada Web site is the place to go for info on all of these. It offers virtual tours (yes, audio and video plug-ins required) of sites as diverse as Winnipeg's Union Station and Waterton Lakes National Park. As far as parks go, you can search for them by province or by name, read up on the ministry's policies and reports, learn about ecosystem conservation, or just get the details you need for the perfect camping trip (including hours of operation, fees, directions, and contact numbers). Same goes for the historic sites. This site may be a tad "governmental" in its presentation, but we love the breadth of information you can access here.

Okay, So Book It!

Do-it-yourself is the name of the game, and these days, you can do an awful lot on your own with just a few megs of memory and a high-speed processor. Whereas travel guides are overflowing with personality, the major online booking sites blend style (in layout and graphics) with their substance (reservations and tickets). They do both to achieve their more utilitarian end — that is, to get you a flight to your destination, a car and bed on arrival, and, finally, a way back home. Oh, sure, most of them provide destination and cruise info, but these niceties definitely take a backseat to the business at hand: booking and buying tickets.

BonVoyage.com

www.bonvoyage.com

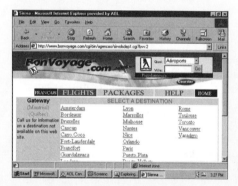

One billet to Vancouver, s.-v.-p!: BonVoyage.com is a bilingual, truly Canadian, and easy-to-use site that offers online perusal and purchase of airline tickets and vacation packages for global destinations. On the downside, you can only book trips departing from Quebec City or Montreal. Still, use this site for everything from week-long all-inclusive resort vacations in Cancun, to a quick return flight between Montreal and Toronto. You also get handy on-site, bilingual access to YellowPages.ca, the online version of The Yellow Pages. A note to English-only Web surfers: BonVoyage.com greets you with a French home page. You will have to click on Entrer (that's Enter!), then click English on the main navigation bar to enable the anglo version.

Canoe Travel

www.canoe.ca/TravelCanada/

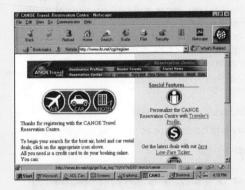

Popular Canadian portal goes global: Canoe is popular with Canadians for a bunch of reasons, including wide-ranging content and a truly shocking array of services. The portal's travel section is yet another good reason to visit. Here, after a simple sign-in process, you can book and pay for airline tickets, car rentals and hotel rooms — all in Canadian dollars. The site also has a host of other services. Try looking for cheap airline tickets using *Java Low-Fare Ticker* or subscribe to *Fare Mail,* an e-mail advisory that lets you know about the latest travel deals. You can also find out more about some of the world's exotic locales (including some right here in Canada) through the *Destination Profiles.* If you're Canadian and you want to use the Net to travel, don't miss Canoe Travel.

Expedia

expedia.msn.ca

Full-featured, multimedia ticketing extrava-ganza: All you can really say about the Microsoft Expedia Web site is that it makes the world look like one terrific place to play. The Canadian affiliate presents all prices in Canadian dollars, although you may find a lot of content geared towards U.S. travelers. The travel/booking component is very serviceable and works quite well, but the truly fascinating collection of features (like info on hundreds of destinations worldwide, travel advice, and audio travelogues) are really where the treats lie. As can be expected from a state-of-the-art site, you need a powerful late-model processor with a slew of plug-ins and Internet Explorer 4.0 or higher at the ready (a prerequisite for using many of the site's features). Expedia is one big online Globe-Trotter's Ball.

Flifo/global

www.flifo.com

Hard-to-beat low fares and an easy-to-use booking system: We felt absolutely compelled to sign up at this site. Maybe the clean, well-lit, uncomplicated layout and graphics (almost Japanese minimalist in design) made us do so. Or maybe the fact that, because of its *FareBeater* search engine, Flifo consistently locates the lowest airfares on the Net. Add to that distinction an itinerary-building and booking system that's simplicity itself, and . . .we're in travel-planning heaven. Online since 1996, the site is owned by Travelogix, Inc., of Houston. In partnership with USA Today and Bell-Atlantic, the company's created a perfect jewel. Despite its American roots, the booking services are available to Canadians, Brits, and Aussies, too.

Sympatico Travel

www1.sympatico.ca/Contents/Travel/

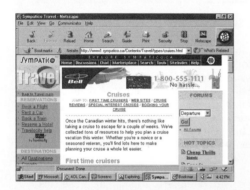

Canada's biggest ISP gets into the act: Sympatico is the reigning giant in the world of Canadian Internet service providers (ISPs). So, as we discussed in the body of this book, it's only natural that this popular portal is jammed with services, including *Sympatico Travel*. On top of allowing you to make your reservations through a partnership with Travelocity.ca, we just like the way the site looks. It's got a huge list of travel-related *forums* — discussion groups — where you can find out what others have to say about their good and bad travel experiences. It's also got advice on everything from destinations to staying healthy while you're on the road.

Travelocity.ca

www.travelocity.ca

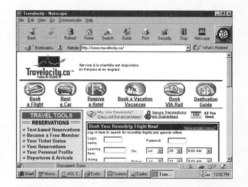

An excellent all-in-one travel booking Web site: Powered by international travel giant Sabre, at Travelocity's Canadian affiliate you find a quick sign-in, pleasant surroundings, and global reservations and booking for all major airlines and car rental systems, as well as thousands of hotels and bed and breakfasts. Yep, you may find a few cheaper deals elsewhere and some specialty areas that this site doesn't cover, but in general, Travelocity.ca is a genuine online travel superstar. The site is thorough and fast, and it boasts several interesting bonus features such as maps, a travel agency locator, a free e-mail newsletter, the *Destination Guide* (which, besides featuring cities and destinations from around the globe, even offers the world-wide *ATM Locator* through a partnership with Visa).

There's also the *Bed and Breakfast Guide* (with listings in Canada and the U.S.) and a *Cruise Critic* (who offers tips, reviews, and picks to plan your next cruise). *Consolidator Fares*, a partnership between Sabre and German Travel's TISS, enables you to reap the benefits of bulk-collective ticket buying in 22 popular markets. Many seats on airlines would go unsold if it were not for the bulk collective ticket buyers. Consolidator's motto is "Think ahead, be flexible, and . . . save." With user-friendly graphics and a very sensible, workable layout, the Travelocity.ca Web site delivers.

The Travel Specialists

The following Web sites may not have everything, but frankly, that's part of their charm. These online travel sites generally concentrate on one area in the travel biz. Most of these specialists, although not all, offer online booking. What they do offer is a variety of travel options to help inspire or fulfill your globe-trotting plans.

CPHotels online

www.cphotels.ca

Go big or go home: As one of Canada's best-known and most prestigious hotel chains, Canadian Pacific Hotels is known for its commitment to service and style. The company's Web site lets you make reservations at all its Canadian and internationally-held hotels, including Banff Springs and the Royal York Hotel. The *Destination Planner* is intended to "help you choose the Canadian Pacific Hotel best suited to your specific vacation, or travel, or business needs." Not bad, eh? Living up to its reputation for catering to customers' needs, CP also has an online *Concierge,* who can answer questions about weather across Canada, convert currencies, or just give you some useful facts about various regions where you might be travelling.

CottageLink

www.cottagelink.com

Lakeside properties with limited responsibility: In a country where summer pretty much equals cottage-going for a lot of folks, it's probably not surprising that such a great site as CottageLink exists. Still, we were surprised at how much it made us want to pack our bags and get to the lake ASAP. The site is easy to use: Just choose a region of the country and click on one of the hundreds of rental cottages available. The photos are simple and clean, and the descriptions of each property are complete. You can also use this site's many related links to find local cottages associations across the country or to get in touch with provincial tourist associations. If you've got to get away, start looking here.

CyberRentals

cyberrentals.com

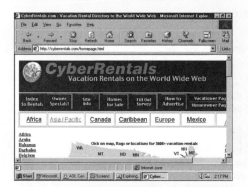

Rent a vacation home in a far-off land:
CyberRentals lists vacation-home rentals
in 20-odd countries (including ours) plus
the entire Caribbean, with pictures, prices,
and booking info attached to each one.
Remember prices are listed in U.S. dollars,
so keep a currency calculator handy.
Shopping around the CyberRentals site is
great fun. It has simple graphics and beautiful, high-definition photos, and it enables
you to contact either an agent or the
owner directly by e-mail. Okay, so here's
our thought: A five-bedroom, two-bath
Country Stone House with pool on the
Cote D'Azur. (No kidding!) At just over
US$1,500 a week, who could resist? Well,
it's fun to look, anyway.

Greyhound Canada

www.greyhound.ca

*Routes, schedules, and fares for buses
across Canada:* For 60 years, Canadians
have been exhorted to "Take the bus and
leave the driving to us." Since 1930, after
Swedish immigrant Carl Eric Wickman and
his partner Orville founded The
Greyhound Corporation, countless millions of travelers have stepped on board
these indispensable steel-wheeled hounds.
The sight of someone's son or daughter
heading off to the big city on board a
Greyhound is quintessentially North
American. The present-day site of
Greyhound Canada is on the World Wide
Web, and it's a clean, bright place with
cheery graphics that gives you schedules
for the fleet's 500 buses heading to any of
the 1,000 Canadian stops from coast to
coast. Next time you're without a car and
you need to get from a small town in Nova
Scotia to Saskatoon, you may be very glad
this site is here.

Hostelling International

www.iyhf.org

*Detailed information about youth hostels
around the world:* This Web site makes the
old wanderlust wax pretty strong, especially if you spent any time in your life as a
goliard (you know — those student trouba-
dours in the opera *Carmina Burana*). Even
if you didn't, you can appreciate that more
than 18 million people a year get together
to share a meal and spin yarns in warmth
and comfort for an average of $12 a night.

Some people, however, share a common misconception about youth hostels: Many weary travelers on a tight budget (including some information-challenged Canadians) think that these hostels are only for young people. Not so — youth hostels are only for people who are young at heart. The Hostelling International Web site, run by the IYHF (International Youth Hostel Federation), is fresh and delightful. It describes in detail 4,500 hostels in 60 countries and provides pleasant graphics, lots of pictures, text in many languages, and, happily, your connection to a host of friends around this world.

RailServe

www.railserve.com

Connections to worldwide train reservations systems: An awful lot of train sites are out there — and an awful lot of trains, too. If travel by rail is your notion of a romantic way to take a journey, this site is the one for you. RailServe, the Internet Railroad Directory, provides a terrific service by assembling informative links from all around the planet in a sensible and legible fashion. Take a look at the original Orient Express at www.wagons-lit-paris.com (the only place where you can arrange a trip on the original Pullmans, by the way) or the exquisitely beautiful Web site put together by VIA Rail (see the listing in this section under *VIA Rail* for details). If speed's your thing, maybe you can settle for a brisk 274 Kph — check out the

schedule for the *Shinkansen* (the bullet train) at www.japanrail.com. Then you have the Durango-Silverton Narrow Gauge Railway and the Northern Star from Mumbal to Nirvana. The possibilities are endless.

The Hotel Guide

www.hotelguide.com/

Comprehensive listing for global accommodations: Well, with 60,000 possibilities, the online Hotel Guide should be able to help you. It's the biggest all right . . . in fact, three times bigger than the next biggest. Now, we're not sure whether the size of the database makes getting around in this site a little slow or if every travel agent on Earth uses it, but it *is* a little slow. (At the same time, remember that it *is* also the biggest online listing for hotels that you can access anywhere.) Anyway, if you're headed somewhere obscure (as many Canadians with wanderlust are), this site may prove invaluable. How many tour guides do you know that list three hotels in Djibouti?

VIA Rail

www.viarail.ca

This great country was built on rails like these: Did you know VIA Rail enjoys 94 percent customer satisfaction on some of its most popular routes? Not surprising if those same people are using the VIA Web site as a starting point. The site is just adorable, with cute icons to guide you to a host of online services. And why shouldn't it be beautiful? After all, VIA is the federal train service for the country with the most stunning and diverse wilderness in the world (if we do say so ourselves). If you want to ride the rails, come here for fare and schedule info, whether you're a leisure, business, senior or student traveler. There's a stunning photo gallery that pays homage to the beauty of this land, and the site has numerous links to tourist information sites, tour operators, and destinations across the country. To book your train tickets, VIA directs you to Travelocity.ca.

WebFlyer

www.webflyer.com

Frequent flyer descriptions and great airline deals: Most of the departments on WebFlyer's Web page involve Frequent Flyer updates of every description, but even for those of us not smart enough to take advantage of these perks, this site has a lot to offer. Yes, this is a U.S.-based site, but the information here is universally appealing to people who can't stop getting on planes. The site's *Deal Watch,* for example, is devoted to the listing of time-sensitive weekly deals on domestic and international flights, hotel reservations, and car rentals. The prices are so good on many of these offers that you may actually think about popping over to Belgium for a three-day weekend. That's plenty enough

reason to drop by this place on a regular basis, and if you are on top of the Frequent Flyer scene, you've found a new home in Bonus Mile heaven.

Other Stuff to Check Out

www.xe.net/currency
www.canadiangeographic.com
babelfish.altavista.digital.com
www.caa.com
www.cyberbeach.net/~solonyka/LCRA/
    main.htm
www.hostellingintl.ca
www.restaurant.ca
www.swap.ca
www.the-wire.com/street/resorts
www.virtual-vacation.com

The Real "Estate" Deal

Ever pound the streets looking for a new place to live — in the winter? This is not one of life's great pleasures. We've certainly got nothing against the occasional open house, but with the advent of online real estate services, you can save the soles of your shoes for the outings you really *want* to partake in. The Web has listings for apartments, houses, commercial properties, and even mortgages that you can peruse at your leisure. So go out and buy a can of Fresh Air 'cause if you're in the market for a new place to live, you've got a whole lotta Web ahead of you.

You Rentin' . . .

The phrase "It's a jungle out there" was probably invented by some poor apartment hunter who just missed out on the last three deals by arriving a hair too late to the showing. Now the showings take place 24 hours a day, seven days a week at your convenience. Apartment renting is a growing online field in Canada, with more and more databases ready to match your needs and means with the right rooms and views.

Canadian Apartments For Rent Online

www.carol.ca

Growing database of apartments for rent: Canadian Apartments For Rent Online — or Carol for short — has about 7,000 combined listings for residential and commercial apartment spaces for rent in Canada. That number includes apartments being rented by individuals (check out the Classifieds section) and buildings run by larger property management companies. By Carol's own admission, its database is still growing, so you might have trouble finding the apartment of your dreams in certain cities. They've backed up their system by including an information request. That way, if you're in the market to rent, Carol might be able to put you in touch with a management company that's got the space you need.

Rent Canada

www.rentcanada.com

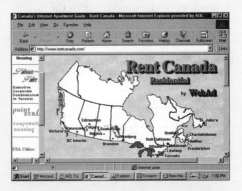

A bit of everything: Like Carol, Rent Canada's site is still a growing site, but we like the way the listings for apartment complexes include everything from photos to floor plans to a locator map to an online application form. Now that saves footwork! Rent Canada also has a classified section where you can either list or read through listings for apartments for rent by individuals. The *Vacation* section lists vacation properties, and *Temporary Corporate Housing* lists upscale short-term accommodations available from large rental companies across Canada — perfect for the business traveler.

Rent.Net

www.rent.net

Widespread listings: Rent.Net is a giant in the world of online rentals. Although geared towards the U.S. market, Rent.Net has a large searchable database of Canadian apartment listings. You can specify your area, price range, and apartment style before submitting your search, which returns listings that include photographs, a list of amenities, and contact info. Rent.Net even lets you compare prices for similar properties so that you can be sure you're looking at the best deal around. Also check out *The Rent.Net Daily Article* on the home page, which offers tips on apartment living — from keeping your kids under control to getting along with neighbours.

. . . Or Buyin'?

Home ownership is no small accomplishment — it isn't referred to so often as "livin' the dream" without good reason. The good news is that your dreams are one step closer to reality, thanks to the wide network of sites on the Web devoted to realtors, home sellers, and home-owning information. And you don't need to rely on the abbreviated descriptions in the Sunday paper, either.

For Sale By Owner

www.forsalebyowner.ca

 $

For independent buyers and sellers: The idea of buying or selling a home without an agent is daunting to most of us — statistics show over 90 percent of Canadians have used real estate agents in the past. But when it comes time to pay hefty commissions, we probably wish we'd given it a try. This unique and welcoming site is designed to facilitate just that. It's got a veritable ton of information for prospective independent buyers and sellers, including a do-it-yourself kit for people who are preparing to sell their home, downloadable legal documents, and tips on how to become a tougher negotiator.

To access all these services, including adding your listing to the site, you need to sign up with For Sale By Owner and pay a fee (about $150). But even without signing up, you can browse the site's housing listings for free. The site also gives you the option of typing in listing numbers you've seen for homes in a few small Canadian newspapers (expect more soon). For Sale By Owner even keeps a database of existing *Services* across the country that are out there to help homeowners and homesellers. Just click on your home province and choose from the list of categories. If you're thinking of going the independent route — or even if you're just a bit curious — this site is an absolute must-see.

HomeScout

homescout.iown.com

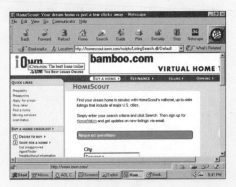

Listings of international homes for sale:
One of the many extraordinary features of
HomeScout's rapidly expanding international real estate database is its sense of
global outreach. HomeScout has an egali-
tarian search engine that enables you to
price out your property in all the world's
major currencies. Closer to home, this site
offers more than 500,000 listings in Canada
and the U.S. Figuring out exactly where
the HomeScout listings are and where
they're not is a little difficult, because it
has an up-front location-specific search
engine; if the site has a list or map of all
offered real-estate locations, we couldn't
find it. Nevertheless, the "Scout" is an
excellent and even affable online real-
estate resource.

HouseSeek

www.houseseek.com

Post it and they will come: Let's dream, for
a moment, about a world where instead of
looking for a trustworthy real estate
agent — or even surfing the Net looking
for home listings — some of the best
agents in the country would come to you.
That dream is a reality with HouseSeek.
The idea is simple: You post on the site
the details of the kind of home you're
looking for, and within 24 hours, a rep-

utable agent gets back to you by e-mail,
fax, or phone with a list of homes. Even
better, for people thinking of moving
abroad, the site has connections to agents
outside of Canada. And it's all free. You
gotta love it.

International Real Estate Digest

www.ired.com

An enormous real estate venture: The only
problem we have with the International
Real Estate Digest's (IRED) massive site is
figuring out where to begin. Our suggestion is to zero in on a geographical locale
of interest to you and then start clicking.
This U.S.-based site has a lot of listings for
properties south of the border, but also
offers 18,000 links to 102 other countries
around the world. So if you'd like to retire
to the Mayan Island Beach Club in Belize
and end your days doing marine biology
research on the barrier reef — by golly,
you can do it! The site reflects an awesome complexity made simple with one
sensible search-engine interface after
another. Endless graphics, multimedia
applications, and interactive programs
make IRED a Real Estate Carnivale. Next
time you go to Paris, use IRED and your
keyboard to book a luxurious furnished
apartment in St. Germain-des-Pres instead
of a $400-a-day hotel room.

MLS Online

www.mls.ca

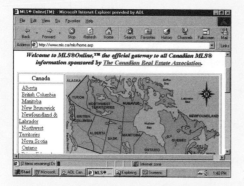

The power of multiple listings: This site, sponsored by the Canadian Real Estate Association, uses the power of a system called MLS (Multiple Listings Service), a marketing tool of the Canadian Real Estate Boards. Whenever you list your home with an MLS-affiliated agent, the listing is automatically made available to other MLS members. MLS Online lets you tap into that enormous database to show you listings for thousands of properties across Canada — be they residential or commercial. We were simply stunned by the access we got here. And each listing comes with a series of icons that enable you to view photos, video, audio, or extra brochures related to the property. We found the icons ghosted, but you can expect more multimedia use in the future.

Marketplace @ VisionQuest

www.mlz.com

Listings and links to boot: The Marketplace site may not be as big as some of the others in Canada, but we like its simplified approach to house shopping. The home page greets you with a list of three options identified by colourful giant ball-shaped icons. Doesn't get much more basic than that, eh? Click on *Listings* to see what

properties are for sale, *Agents* to find someone who can help you sell your home, or *Classifieds* to list or browse for stuff in a range of categories (not all home-related).

The downside to Marketplace is that listings sometimes have just a brief description of the property, followed by a contact number or e-mail address. You have to make the effort to find out more. You can add your own listing to the site either for free (for a very simple listing) or for somewhere between $30 and $50 (if you want something a little more eye-catching). You can even pay for your listing online by using your credit card. Marketplace uses a secure server to ensure transaction safety.

On The House

www.mmaweb.com/onthehouse/

Directory takes step closer to home owning dream: While On The House is a U.S. directory, it also has a pretty impressive set of Canadian links for most of the provinces. Choose a province name and then browse through links for real estate agencies and other homebuyers' services. This site is ideal for people just beginning their home buying search.

The Canadian Real Estate Pages

www.realestate-canada.com

One-stop home-buyers' shop: Whether you're buying, selling, renting, building, timesharing, or even just moving, The Canadian Real Estate Pages site is a good place to start. Here, you can read up about the real estate industry in Canada, access a list of contractors, browse houses for sale or rent, look for a mover, or link to a real estate agent. Although you have the option of listing your home at the site, we found most of the listings were for real estate agents rather than individual properties. If you want to keep your finger on the pulse of a local real estate scene in a given town or city, this site's a good guide.

Shopping for an Online Mortgage

After you find the perfect house, you need to think about how you're going to finance it. You can find a wide array of sites that are willing to help you pull it together. Information abounds on any topic necessary for either first-time buyers or refinancing homeowners. Many sites offer mortgage calculators, interest-rate watchers, and other tools of the modern information age to get you in that snuggly little home — or the castle around the bend — that you've always wanted.

Canoe Rates

www.canoe.ca/Money/

A site we love gives us the lowdown: Before you even think of applying for a mortgage, you probably want to have an idea how much it will cost you, right? Well, look no further than the popular Canoe portal. Its rates page has a mortgage section that includes *Variable, Open and Convertible Rates, closed Mortgage Rates,* and *closed Long Term Mortgage Rates.* Canoe's sources include the Big Five banks (Bank of Nova Scotia, Royal Bank, CIBC, TD Bank, and the Bank of Montreal), as well as a host of smaller institutions, credit unions, and lending houses. The site also

offers a *Mortgage Calculator* that gives you an idea of how much your monthly payments will be, depending on the total amount of your loan, the rate and the number of years you'll be paying. Finally, Canoe can help you understand the costs associated with mortgages that compound on a semi-annual basis with the *Mortgage Table Generator.* To get to Canoe's rates page, start at Canoe Money (the URL listed above), use the main drop-down menu to find Rates, and click on Go!.

Canada Mortgage and Housing Corporation

www.cmhc-schl.gc.ca

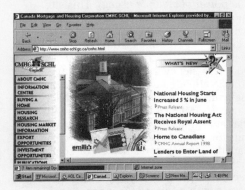

Everything you ever wanted to know about mortgages but were afraid to ask: The federal government's Canada Mortgage and Housing Corporation (CMHC) has been making it easier for Canadians to access housing since the end of WWII, when the government helped finance homes for returning war veterans. The CMHC's mandate has changed somewhat since then. It's now in the business of insuring mortgages, developing the Canadian housing market and addressing the housing needs of groups like Native peoples, disabled people, and elderly people.

The CMHC has posted many of its publications to its site. You can download

Homebuying Step-by-Step, a series of documents that explains just about everything involved in financing your home (you need an Adobe Reader plug-in to view these), or read up on a CMHC software program called *AffordAbility*, which analyses any home purchase you are considering. Although you can't download *AffordAbility* directly from the site, you are provided with a toll-free ordering number and a list of stores that sell the program. The site's also got information on *emili*, an electronic application form for the CMHC's mortgage insurance. You can find out about emili at this site, but to use it, you need to go through a mortgage officer at one of the CMHC's approved lending institutions.

i\money

imoney.com/mortgages/index.shtml

If you can't find it here...: When it comes to online financing in Canada, i\money is tops. (No wonder Sympatico and MSN.ca use it to power some of their financial services pages.) At the i\money *Mortgage Centre,* you find a host of online services, including these very cool ones:

- *Mortgage Rate Alert:* Sign up to receive an e-mail alert when mortgage rates change.

- *Mortgage Reminder:* Let i\money know when your current mort-

gage is up for renewal, and you get a reminder via e-mail.

- *Mortgage Qualifier:* This service lets you calculate the maximum loan for which you would qualify using two popular lenders' formulas. For this service, you need to know your gross monthly income and expenses.

- *Mortgage Application:* Link to online mortgage applications from several top Canadian lending institutions. (i\money does not lend money itself.)

- *Compare Mortgages:* Find out whether you're getting the best rate by comparing mortgage costs from two different lending institutions.

- *Mortgage Info and FAQs:* Spend some time browsing through an impressive array of facts, tips, and answers to your questions about mortgages at the i\money Mortgage Centre.

Sympatico Mortgages

www1.sympatico.ca/Contents/Finance/

Help finding the right lending institution: As we mention previously, Sympatico has a partnership with i\money, and many of the services overlap, but you should still visit the Sympatico site for its links to a number of Canada's top lenders, including the Big Banks and credit unions.

Other Stuff to Check Out

www.cba.ca
www.chba.ca/buyinganewhome/
    buyinganewhome.html
www.century21canada.com
www.homesandcottages.com
www.openhouse.com/active/chat.asp
www.royallepage.ca
tenant.net
www.westfortcu.on.ca/FINANCE/HOME-
    FACT.HTM

Second That E-Motion

You can research and buy all manner of transportation on the Web these days. Shopping for a car online turns out to be one of the top uses for e-commerce. And if you can comparison-shop for a car, why not a boat or a plane? The Web brings all kinds of vehicles to your desktop, and all you need to do is drive that pointer around the screen and stop for the occasional click.

After perusing the sites in this section, you're not going to think of the Internet as just the Information Superhighway — it's gonna be the Super Sealane and the Super Jetstream as well.

One If By Land . . .

A car is an extraordinarily complex machine that almost everyone takes for granted. Everyone, that is, except anyone who's in the market for a new (or used) auto. If you're shopping for some new wheels, you need all the information you can get your hands on — and through the Web, you can get your hands on a ton of data. Blue book prices, feature comparisons, reviews, photos — you can even find auto-related Web sites that enable you to take a virtual-reality test drive. So what're you waiting for? Slip on those racing gloves and rev those engines!

Autobytel Canada

www.autobytel.ca

Wide dealership database from which to choose: Autobytel is a Canadian affiliate to a U.S.-based site, so prices are in U.S. dollars, but its services are still useful to people on this side of the border. Autobytel gives you extensive model and pricing information on both new and used cars. When you use the site's online buying component (which asks you to submit a highly specific request form), one of 2,700 Autobytel Accredited Dealers gets back to you within 24 hours with a deal! The concept is audacious; the database is enormous; and the postal code-based search engine is effective.

Automobile Journalists Association of Canada

www.ajac.org

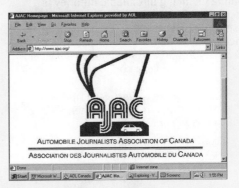

They've got the scoop on the best buys: Who better to turn to when you're thinking of buying a car than the people who write about them for a living? The Automobile Journalists Association of Canada (AJAC) Web site keeps a list of their *Car of the Year Award Winners* in categories like *Best New Family Sedan* and *Best New Sport Utility.* Winners are listed with photos and details of how they won (including price and ranking). The site also has an index of Canadian and non-Canadian automobile manufacturers and their Web addresses. This site may not be as pretty as some of the others — after all, it's run by journalists — but it's a good place to get info on cars and news about the auto industry.

Autoweb.com Canada

canada.autoweb.com

Nice range of auto-buying support components: A Canadian affiliate to the original U.S. site, Autoweb.com Canada is a spread-out kind of site that features a little something for everyone in the car market. First, a *New Car Showroom* offers specs and reviews of all the latest models. You can also try the used-car search engine. Some of the links at this site aren't as helpful to Canadians. Still, we really like the searching capability, which provides local listings. After you find a car you like (prices are in Canadian dollars) and fill in

your personal information, you can submit a request for more information from the seller. You can even ask questions about the vehicle you're considering. The dealer gets back to you within 48 hours by phone or via e-mail with the answers.

Autobynet

www.autobynet.net

Serious site for serious car buyers: You know it's the real thing when a site advises you not to use its services until you're ready to buy or lease (as in, that day or the next). Not only that, but Autobynet also pleads with you to educate yourself on the car you want (and it offers quick links to many of the major car manufacturers to help you do this). The reason for the serious tone is that, once you submit a *Purchase Request* through Autobynet, its agents assume you are serious about buying that particular car ASAP. That means one request per customer only, and the more specific you can be about what you want, the better.

Within 48 hours of submitting your request, an Autobynet agent calls you on the phone to quote you a wholesale price and a finance package for the car you chose. If you like it, the car is yours. All that's left for you to do is pick it up or have it delivered.

Bowes Publishers Ltd. ClassEFind

www.bowesnet.com/classifieds

Local newspapers act as car-buying aid:
Bowes Publishers Ltd., which owns many
of this country's smaller newspapers,
gives you access to the combined breadth
of their classified sections through its
ClassEFind search engine. You never know
what kind of deal you can find close to
home or a little further away.

CAA Online

www.caa.ca

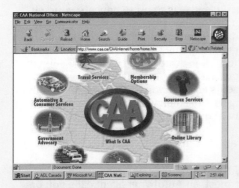

*From the people who provide you roadside
assistance, a super site:* There's something
implicitly trustworthy about the CAA site.
It's nice to look at, but probably the trust
has more to do with the organization
itself, which has thousands of members

across Canada. At the CAA Online, you
can look over the entire array of CAA
membership services and then buy your
membership online. The site has a new
section detailing the latest stats on driving
costs. You can also access the group's
travel and insurance services. Also check
out the additional features — like the
Online Library, Traffic Safety, and the
Government Advocacy sections. Read
through this stuff, and you'll be closer to
the kind of informed driver we want
speeding alongside us in traffic.

CanSell.com

www.cansell.com

Classifieds site with auto listings: One way
to look for a car online is through a site
dedicated to classified ads. CanSell.com is
a good one to try. Just use the maps to
specify what area of the country you want
to look in and browse the listings. Some
will have photos attached, though many
don't, and the accompanying descriptions
are often short, but if you want to buy
used and local, you'll still want to take a
few minutes to check them out. If you're
planning to sell a car using CanSell.com,
you have to go through a sign-up process,
and you're charged a fee for the listing.

CarClick

carclick.canada.com

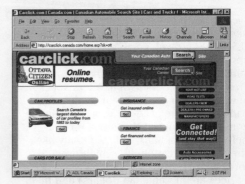

Using the power of the Southam newspaper chain to look for good car buys: Southam Inc. owns some of the biggest daily newspapers in the land. So it has consolidated the classified listings from a number of those papers and built a site where you can search them. The result is CarClick. This site is relatively new, and as time goes on, the number of newspapers that feed the listings are likely to increase. But already, you can find over 5,000 listings for cars updated daily including cars for sale, auto services, accessories, dealers, and recreational vehicles. Some listings come with in-depth profiles, although many don't. CarClick also has a *Finance* section, where you find links to major Canadian lenders. All in all, the idea behind this site is very smart (that is, drawing on up-to-date newspaper listings), and that makes it worth the visit.

DealFinder

www3.sympatico.ca/dealfinder/

It ain't fancy, but deals it does find: DealFinder is not a graphically enhanced site — at all. And you are only given a few options: You can read testimonials about the service, check out the FAQs, or use the new car-buying service. But what a service! DealFinder acts as a runner for car buyers. You enter your specifications, including the type of car you want and where you live, and for a fee (about $120), DealFinder looks for a few good possibilities at the best possible price. From that list of options, it's up to you to pick out the car you want. Once you do, DealFinder makes all the arrangements for you to get down to the dealer's office, sign the paperwork, and pick up your vehicle.

Drive On-Line

www.driveonline.ca

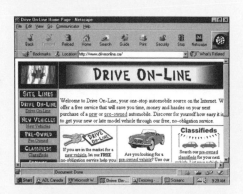

Impressive info and adequate listings: We like the look of this site with its cheery home page. We also like the range of services, including a *Maintenance Reminder*, which fires off an e-mail to you whenever your car needs a tune-up. (Now, why haven't any of the other sites we looked at thought of that?)

The site includes a classified section for people in the market for a "pre-owned" vehicle (a charming term for "used"), dealership, and manufacturer links. But the site's central service — which is, by the way, free — is reminiscent of some of the others we've described in this section. You can submit info about the kind of car you're looking for and Drive On-line submits your query to its 60 affiliated dealers. It then comes back to you via e-mail or phone with cars that closely match your criteria. Remember this service is free and submitting a *Purchase/Lease Request* at this site does not oblige you in any way to actually buy a car.

The Auto Channel
www.theautochannel.com

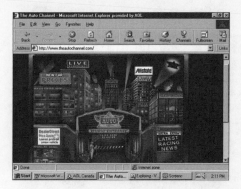

A high-end multimedia all-vehicle exploratorium: Probably the first thing you need to do after you enter this amazing site is to hit the *Tech Info* feature, 'cause you're gonna need to download about a million plug-ins to view everything that this site has to offer. Beautiful and somewhat bewildering, The Auto Channel is a multimedia extravaganza that encompasses all of humankind's moving machines. To facilitate a tour of the site, make sure that your equipment and software is top of the line, latest version, and cutting edge. You can tool about on this site with version 3.0 browsers, but anything less can't guarantee entrance. You may find that you can easily get lost in the kaleidoscope of color and sound that The Auto Channel offers, but you're probably enjoying it the whole time. Streaming video and audio, slide shows, photo galleries, a VR Library, chat rooms, message boards, and links to links — everything's here within the film-noiresque borders of The Auto Channel experience. While this is a U.S.-based site catering to that market, we can't resist directing you there because of the beauty of the design and the breadth of general information.

Two If By Sea . . .

As any current or prospective boat owner can tell you, buying anything that floats is

a major investment of both time and money. The online boat-seller's market is about education as much as selling a specific boat. Not only can you get a terrific sense of what's available (and at what price), but you can also get in touch with the vast network of fellow sailors and suppliers who are also on the Internet.

Aboard
www.aboard.com

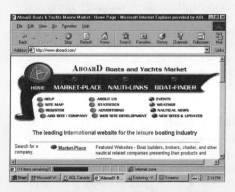

Multilingual site for international boat shopping: The Aboard Network is the product of a U.K. firm, based in London, with its eyes on all seven seas and five oceans. An astonishing collection of international mariner links are presented in English, Spanish, or French versions. The site is divided into three main categories:

- *The Market-place,* where boat builders, yacht brokers, and other maritime-related companies present their wares at a sort of cyber High Tea.

- *Nauti-Links!,* with 4,248 marine-site links and 7,810 marine companies represented (at their "nauti-est," ha!).

- *Boat-Finder,* where one may, if one's so inclined, browse Aboard's substantial files for new and preowned motor and sailing boats.

In summary, this site is nothing less than a jolly good show.

BoatNet

www.boatnet.com

Excellent descriptions and photos of high-end boats of all kinds: This site is a great online aquatic resource, with features to attract boaters of every stripe. In particular, check out *Scuttlebutt* and the *Calendar* where you can see what's coming up in the boating world (or let the world know through the Net what event you're planning). The *Boats for Sale* department obviously caters to a seriously upscale clientele, but BoatNet is also an extremely well-put-together site with a search engine that divides the world first into regions and then into power and sail categories and, finally, presents supremely detailed descriptions of the seacraft that it offers (many displaying full-screen photos that should have you soon yearning for a high-seas adventure). The prices may be in U.S. dollars, but the boats are beautiful and some of the listings (check the *Great Lakes Region*) are either posted by Canadians or will appeal to Canadians living near the border.

Boat Trader Online

www.traderonline.com/boat

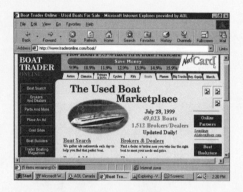

More listings than anyone else in new and used boats: As of this writing, you could find 37,670 boats for sale on Boat Trader Online, the Used Boat Marketplace. Our guess is that this company, with its links to about 1,500 boat brokers and dealers, has a few new boats bobbing around as well. Boat Trader Online offers a lot of useful maritime links and features. Stop by *The Boat Bookstore,* for example (offering reference, maintenance, design/shipbuilding, and travel books). Bright, cheerful graphics and a flexible search engine make this site an important port of call for those who're all at sea about where to find their dreamboat. The only shortfall is that the ads are most often photoless and brief, but such quantities of watercraft compensate more than adequately for this slight failing.

Classifieds2000

www.classifieds2000.com

Straightforward and easily searchable classifieds: The boat-for-sale ads on Classifieds2000 are extensive and presented with the same simplicity and easy-to-access style that typify all its online services. A diverse array of watercraft appears for sale here. Most listings are by Americans in U.S. dollars, but we found plenty of Canadian listings, too (yes, in Canadian currency).

Computer Boat Search

www.computerboatsearch.com

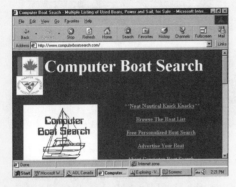

Impressive Canadian site with lots of listings: There are over 3,000 boats listed for sale at Computer Boat Search, including powerboats and sailboats. But that's not all. You can also buy motors and trailers, browse the excellent marine-related links, or conduct personalized boat searches. We especially love the listings under *Nautical Knick-Knacks*. Excellent listings. Excellent site.

And Three If By . . . Air?

This subject is definitely cross-referenced with the "Who'd a thunk it?" category. Imagine shopping for an airplane on the Internet! Well, if you think the idea through, it's really not as crazy as it may seem. Most planes transfer from one technically savvy owner to another, either of whom you may find almost anywhere on the planet. Sounds like a recipe for Web interaction to us. Even if you're not in the market right now but just want to see some great shots of magnificent flying machines, you can't go wrong by perusing any of these sites.

Classifieds2000

www.classifieds2000.com

Great for both dealer and privately owned planes: Classifieds2000's aircraft listings range from hang gliders to corporate jets. The Web's largest classified-ad site lists flying machines from around the planet. Its complete search engine enables you to specify whether you're looking for new or used aircraft from a dealer or a private owner.

Global Aviation Navigator

www.globalair.com

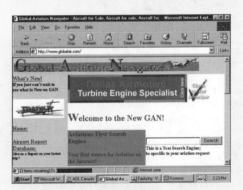

International catalogue of airplanes with excellent value-added features: The Global Aviation Navigator has an extremely well designed search engine, a pleasant graphics style, and a medium-sized (as the world of online plane buying goes) database. The Global Aviation Navigator has many other virtues besides its classified-ad component.

The *Aviation Internet Directory* is an outtasight congregation of links for business and commercial aviators, offering global weather conditions, insurance info, airport data, pilot services, dealer listings, extensive technical support, flight schools, and more. Although the site is not tops in the photo department, you find a great collection of used aircraft listings from every continent.

Trade-A-Plane

www.tradeaplane.com

 $

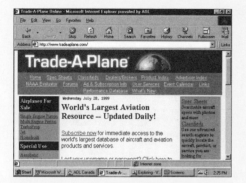

Giant database of planes online: "World's Largest Aviation Resource," states Trade-A-Plane, "Updated Daily." Sounds good, but it's going to cost you to see that 5,000 aircraft database — US$29.00 for a year-long online subscription. Not being a subscriber, we were unable to enter the clubhouse, but from all outward appearances, and from Trade-A-Plane's reputation in the industry, we'd say that anybody searching for the perfect high-altitude transport would be wise to shell out the dough for this one.

Other Stuff to Check Out

www.consumerreports.com
www.islandnet.com/~canev/
www.rvgazette.com
www3.sympatico.ca/bob.wheaton/
    home/cobra/
www.vru.com/carshow/
www.allaboutaero.com
www.beforethewind.com
www.bluenose2.ns.ca
www.sailing.ca
www.aviationworld.net
www.infomart.net/av/
www.grailworks.com/adanac/

Just what is it about electronics that makes them so . . . well, so all-consuming?

Consuming Electronics

Ask any gadget lover why he or she loves power toys so much and the first response is usually "It's not a toy; it's a tool." Actually, it's probably both a tool *and* a toy — and that's one of the reasons why consumer electronics are so compelling. Whenever you can accomplish a necessary task in a cool fashion, you feel cool yourself. Web sites featuring consumer electronics almost by definition need to be the coolest around. Stop by any of the sites that we list in this section to get an exquisite taste of the future. Consume away!

Picking Up Some Hardware

The electronics industry calls its biggest fans *early adopters* because certain folks feel compelled to be the first on the block to have the latest and the greatest items available. The Web, however, is a great feeding ground for both early adopters and late bloomers — for everything from the zippiest hardware system and hottest software to anything that has a circuit board or emits a beep. Online shopping for computer hardware has really taken off, and comparison-shopping is one reason: Checking spec sheets online is easy. Price is another reason: You find on the Web some of the best hardware deals anywhere. Ready to sign some adoption papers?

Those fabulous computing machines

Bid.com
www.bid.com

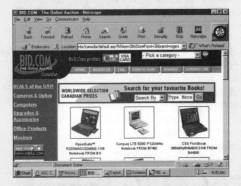

Online auction house offers hardware galore: The main advantage of looking for computer hardware through an online auction house is simple: cost. Depending on who's out there bidding against you, you can walk away from an auction with some very hot deals. As well, the stock is always changing. So if you can't find the computer package, notebook, or component (monitors, keyboards, and so on) you're looking for today, come back tomorrow. On any given day, Bid.com has a very extensive array of new computers on its auction block to suit almost any need on block. And since this is a Canadian site, you find prices that make sense and can get simpler shipping arrangements. To use Bid.com, brush up on the rules and regulations of auctions. Don't worry though, once you get the hang of them, they're easy.

Compusmart
www.compusmart.com

Wide selection and good prices: Compusmart has a nice, uncluttered Web site where you can find all sorts of computer goodies at really good prices. In fact, Compusmart claims that if you can find a cheaper deal on the same product they're offering (in Canadian dollars and including shipping costs), they'll match it. Not bad, eh? Given that the site recently offered a month-long free shipping campaign, its commitment to low prices seems genuine. We also like the fact that shipping takes place in a hurry (as little as two days for some cities), and that returns can be made in person at one of Compusmart's 17 locations across Canada.

Dell Canada

www.dell.ca

Configure your own system online: With annual sales reaching 12 billion, Dell Computers is a major-league player. Its online store is terrific — it communicates everything you need to know in a way that we can describe only as crystal clear. The *Build Your Own System* feature (which applies to every system for sale) is filled with options and is easy to operate. Start with a *bundle* and configure the computer to your own personal specifications. The feature includes a more complete range of products and peripherals than we've encountered in most other similar systems. You can purchase (or lease if you're a qualified applicant) all Dell computer systems online.

Future Shop

www.futureshop.com

Canadian online super store: Future Shop is known across Canada for its big size and low prices. That reputation should remain intact for Net junkies as well, judging by the store's excellent Web site. Every kind of hardware your cyberheart could desire is available for sale online. After a brief sign-in process, you can place your orders through a secure server, and deliveries are speedy for most Canadian cities. One unique feature in the store's hardware aisle is *Compare,* which lets you do just that: compare two or more brands of hardware. This comes in handy when you find yourself deciding between two similar components. For example, in the category of monitors, we can create a chart listing all the specs for several 17-inch models, showing for each model a photo, price, display size, warranty, and more. Other notable features here include the *Power Search,* which helps you navigate through Future Shop's merchandise to find just the product you want, and the electronic *Coupons.* Best of all, you can get a heck of a lot more than just computer hardware at Future Shop online. We could have written this store up in several directory categories including software and electronics, so be sure and check it out.

IBM Canada

commerce.www.ibm.com/ca/

Top-quality merchandise at reasonable prices: Well, we couldn't possibly leave out Shop IBM could we? These three letters are synonymous with computers the world over. Its online store features the Aptiva Series home computers and ThinkPad notebooks — terrific systems that offer great technology at an extremely reasonable price online. Take a look around this site, and you can see that the excitement is still with this company. IBM computers are sold everywhere, by everybody, but you still may decide to buy your PC directly from the source.

JC Sun

www.jcsuncanada.com

Discount computer dealers: JC Sun isn't the most aesthetically pleasing site out there, but you can find a range of new computers and components for got-to-go prices. The site is enabled to take online orders, or you can call in your purchase by using the toll-free number. We found some of the functions at this site confusing. For example, the shopping cart is small and easy to overlook (it's on the top right-hand corner of the home page), and the *Bargain Deals* seem to be listed in U.S. dollars only.

Microson.com

www.microson.com

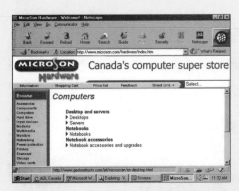

Bilingual site for computer lovers: What we like best about Microson is that it's a truly virtual store. Unlike most Canadian shopping sites, the site is not connected to a brick-and-mortar store anywhere. Based in Quebec, Microson is a direct online sales company. Because their overhead is very low, their prices are too! You can even sign up to receive an e-mail keeping you up-to-date on Microson's weekly price list. The site is also nicely designed, with a simple, colourful layout; easy-to-use navigation bar; and helpful symbols letting you know how quickly you can expect to receive your order.

Speaking of orders, the online order form is also simple, and shipping costs $10.95 for most purchases. Orders are sent out via Purolator, usually the same day you order. One major drawback to Microson's site: You'd better know exactly what you're looking for when you shop here, because products are not accompanied by any description (other than basic specs).

OA Books

www.oabooks.com

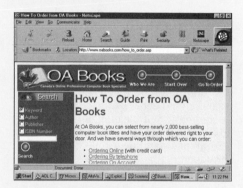

Figure out how computers work before you buy: So what if you can't buy a motherboard or a monitor here? We decided to include this site because (without bragging) the computer book industry has grown immensely — and with good reason. As technology changes, you sometimes have to do a bit of homework to stay on top of things. OA Books, operated out of Edmonton, has an excellent selection of computer-related books, including such topics as Internet design, spreadsheets, word processing, and yes, books that explain how all your computer's components work together to make the magic happen! You can search for books by subject, author, publisher, or ISBN number, and after you've found one that you must have, you're asked to log in before checking out!

Audio, video, and beyond

Whether music, video, or music videos are your thing, you can't go wrong with a visit to these Web sites. Being an informed shopper is essential when you're in the market for high-tech toys, and almost all of these sites offer data galore. And with the low prices available on the Web, you'll need to add on to the rec room to handle all the goodies you can find here.

GadgetBoy

www.gadgetboy.com

Right-on reviews of a broad range of consumer electronics: Whom can you depend on to give you the straight skinny on consumer electronics as diverse as an electronic breadmaker and the latest in digital cameras? Gadget Boy, of course. The site's opening logo says it all: "Product Reviews with Attitude!" You don't find every make or model under the sun on this site — just those that promise to be exquisitely cool. (Whether they actually make the grade is another matter.) Gadget Boy doesn't pull any punches, and the reviews you find here are frequently hilarious. New product reviews can change several times a month, and all the old reviews are archived. Gadget Boy also keeps a keen eye on the convergence market (where computers and televisions dare to mingle). This site is a must-browse for the hard-core electronics aficionado.

Henry's

www.henrys.com

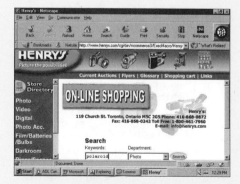

A photographer's dream, and good prices too: We'd be hard-pressed to find something negative to say about this Web site. Henry's has an enormous range of cameras for sale online, including traditional 35mms, video cameras, digital cameras, and even used cameras (where the real steals are). Of course, each product comes with a good description and photograph. Other features include *Current Auctions,* a service that takes you directly to Henry's products on the auction block at eBay, the online auction giant. There are also online flyers that you need a reader program like Adobe Acrobat to read. They're worth checking out if you're waiting for a sale price before taking the plunge.

Home Automation Systems, Inc.

www.smarthome.com

Multimedia site featuring the latest in electronic gizmos for the home: Home Automation Systems features thousands of electronic items of the most eclectic nature. To get the full experience, first listen to the RealAudio sales pitch (pleasant and brief) and then click the SmartHome Guided Tour and follow the arrows through a highly amusing and fascinating trip into the computer-operated Home of the Future Today. Available on the site are all manner of timers, light switches, and appliance automators — and all can be programmed by your home computer.

Here's just a tiny hint of what's in store: You and your significant other are in Lausanne, Switzerland, for the annual SpargleFest. Your mother-in-law needs to get into the house (back in Kelowna) to play with the cat, and you forgot to leave the keys. You call home, and through a combination of verbal and numerical instructions with the X10 Telephone Responder, you tell the porch light to go on (Smart Switch) and the door to unlock (Video Door Intercom), you feed the cat (Automatic Pet Feeder), change the litter box (Automatic Self Cleaning Litterbox), scare away that big dog from next door (the Scraminal), and heat the jet-spa (Thermostat Setback Controller) to just the right temperature for Mom. Then, after she leaves, you instruct the house to go back onto a preprogrammed house-activity plan (Home Automation Interface). It's all here, and you can purchase it all online.

Leisuredome

www.leisuredome.com

All types of electronic musical instruments in a beautiful setting: This exquisitely crafted British store is a site for sore eyes. Every step of the way, the Leisuredome beckons you on. The Leisuredome is dedicated to satisfying your most (or, rather, most of your) instrumental needs. Featuring electric and acoustic guitars of all sorts, from Jimi Hendrix Signature Series Fender Stratocasters to handcrafted Yamaha classical acoustic guitars that may have pleased Segovia, the Leisuredome is a fabulous musical destination.

Aside from its guitars, the Leisuredome sports various keyboards, amplifiers, DJ equipment, and instrumental accessories. This site sells online and apparently ships to every location on earth that has a computer or a landing strip. Although prices are all in English pounds, you do find a currency calculator on-site. Beautiful graphics and the photos of the instruments are nothing short of delicious. Pop on over like a good Web surfer and have a look for yourself.

Rent Express

www.rentexpress.com

One-stop cell phone rentals for travelers: The good people at Bell Mobility have come up with a very good use for the Net: a site where people on the move around the globe can reserve rental cell phones. That way, wherever you land, you have access to reliable local cell phone service. Depending on your needs, that phone can have a local number, provide international access, or even access satellite services. Canadians can choose to pick up their rental from a counter at one of Canada's major airports, or for a charge, you can get the phone delivered to your front door *before* you leave home. This service is primarily designed for business people, so it isn't cheap. Still, if you do a lot of work on the road, it's probably worth the cost.

Sony

www.sony.ca

Digital cameras, accessories, and much more: Sony's Canadian online store is another site that fits into more than one category of this directory: You can also buy top-quality Sony computer hardware here. We thought we'd include it in the electronics category though, because this site has an extensive range of digital cameras as well as WebTV consoles — two

products that give you a taste of what's to come in the multimedia world.

To start your spending spree, click the *Buy Sony Online* icon at the Sony Canada home page. After you're in the Sony Store, you find several main categories. For digital cameras, choose *Digital Imaging* from the main navigation toolbar. We particularly enjoy exploring the Handycam accessories. You can find some very cool things in this category, including digital photo frames and a digital still camera that pulls photos out of your home videos.

Prices at the Sony Store are listed in Canadian dollars, and you can have your purchase shipped anywhere in the country overnight or by ground delivery (three to seven days).

The Best Software Anywhere

Selling software on the Internet? Hmmm, why does the term "no-brainer" spring to mind? If you're interested in a specific piece of software, you're likely to find that:

- You can view a demo or screen shots with full backup, such as game hints or spec sheets.

- You can download a trial version to give the program a spin and see how it plays. Depending on the manufacturer, the trial can be either time or feature limited.

- You can download a complete version with online help. The rising cost of paper manuals has forced development companies to embrace the all-electronic version of a program with unbridled joy.

- You can order a program online cheaper than you can get it in a store.

Okay, so you don't get the satisfaction of unwrapping the box and leafing through the manual while you're driving home.

(What? You don't read and drive at the same time?) But you do get to jump up and down after the package arrives, and that's almost the same thing.

BetaNet

www.betabeta.com

Before software companies release a commercial program, it goes through several phases: The *beta* is the version where the features are set and the program is stable enough to be tested. At BetaNet, the whole dad-blamed site is dedicated to testing your limits — and we mean by that, of course, the limits of your CPU. Hundreds of beta programs await your download, all free, and the only guarantee they carry is that you're not going to be bored testing them.

Some fascinating stuff, fresh off the drawing board, is waiting patiently out there in BetaLand for your perusal. So if you wanna be the first on your block to boot it up, BetaNet is just your poison. A note of caution: Beta programs almost always have bugs that can cause the program to malfunction. Caveat Downloador.

Business Depot

www.businessdepot.com

Excellent selection at excellent prices: With over 130 stores across Canada, Business

Depot is already the country's largest supplier of office products. Now, it's building an equally strong reputation online. The download store has over 130,000 titles in categories like business, desktop publishing, education, entertainment, and more. Whatever your interests, kick back and browse through the titles. You'll like what you see. To download a software program, you first have to go through the secure online order page. After you buy the product, Business Depot walks you through the download process. Programs that are not downloadable can also be purchased online. You just have to wait a couple of days while the company ships them to you.

Corel E-store

www.corel.com

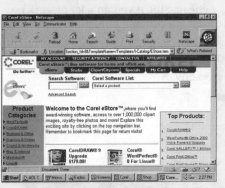

Canada's leading software designer has programs to ship and download: Corel, based in Ottawa, has become a world-leader in software development based on the success of programs like WordPerfect and CorelDRAW. The company's also become a media darling because of its ever-shifting fortunes and its flamboyant owner, Michael Cowpland. At the E-store, you can buy the company's latest software offerings. You can purchase and download some pretty impressive image packages in the *Corel Studio*. And don't forget to check out the *Freebies!* One drawback to the E-store? Prices are in U.S. dollars. But shipping is done within Canada, so you won't face any hidden cross-border charges.

Download.com

www.download.com

A lot of free software — and some you have to pay for too: Part of the CNet family of sites, Download.com is one of the most popular destinations on the Web to go for software downloads. Why, you ask? Well, because there's a heck of a lot of freeware here.

Choose from the long list of categories, including business, education and games. After you enter a category, you see hundreds of listings. Demos, freeware, and shareware are clearly marked as such. So are programs that you need to pay for. Click on the product name for a full list of specs, including download time. Also worth a browse are the site's daily features, the *Most Popular Downloads*, or Download.com's own top picks. An altogether fabulous place for software lovers.

Shareware.com

www.shareware.com

Excellent organization and a great selection: A good search engine is a thing of beauty — and, therefore, this site has beauty galore. One of CNet's extended family, Shareware.com, with its quarter million files and great organization, is an online asset worthy of serious consideration. Search by platform or subject and then link-jump over to sister service Download.com and browse by category for a fine example of glorious abundance. Both sites make hefty use of mirror download sites around the globe. For the fastest results, make sure that you pick the download site nearest you.

Shareware Junkies

www.sharewarejunkies.com

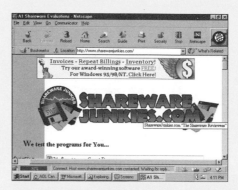

Great reviews, program testing, and additional coverage of shareware authors: After you land on the Shareware Junkies site, surf on over to your appropriate operating-system database; from there, it's browse, baby, browse. You find excellent reviews of the multitudinous downloads available in many categories, such as games, graphics, Internet, miscellaneous, and utilities. Don't miss the site's *Steals and Deals* software store for bargains on software and computer-related books.

The Edutainment Catalog Online

www.edutainco.com

Excellent selection of entertainment and educational software for the entire family: The Edutainment Catalog specializes in commercial and educational games and interactive learning programs. Your child's face will light up to see the broad choices available. The site offers a wonderful search engine that enables you to specify the manufacturer — we guarantee that you're going to be amazed by this list — the age (1–18; for adults, choose 18), and subject of interest for the software you want. Every search we launched came back loaded with possibilities. Keep in mind: This is a U.S. site, and the prices are all listed in U.S. dollars. Still, we highly recommend this site for those interested in finding the kids delightful alternatives to more passive media.

Tucows

www.tucows.ca

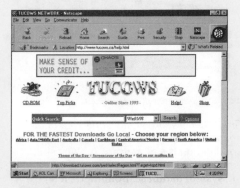

One of the broadest collections of Internet-related software: With affiliates worldwide, Tucows may well fulfill its acronym to become "The Ultimate Collection of WinSock Software." After you first enter the Tucows site, you need to choose the mirror site closest to you. The chart not only shows its worldwide locations, but also how frequently the site updates. After you're inside, select a category and then browse through the capsule descriptions of the featured software. If you're looking for any kind of Internet utility — amateur or pro — you can find it on Tucows.

ZDNet Software Library

www.hotfiles.com

Terrific editorial overview of an extensive software collection: ZDNet, with about a zillion features and a number of exclusives, is, to put it briefly, a blast! Head to your platform and go for it. Make sure that you check out the annual *Shareware Award*

results. Award categories include Coolest Waste of Time, Biggest Bang for No Bucks, and Game Most Likely to Make You Buy an Abdominal-Workout Product. ZDNet features a *Download Basket* that enables you to mark up to 10 different titles for later retrieval. All the software offered on ZDNet is reviewed and rated; file search results display both the file's review rating and its implicit rating, the latter based on the number of downloads.

At Your Service

If the '90s have taught us anything, it's that we are not alone. No, we're not talking about Area 51; we're talking about this shrinking ball of soil called Earth, where every innovation in communications brings the rest of the planet into your living room, onto your desktop, or into your cellular. If someone told you ten years ago that you'd be shelling out about $240 a year to maintain a constant link to a worldwide computer system, we doubt you'd have believed her. A lot of companies are out there vying for the right to bring you and other planeteers closer together — and guess what? You can find them all on the Web, where you can check out their qualifications, sign up, and get customer support around the clock. Telephone, television, and Internet services complete the consumer-electronic equation that connects you and your hardware to everyone else and all their hardware.

Hello, Operator?

Not surprisingly, the Web offers an excellent way to sort through all the various options when it comes to long-distance phone plans. Rest assured that should you ever really want to know the details of all the available calling plans — and pick one for yourself — you can do it on the Net.

Bell Canada

www.bell.ca

It's big and it's good: Bell Canada's Web site is so full of services, it might take you a while to explore every nook and cranny. Aside from enjoying the design of this welcoming site and its easy-to-understand commands, here are some of the things you can do there:

- View or pay your phone bill electronically.

- Shop at Bell World, an online emporium for phones, pagers, phone cards, Internet hook-ups, among other things.

- Read up on long-distance savings plans and sign up electronically.

- Access some pretty interesting information about Bell Canada through its press releases and archived newspaper articles.

- Learn how to wire your home for telephone service.

- Check out the special rates available to students.

- Use Canada 411 online to locate a business or residential number.

Sprint Canada

www.sprintcanada.ca

Many service plans detailed by an interactive planner: Another big competitor in the Canadian long-distance market is Sprint Canada. The company's Web site is beautifully designed and acts as a full-service online facility. You can find out all the benefits of each long-distance savings plan. When you find the one for you, you can sign up electronically. The *Plan Wizard* helps you compare plans depending on your needs, and the *Customer Service* option links you to a number of online services including FAQs and account management. The site also has a link to The Most Online, the company's Internet hook-up counterpart and full-service portal.

Wanna Watch Some Tube?

You know you're spending too much time looking at the television when you wake up in the middle of the night and an answer for the TV Guide crossword pops in your head. Not that we've ever done that. But we have taken a break from our awesomely busy days to browse on over to a TV listings Web site to see what's on tonight. And, come to think of it, what is a six-letter word for an '80s nighttime soap opera featuring Larry Hagman and Patrick Duffy? Be back in a bit. . . .

Canoe Television Jam!

www.canoe.ca/Television/home.html

TV listings and up-to-date entertainment news: Canoe has linked up with Jam!, the specialists in online TV and entertainment information, to provide complete Canadian TV listings. To access them, you need to sign up to the site and include your postal code. You can get more details about what's coming up on the tube for a particular week by reading the Jam! *Recommended TV Viewing.* Another fun feature is the ratings area for both Canadian and U.S. TV programs — some people know exactly how close their favourite show is to being cancelled! Finally, don't miss the Jam! Showbiz news headlines and features. You are a member of a celebrity-obsessed culture, after all.

CBC Television

www.tv.cbc.ca

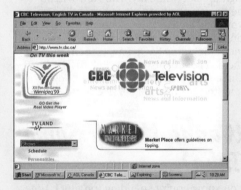

Serving Canadians from coast to coast: You grew up with it, and it's still going strong. CBC Television has a wonderful, interactive Web site that gives you a synopsis of all its programs, as well as the main network program schedule and links to other CBC properties like CBC Radio and CBC Specials. We also like the *Personalities* feature where you can read profiles of some of the best-known faces on Canadian television. Highly recommended for TV junkies and Canadian nationalists alike.

CTV

www.ctv.ca

The private network with a lot of good shows: The gateway to the CTV Web site is a beautiful image which gives way to a good variety of online options. You can browse *CTV Entertainment, CTV News,* and *CTV Sports* for program listings and upcoming highlights. You can even e-mail some of CTV's national reporters with story ideas or feedback. We enjoy the *Corporate* section because it lists all the network's local affiliates across the country — another way to feel connected.

TV Guide Live

www.tvguidelive.com

You buy it on the newsstands; now use it online: TV Guide is an immensely popular source for Canadian TV listings. Now, you can sign up for your subscription online at TV Guide Live and enjoy a plethora of nifty options. Not only can you browse TV listings, but you can also actually customize the grid that appears, based on your preferences. Couch potatoes everywhere are cheering, we're sure. You find daily *Top Picks* by TV Guide's television writers, *Star News and Celebrity Gossip,* online recipes by the current *Celebrity Chef.* You can even enter contests. If you love TV, you absolutely must give this site a try.

The Internet Connection

We think it's a safe bet that ten years ago, no one ever asked who your Internet service provider (ISP) was. Ten years ago the Net hadn't taken over our lives or brought a rich, but confusing, bounty of information to our door. Today, the marketplace is just jumping with all kinds of companies vying to usher you into the next century. All the sites listed here are viable choices. With so many options, it's a good idea to make ISP's middle name — service — your deciding factor.

@Home

www.home.com

Cable access to the Net @Home: In Canada, there are several ways to connect to the Internet using an ISP. One relatively new way is through your cable hook-up instead of your phone line. The Canadian version of this service is called @Home. The URL we've provided above is for the U.S.-based parent company. You can also find out more about @Home services by going to the Rogers@Home Web site at rogers.home.com or to Shaw@Home at shaw.home.com. Depending on which of these companies you subscribe to, you have access to a slightly different version of the Canadian @Home portal. Whichever way you get to it, the site is excellent — including a good Canadian shopping channel.

AOL Canada

www.aol.ca

The largest online service in the world: AOL Canada, operated by America Online, Inc. the world's leading online service provider with more than 17 million members, is an interactive online service tailored to the Canadian marketplace. Sure, AOL has its problems (like annoying spam attacks and heavy user-traffic congestion), but it also has plenty of virtues: Endless features; major online partnerships; easy, effective e-mail; instant message transmissions; and the biggest member directory in the biz. AOL also features a complete built-in Web browser — a special version of Internet Explorer so that members have a seamless experience moving from AOL-only areas to the Web. Not that AOL Canada can afford to rest on its laurels — not with the World Wide Web of competitors gunning for it.

CompuServe for Canadians

www.compuserve.ca

Great technical resource with extensive information and file database: With two million members at home, in the workplace, and around the globe, CompuServe is one of the founders of the online service industry. Even though CompuServe was acquired by AOL, it is maintained as an independent service, offering unparalleled depth and breadth of content, premium services, hundreds of Forums, and access to the Net. CompuServe also offers a comprehensive yet easy-to-navigate Web portal for CompuServe members and Internet users, available at www.CompuServe.com.

Internet Direct

www.mydirect.com

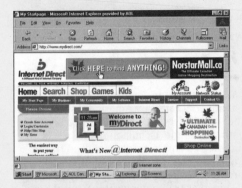

Canadian ISP makes good: There's something really appealing to us about Internet Direct, one of Canada's leading nationwide ISPs. Maybe it's the fact that the company was started here and has grown so nicely. Maybe it's the friendly Canadian feel it's achieved at its Web site. Whatever it is, we like it. The portal offers shopping, downloadable games, and online customer support. Check out the Company History to read about how a young start-up became a player in Canada's budding e-commerce scene.

Netcom Canada

www.netcom.ca/homeport

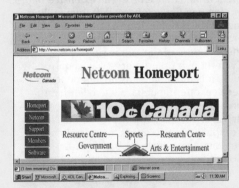

ISP partners with world giant AT&T to offer hook-ups: Netcom is the Canadian presence for telecom giant AT&T. This ISP is available to people in most major centres. Even non-members can use the main Web site to access a number of quick services there, including a giant directory of links (on things like weather, arts and entertainment, search engines, and basic info on the Internet). For some reason, Netcom's online registration page is hard to find (get there directly by using the URL `www.netcom.ca/software`). Still, after you get there, you can start the hook-up process lickety-split.

Sprint Canada

www.sprint.ca

Popular in the long-distance market; popular ISP, too: Sprint Canada, which offers Internet access across this fair land, has an excellent portal site with a number of channels, including shopping, travel, news, careers, and more. You can sign up for your dial-up access here or just browse around. An online chat room is available, and we like *The Vault,* where you can find a bunch of links to sites for kids, including some excellent Canadian sites.

Sympatico

www1.sympatico.ca

There's no place like home: Sympatico is the biggest ISP in Canada, with over 600,000 member households. Although you can sign up at the portal for traditional dial-up Internet access, consider trying Sympatico's new (and more expensive) High Speed Edition. The edition uses new technology enabling very fast, unlimited access to the Net over your phone line at the same time letting you receive calls and faxes. Find out all about your lower- and high-speed options at the Sympatico portal, which also assembles an incredible array of services and information available to both members and non-members.

The Online Shopping Directory

It's the Good Life, Online!   D-43

Suffice it to say, you're getting your money's worth by dropping by the portal.

Other Stuff To Check Out

www.egghead.com/store/ent/
eggs_portal.browse
www.cendirect.com
www.geocities.com/TelevisionCity/9544/
index.html
www.psinet.com
www.sysopt.com

It's the Good Life, Online!

How do you know that you've arrived? The amount of leisure time you have is one major clue. Another is purchasing goods not because you need them but because you *want* them. A lot of items sure are available online to start you salivating — and we're not just talking about gourmet food and drink. Name the activity or commodity that gives you pleasure and enriches your life, and you're likely to find not just one but a host of Web sites waiting to offer you the best available in the field. And why not? You've worked hard; you deserve it — so kick back and surf your way through a little bit of luxury.

Some Cool Stuff for the Home

Wanna spiff up the ol' castle? Whether you're looking for turn-of-the-century tableware for 18 or some classical sculptures to spread about the front lawn, you can find all manner of housewares online. We're real furniture-store hounds ourselves — easily spending hour upon hour trying out the different chairs and recliners. Although the Web hasn't quite figured out how to convey the sensation of an Italian leather–covered LaZy-Boy, you can certainly narrow down your choices with

a little judicious online browsing. If, on the other hand, the kitchen is more your little bit of heaven, you can find lots to like online in that area, too.

Avalon Garden.Com

www.avalongarden.com

Terrific array of outdoor garden sculptures: Avalon Garden.Com offers birdbaths, fountains, planters, and architectural elements galore. You can pick up a lot of attractive, entertaining, and reasonably priced accents for your garden, terrace, windowsill, or kitchen wall from Avalon Garden.Com's beautiful online sculpture garden. Whether utilitarian or decorative — or, quite often, both — all items have pictures and descriptions and are available for purchase online.

Canadians take note: This is an U.S. site. Prices are in U.S. dollars and shipping costs to bring your purchase home will be bigger than those advertised on the site.

Bocabec Twiggery

www.twiggery.com

Truly beautiful twig furniture: At the Bocabec Web site, you're greeted with a series of giant, colourful photographs that made us fantasize about having twig furniture in our own backyards. This furniture is hand-made by a New Brunswick artisan, so you have to make direct contact with her via phone or e-mail to place your order. Shipments are available for a cost, depending on the distance.

Kitcherama

www.kitcherama.com

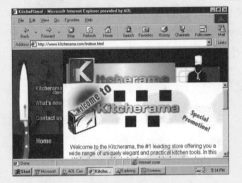

A bilingual site with excellent products: Kitcherama must be serious about kitchen products because they put a razor-sharp knife on their home page. The company, based in Montreal, has a large online catalogue of beautifully designed, higher-end kitchen tools, including everything from knives to wine openers. The photos are sharp, and the descriptions complete for all items. To order, call the toll-free number (Kitcherama doesn't yet have an online order form). Take the time to read the maintenance information to learn how you can keep your kitchen supplies in tip-top shape.

Pioneer Handcrafted Log Furniture

www.pioneerlogfurniture.mb.ca

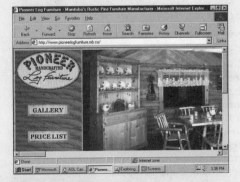

Old-fashioned Canadian handiwork: If you're looking for beautiful wood furniture, look no further than Pioneer Log Furniture's Web site. You can view an extensive selection of wood products including tables, chairs, and sideboards. You can also submit your order online. Our only problem with the site? Even though it's Canadian, it caters to an American clientele, meaning prices are listed in U.S. dollars. You need your currency converter for this one.

Sears Canada

www.sears.ca

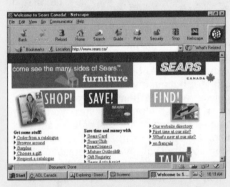

Long-standing catalogue company goes online: Sears Canada has done a very smart thing by getting online in a big way. You can buy almost anything here, including a wide variety of home products and furniture. You can order in a number of different ways: online, by calling the toll-free ordering number, by printing out your order form and faxing or mailing it, or by cross-referencing the item's catalogue number with the old-fashioned seasonal catalogue that comes to your door. This site is one of Canada's premier online shopping stops, and we highly recommend taking a look around.

The Anywhere Hammock Chair Company

hammockchair.hypermart.net

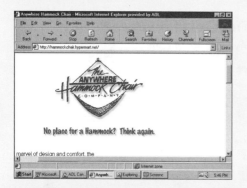

A hammock you can hang just about any-where: True, this site's not exactly an online emporium; it sells only one product: the Anywhere Hammock Chair. But come on! Who doesn't want one of these things? We like the cute pictures showing different hanging styles, and the secure online ordering form. You can also call in your order or send it in by fax or mail.

The Chef's Store

www.chefs-store.com

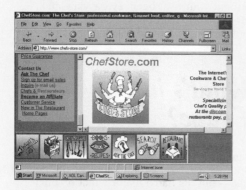

A one-stop shopping site for kitchenware and accessories: Combining fun graphics and first-rate products, The Chef's Store enables you to build the kind of kitchen

that can make you weep for joy. Of the many excellent features on this site, *The Chef's Kitchen* is particularly nifty. You choose among *The Basic Kitchen, The Well-Equipped Kitchen, or The Chef's Dream Kitchen;* then just sit back and peruse merchandise from the top manufacturers in the trade. The Chef's Store also offers recipes, shopping advice, online ordering, e-mail updates, and a thorough search engine. Although this U.S. site lists prices in U.S. dollars and you have to ship your purchases over the border, we think you'll appreciate the incredible selection here.

Stocking the Virtual Cellar

Remember the first time that you tried a special wine or liquor and hated it, and someone said, "It's an acquired taste." We can assure you that you can find a lot of tastes you'd like to acquire while browsing online. One of the major benefits of reading up about wines, spirits, and beer is the terrific amount of information available that can help you educate those taste-buds. So name your poison and spend a little time in our virtual cellar, where the good stuff is just waiting for you.

Canadian Iceberg Vodka

www.icebergvodka.net

They actually make this stuff from icebergs!: It's true. They use water from iceberg parts, called "growlers" to make their vodka. Go to this site to find out more about a unique Canadian product. There's also quite a substantial number of drink and food recipes that use Iceberg Vodka as an ingredient. Submit a recipe via e-mail, and you can win a free T-shirt! Cool. Well, very *cold*, actually.

Discovery Wines Online

www.discoverywines.com

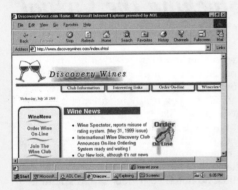

Wines of the world sold online to residents of B.C.: It's not our policy to include sites available to only some Canadians, but we think Discovery Wines is noteworthy enough for a few words here. After you join the Discovery Club, you're notified monthly of new wine selections. You can then order some truly elegant wines (some in limited supply) online and have them delivered to your door.

Did we mention you have to live in B.C. to use the service? Yeah, we're bummed too!

Mike's Hard Lemonade Online

www.mikeshardlemonade.com

A fun site by the company that's cleaning up on the popularity of spiked lemonade: The

content may not be deep, but the people behind Mike's Hard Lemonade have brought you a good-looking and fun-to-browse site. If you're of legal drinking age, you can also download screen savers. Fun site for a rainy day.

The Canadian Beer Review

www.canbeer.com

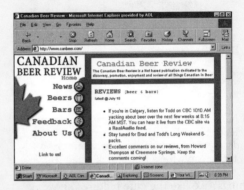

All the latest on Canadian beer: Surely you're not surprised that in Canada there would be a site like this one! The Canadian Beer Review is dedicated to promoting and educating the Web-browsing public about Canadian beer. Yep! You can find out about beer-related events, read news reports about the beer industry, and sample the up-to-date reviews. You can also submit your own beer review via e-mail. We think the list of bars is a good idea, but so far, it's limited to a handful of provinces.

What's in the Fridge?

"Food, glorious food!" Neither of us can remember where we first heard that song — we don't even remember the musical — but it's had a major effect on our lives. And now, our search for ever more glorious food has been simplified tremendously with the available sites on the World Wide Web. Luckily, we can now satisfy our cravings with a modem connect here and a mouse click there — and you can, too.

Belgian Chocolate Shop

www.giftex.com/belgian

The best in Belgian chocolates offered for your sweet tooth or as a gift: You've got your boxed chocolates, your nut clusters, your dark chocolates, your milk chocolates, your sugarless chocolates . . . the list goes on at this site. And they're all made with Belgian chocolate. The site also offers exotic chocolate products, including chocolate-covered ginger and chocolate-covered orange peels, as well as chocolates shaped as cigars or white-chocolate golf balls. If it's a gift your sending, you can choose to send your chocolate in a cup or themed tin and personalize a card online with it.

Black Bear Company Store

www.blackbear.net

An excellent taste of wild salmon from the Charlottes: Salmon connoisseurs living anywhere in the country can sink their teeth in hand-filleted and traditionally smoked salmon from the West coast. This family-run business has smoked salmon for many of Vancouver's premier hotels and restaurants. Various King and Sockeye salmon are prepared with secret family recipes and can also come in gift boxes.

Grocery Gateway

www.grocerygateway.com

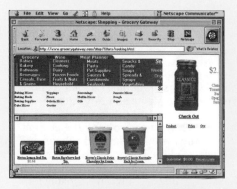

High-quality food items delivered to your door: If you live in Toronto, Grocery Gateway gives you access to thousands of perishable and non-perishable grocery items via Longo's, a Toronto supermarket chain known for high-quality fruits and vegetables. After you register, the variety is spectacular, from basic milk and eggs to hard-to-get brands and organically grown food. They even offer wine (with proof of your age, of course).

Other features include a *List Manager* that stores a list of your weekly purchases to save time on your next visit and *Meal Planner* with recipes including ingredients that you find in the store. Payment options are fabulous, as you can pay at your door with cash, cheque, credit card, or even debit card!

Lobster Direct

www.lobsterdirect.com

Everything you need to enjoy lobster from the cold waters of Atlantic Canada: This site offers live Maine and Nova Scotia Lobster and smoked salmon, as well as the utensils you need to cook the critters. Also on the menu are smoked salmon and special gift ideas. For you lobster novices, Lobster Direct provides the do's and don'ts of eating, storing, and cooking lobster and lets you try mouth-watering lobster recipes. The ordering process is a snap, and Lobster Direct delivers across Canada — it even throws in lobster bibs and lobster jokes you can tell as "yer crackin' a claw."

The PeachTree Network

www.thepeachtree.net

One of the first online grocery shopping sites to service Canadians nationwide: The PeachTree Network is essentially a group of independent, local grocers that provide delivery of perishable or non-perishable items right to your door. Some of the affiliates (which also have their own Web site) include AM Foodfare, Web Grocer-e, and Food for You. This cyberstore has a number of different virtual aisles, apart from food products (such as health and beauty and pet products), enabling you to choose from thousands of items representing an extensive choice of brands. You can also save your regular weekly purchases on the site to make your next visit faster. A shopping-cart feature makes filling up a cinch. The site is a lively, colourful, fun place to visit.

Sunterra Market

www.sunterra.com

The Online Shopping Directory

It's the Good Life, Online! D-49

Some of the best fresh items available delivered from the farm to your door: This neighbourhood store in Calgary hosts one terrific online site and lives up to its slogan, "Your Fresh Food Connection." The Sunterra Market brings the European style market to the fingertips of Calgary residents. You can access more than 9,000 grocery items, including produce brought to you directly from growing areas, flavourful meats from the store's farms, imported and domestic cheeses, sandwiches and deli meats, and breads and desserts from its in-store bakery. The site even includes a Tobacco department. You also have the option of picking up your order rather than getting it delivered. Other features include a catering service as well as a section, *Explore Sunterra,* that allows you to learn cooking tips, view recipes, and get to know the family that built this store decades ago.

From Movies to Music and Back Again

For better or worse, few things in our culture are more influential than popular music or movies. At the same time, both art forms have an astonishingly broad range of styles. After all, the simple fact that music has room for both Johann Sebastian Bach and Snoop Doggy Dog is pretty amazing. No matter what your taste — in movies or in music — you can find it online. Movies in Canada are, for the most part, available online for sale only. Music, on the other hand, is definitely moving into a try-before-you-buy mode online. Feel free to listen to your favourite artist's latest tunes via streaming audio the next time that you drop into a Web music parlor. Who knows? Maybe "gangsta fugues" are gonna be the next musical rage.

CD Plus

www.cdplus.com

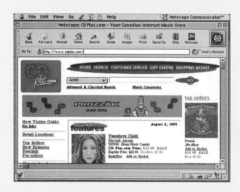

Excellent search options guide you through its enormous database: We can see why this site is confident enough to bill itself "Your Internet CD Source." This site is the online sister of the business that has more than 100 stores across Canada that operate under such trade names as AVE Entertainment, Music Baron, and Music City, as well as CD Plus. Browse through its 28 music categories or fire up its incredible search engine that lets you search for music, using any combination of artist, album title, soundtrack, song listing, album label, composer, performer, instrument, and so on.

Other features include *Hot Sales* and *Top 20* charts (with purchase links); a *Pre-Order* department for upcoming releases; links to six major record distributors; and *Ask the Wizard,* a cool feature that answers a question you submit if, say, you're looking for the whereabouts of a band from yesteryear or want the lyrics to a favourite song. In addition to the descriptions, song list, and cover art accompanying each listing, you also find a list of *Other Albums* that the artist recorded. And with some, you can tune in to a promotional clip of a song. And the site also plans to sell digital music online!

HMV

www.hmv.com

A multi-featured online music and video extravaganza: Entering this site is as exciting as walking into one of its stores in the physical world. You find an extensive collection of music CDs in categories ranging from your standard Rock and Blues to the eclectic like Francophone and International offerings. Beyond the tunes, check out listings for karaoke, self-improvement, and spoken word CDs, as well as a wide selection of VHS/DVDs. You can also find *New Releases, Bestsellers,* and CDs on sale.

Each CD listing includes its track listing and cover art, as well as the artists' biography and discography. What blew us away is the site's audio visual elements. Watch the performance of a band that played at an HMV store or check out a live broadcast of famous artists through its link to Virtually Canadian, a gateway to online music channels.

SamsCD.COM

www.samscd.com

Low prices on a wide selection: Sam The Record Man has taken to the Web, offering more than 300,000 CDs and cassettes as well as VHS and DVD titles at some of the best prices we've seen online. You can even find a special section for CDs under $10. After you browse the site's categories or use its search engine to select a CD, you can view that CD's cover artwork and track listings. With some, you can listen to RealAudio sound clips — and if you're not plugged in, you're one click on your way to downloading a RealAudio Player. You can also check out which popular Canadian artists are touring near you. With free registration, you can join *My Sams* and tap into a wealth of music info, including artists bios, music news and gossip, and CD reviews both current and archived.

Columbia House Canada

www.columbiahousecanada.com

Club deals combined with online advantages: Most of the features offered by this world-famous club are now available online. The basic club deal is that you get 12 CDs for free as long as you buy six CDs at the regular price over the next two years. You can search the complete Columbia House Canada Music Catalogue — which includes 6,000 titles — five different ways and then listen to audio clips from select CDs. Browse through CDs in sections including *Essential Collection, New Releases,* and *Hot Picks.* And check out the *Best Album You've Never Heard.* A relatively new feature is a *Video Library,* where you can purchase episodes from 60 classic TV shows. If you're a member of Columbia House Canada's video club (out there in the mail world), you can respond to your club mailings online.

Videoflicks.com

www.videoflicks.com

A wide selection of movies plus a review of each film: Launching from the success of Videoflicks' chain of some 30 video rental stores throughout southern Ontario, this site was chosen by *The Globe and Mail* 's *Report on Business* as one of the top 25 sites on the Net and receives more than 14 million hits a month. You can search for a VHS/DVD movie by title or person, or you can browse through 13 categories that index more than 65,000 titles. Select a movie and view its box cover, read a synopsis, and check out movie reviews from fellow buyers around the world before dropping the selection in your shopping cart.

It's hard to imagine that you won't find the movie you're looking for here, whether it appears in one of the sites many lists, including the *Top 10 VHS Releases,* or the American Film Institute's list of *America's 100 Greatest Movies.* But if you do come up empty-handed, click on over to the *Auction* section. You can also subscribe to movie-related newsletters and play the site's weekly movie trivia test for a chance to win a prize.

Videomatica

www.videomatica.bc.ca

A cornucopia of mainstream and off-the-beaten-path films: This site has one of the largest collections of VHS/DVD films we've seen on the Web, offering movies that you simply won't find at your corner rental store. The Vancouver store was created in 1983 for film buffs and made its name peddling films that were made in more than 50 countries from Albania to Zimbabwe. But it also offers mainstream, albeit unique, films as well, including French Canadian, silent movies, musicals, the World's Worst Movies, Japanese animation, and BBC/A&E/PBS documentaries. You can search for a film by title, actor, or director, or you can browse through a comprehensive catalogue of categories and view, in most cases, the video box. And those of you living in the Vancouver area, you can even rent a movie online.

Nothing Quite Like a Good Book

We're not asking for a spot on *Oprah,* but we're ready to admit we have a problem — we're book-a-holics. In fact, there's no scarier feeling than coming to the end of a book and realizing there aren't any new ones on our shelves to crack open. After discovering the incredible diversity and fantastic convenience of online bookstores, we've fallen even further into our addiction. Not only can we get the newest bestsellers cheaper and with less hassle online than in a regular bookstore, but we can also get all the hard-to-find and out-of-print books we could ever handle. And for the times we can't read — whether we're driving or going for a run — we can listen to any one of the wide variety of audio books available online. If you're a book addict as we are, online shopping is going to make you happy. Too happy.

Aaronbooks.com

www.aaronbooks.com

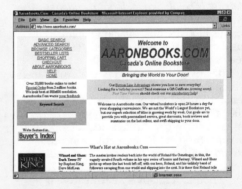

Books with a twist on personalized service: The Canadian site readily admits it's not the world's largest bookstore, but its 50,000-plus stack of titles continues to grow. It has the standard search features that you find on most booksellers' sites: You either can browse through its catalogue to find a specific book or use its search engine to search by author, title, subject, or keyword. You can find loads of information for each book, including a summary and often professional and customer reviews. But it's the personal service that makes this site excel.

The site provides tips to help you narrow your search, and if you still can't find what you need, the staff helps you get it. And what really tickles us is its *Gofer* service (which was in the works at the time of writing). After you register, the Gofer robot gets to know your buying habits, searches out your favourite subjects, and presents you with a list of the latest books. Now that's service!

Audio Book Club

www.audiobookclub.com

A huge selection of audio books and a terrific bargain: Books on tape are big business these days, and this site is the place to get 'em — 70,000 titles, including bestsellers, fiction, nonfiction, self-help, business, and how-to books, read by authors, experts, actors, and celebrities of every stripe. The basic club deal is that you get four for a penny (that's American to you Canucks) and then buy four more at full price within two years. You find lots of RealAudio samples available online at this site. And check out the site's _Old Time Radio_ feature. You can listen to original radio broadcasts from the 30s, 40s, and 50s and then hop on over to the order desk.

Chapters.ca

www.chapters.ca

A huge selection of books at competitive prices and more: Chapters.ca is one of the main Canadian rivals to Amazon.com, offering more than 2 million titles of books — but a whole lot more. The site also peddles a wide selection of VHS and DVD offerings, software, and CDs. It offers easy-to-use search engines, including an _Advanced_ engine that lets you find books not only by the standard author, title, keyword, and ISBN, but also by price and format of the book, such as paperback, hardcover, and audio. You can also browse through bestseller lists and books recommended by Chapters staff, including reviews by buyers like you. You can even pre-order books for upcoming release. The site also has a _Bargain Books_ section, as

well as a nifty _Gifts_ centre that offers suggestions on books for a particular occasion.

ChaptersGLOBE.com

www.chaptersglobe.com

Books with a broad range of literary information: This site is the online product that emerged when one of Canada's largest book chains joined forces with Canada's national newspaper, _The Globe and Mail._ While Chapters.ca is geared to the general consumer, ChapterGLOBE.com is home to book lovers who want literary information as much as the books themselves. The site has the standard, easy-to-use search engine, plus you can find books in the _Bestsellers_, _Awards_, and _Bargain Books_ sections. Book enthusiasts can do any of the following at the site:

- Enter the _Community_ area and read up on the latest book-related news from _The Globe_

- Find out what book signing event, workshop, or literary festival is coming to their local community in a calendar of _Events_

- Enter _Interviews_ and listen to audio clips of interviews, readings, and discussion groups

- Tap into information on 20,000 authors, including 2,500 Canadians located in the _Author's Centre_

You can also join in on a forum hosted by someone involved in the literary community in the site's _Discussions_ area, where visitors can post their thoughts on a particular topic.

The Cook Book Store

www.cook-book.com

A wide selection of some of the best books on food and wine: On this site, you can find the same great food and wine books that earned the Toronto-based store the Canadian Bookseller of the Year Award from the Book Publishers' Professional Association in 1997. And if you can't find a book there that's still in print, the staff helps you find it — plus answers any cooking questions you may have. Other features on the site include the following:

- *Resources* provides links to cooking-related sites, directories and ezines

- *Recipes* lets you test out sample recipes from books you can purchase on the site

- Calendar listings alert you to upcoming author signings or tastings at the store

DH Audio

www.dhaudio.com

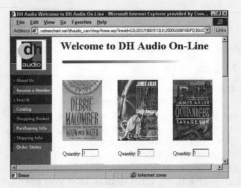

A wide selection of audio books that you can purchase within Canada: The relatively low prices here make this site definitely worth checking out. DH Audio has been in the audio books publishing business since 1980 and offers a Canadian section at its site where you can choose from 600 titles in 20 different genres. Categories include *Romance,* featuring popular *Harlequin* novels; *Financial,* including money facts from Bloomberg; and *Thrillers,* offering classics such as *Psycho* and *Dracula.* DH Audio also has an Order Status feature for members to keep track of their deliveries.

Greenwoods' Bookshoppe

www.greenwood.com

Reviews plus an entertaining interactive feature: Greenwoods' Bookshoppe is an independent bookseller based in Edmonton that has been serving our friends in Alberta for 20 years. Now, its online shop lets the rest of Canada tap into its 60,000 titles on hand and gives access to millions more. Its staff members love books, so you're treated to reviews — but only on those books that get a thumbs up. The friendly people here also help you locate a book you can't find (for a fee). And if you prefer some listening pleasure, enter the site's *Radio Active* section, which broadcasts the CBC Radio show of the same name, when founder Laurie Greenwood joins the show to review new releases each Tuesday. You also can easily become a member of the Radioactive Book Club and receive the newsletter via e-mail, snail mail, or fax.

Indigo.ca

www.indigo.ca

Great discounts with easy to use search engines and lots of extra features: Indigo's online sister has made the same splash on the Net as the book seller did in the real world when it opened its doors in 1996. The site offers the standard online book-seller search engines, letting you search by author, title, subject, keyword, publisher, ISBN number, and publication date. The site also helps you find hard-to-find and out-of-print books, provides order tracking to check up on delivery of your orders, and suggests a wish list of books that you can compile and buy from. Other special feature include an *Awards* section with scores of journalists' reviews of award-winning books; various lists of *Bestsellers*, including Oprah's Picks; as well as a major *Indigo Kids* department.

If you can't be there, enter *On @Indigo* and pick any one of its three channels to listen to author readings, read an article about the author, or access a transcript of a dicussion he or she had. We highly recommend you take a break at the *In Fun* section — read your Horoscope and see what

advice columnists Nick and Nora have for confused souls.

How 'bout Some New Threads?

You don't have to be a fashion victim to want decent duds. Luckily, help is on the way for even the most stylishly challenged. Online clothing stores take away the agony of pawing through rack after rack, only to find just the right item — in just the wrong size. If you shop for a new suit or skirt on the Web, designer or otherwise, you know what's available before anyone can say, "It's you!"

Canadian Heritage Company

www.cdnheritageco.mb.ca

For those who want to keep warm and look good: The Canadian Heritage Company Web site stands out for a number of reasons. We like the soft-focus drawings on the home page; the complete online ordering; and the outerwear that makes us believe we could keep warm year-round — even during a Winnipeg winter! You can get more than coats here though. You can find accessories too, like gloves, footwear, and gear. Choose from men's, women's, or children's merchandise at this top-notch Canadian site.

Club Monaco

www.clubmonaco.com

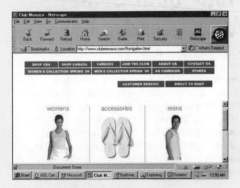

The kids are hip to this so you should be, too: Club Monaco's one of Canada's biggest retail clothing success stories. It also happens to sell some of the coolest clothes around, and the beautiful, minimalist style of the company's Web site reflects its philosophy of simplicity and elegance. Check out the latest men's and women's clothing collections, accessories, cosmetics, and designer products for your home. Yes, you can buy online and yes, the server is secure.

Holt Renfrew

www.holtrenfrew.com

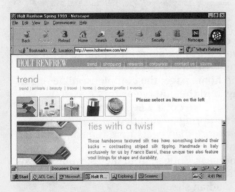

The crème de la crème: If you've ever walked into Holt Renfrew, you know this is a store for people with highly developed fashion sense — and some serious money to spend. The company's Canadian department stores are overflowing the top names in designer brands. Holt also carries several versions of its own signature line of clothing. At this Web site, you can view and buy selections from that line (which is not nearly as expensive as you might imagine). Other cool features include *Trend,* where Holt highlights some special merchandise, and the *Designer Profile,* where you can read about one of fashion's rising stars.

Mark's Work Wearhouse

www.marks.com

For the man or woman who needs everything: Mark's Work Warehouse is a great store. You can get really good quality work and casual clothes at reasonable prices. So we forgive the company for the fact that you can't complete an order (with credit card info and so on) online at its Web site. If you don't live near a MWW store, you can e-mail in what you want. They'll make arrangements to get the stuff to you (which is, we suppose, a pretty good compromise). Alternatively, you can browse the online clothing listings and either show up to the store in person or use the toll-free order number.

Oxygen

www.oxygen-o2.com

The Online Shopping Directory

It's the Good Life, Online!   D-57

Now we're getting so hip it hurts: If you really want clothes with some zing, you've got to take a look at Oxygen's hyperstylized, graphically enhanced Web site. You'll think you're looking at a Vogue spread! A very limited number of clothes are for sale here, organized into outfits you can buy through a secure server. (The site mostly exists to promote the actual Oxygen store located in Calgary). And with designer names like Patrick Cox, nothing here comes cheap. But are those some sweet outfits or what?

Pacific Trekking Company

www.pacifictrekking.com

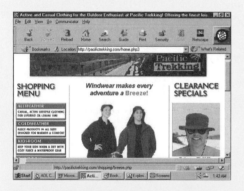

It's warm, it's Canadian, it's outdoorsy: That pretty much describes the essence of Pacific Trekking, a company that understands Canada's perpetually changing and harsh climate. Here, you find *Allweather* gear, *Coldweather* gear, *Children's* gear, *Rain* gear . . . you get the picture. You can also find fleece blankets (so warm!) and accessories like hats. And here's a bonus: If your online order comes to more than $100, Pacific Trekking ships it for free. You can also join the company's e-mail list to get news about upcoming promotions and new merchandise or check out the size chart — a simple and useful tool that's surprisingly rare among online clothing retailers.

Don't Forget to Accessorize!

When the expression "It's the details that count" was invented, we imagine the inventor was probably talking about accessories. You can wear the most killer outfit this side of 5th Avenue, but if you don't have the shoes to go with it, you're not going anywhere! And while we're on the subject, how about a matching wallet or bag? The Web excels at providing the most unique shops with the greatest boutique items — all designed to help you make the fashion statement you've been trying for all your life . . . or at least to help get you some cool shades.

Deelightful Lids

www.deelightful.com

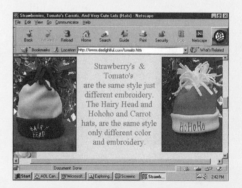

Truly unique fleece hats: We've never seen anything quite like these quirky, handmade hats. How 'bout a bright red tomato-shaped lid for your three-year-old? Thus the name "Dee-lightful," we suppose. Actually, the name really comes from the site's creator and the hat designer herself Dee Beattie, who started her business by popular demand — people kept asking her where she and her family were getting their great hats! These days, Dee's Web site sells her complete line of children and women's lids, as well as embroidery. You can custom order a special hat, and Dee even sells to U.S. shoppers. Orders can't be processed online here, so you have to print out your form and mail it.

Flax Blue Ties

www.flaxblue.com

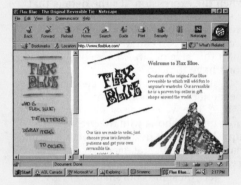

There's nothing like a man with a wacky tie: You can buy exactly that from Flax Blue Ties. The company's claim-to-fame is that its ties are made to order and reversible, so you get twice the wearability for the same price. We took a look around and with some very unique patterns, including *Jungle* and *Holidays* themes, these ties appear to live up to their billing as adding "fun to anyone's wardrobe." Oh yeah, you can also order online.

John Fluevog Shoes

www.fluevog.com

Shoes for the stylishly inclined: If you've ever seen a pair of Fluevogs walking down the street, you'd remember them. John Fluevog is an internationally recognized shoe designer who always seems to know how to strike the balance between whimsy and style. His leather shoes have been worn by the likes of Madonna! Characteristically, the company's Web site is both hip and useful. You can order from the entire Fluevog catalogue here, and all the shoes come with a big photo and charming Fluevog-esque description.

Pull Up Our Sox

www.sox.org

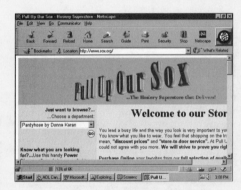

Deals on all manner of hosiery: Now this is a site every woman will love. It's got a fantastic selection of socks, tights, and pantyhose by designers like Donna Karan and Calvin Klein, and it offers these products at really good prices.

Watchcan

www.watchcan.com

Upscale watches for every taste: Watchcan sells Swiss watches designed by Lucien Piccard. You can find literally hundreds of selections here, from men's and ladies' gold watches to specialty pocket watches, pendant watches, and chains. Each style comes with a full description and beautiful photo so that you know exactly what you're buying. If you're looking for a special watch for that special someone (even if that special someone is you), check out Watchcan.

Other Stuff to Check Out

www.bernardcallebaut.com
www.hickoryfarms.com
www.iga.net
www.rogerschocolates.com
www.pcbaskets.com
www.bmgmusicservice.com
www.chapters.ca
www.megatunes.com
www.cascadiabooks.com
www.chbooks.com
www.rustique.ca
www.towerrecords.com
www.enews.com
www.yahoo.ca/reference/libraries
www.roots.com
www.servicemerchandise.com

Great Pastimes

Although the Net can truly offer you some of the most exotic merchandise on Earth, sometimes the best finds are the simplest. A beautiful postcard, an inventive toy, some outdoor camping gear — most of these items you can also buy at the local mall, but the fact that these and other goods are now available on the Web shows just how pervasive online shopping has become. The Web is now an excellent source for goods that you use to pursue leisure activities and not just a leisure activity itself.

As the Web becomes more and more integrated into your daily life, you're likely to use it to support your everyday lifestyle as well as your work. In this section, you not only find sites with great deals on things to buy, but you also find wonderful leads for things to do. Sporting events, performances, museums — the full range of fun is online right now.

Family, Friends, and Fido

Me. Me. Me. Every Web page talks about how you can follow *your* desires and track down just the gifts that *you* want. But how about taking care of some of the significant others in your life? Your kids, your folks, your friends, your pets . . . you get the idea. Online shopping is practically made for gift shopping, especially if you consider the alternatives. (Remember last holiday season?) So get online and follow our lead to some terrific sites, guaranteed to make someone near and dear to you extremely happy.

After all, you've got a birthday coming up, don't you? Sometime in the next year? And everyone remembers the Golden Rule — especially around gift-giving time.

Keepin' the Kids Happy

Had a tough day? Think about the last time your kid started jumping up and down with excitement. Smiling yet? How about when you surprised your offspring with the toy that made them say "please, please, please." Feel better? The sites in this section are sure to give your child a grin from ear to ear — and that's a pleasure that spreads very easily.

Bear St. Canada

www.bearst.com/canada

Stuffed animals ordered online: Gotta Getta Gund? This is a good place to find one! For those who don't know, Gund is a manufacturer of plush toys, and Bear St. Canada offers a mind-boggling assortment of them, each with its own special identity. If you're into cute teddies, you can't go wrong exploring the hundreds of photos posted to this site. There's even a *Fuzzy Finder* search engine so you can locate the exact stuffed bear, dog, bunny, or whatever you're looking for! We really enjoy the *History* option, where you can learn about the entire 100-year history of Gund toys. Use the online order form to order your cutsie-wootsie toy, but remember, prices here are in U.S. dollars, and Canadian taxes apply to your purchase.

Camppage.com

www.camppage.com

Summer camp central: Maybe you can't get away for a month or two to expand your horizons, but your kids can. And the CampPage guide is just the place to find your offspring's perfect summer idyll. The listings here are mostly for traditional camps (canoeing, swimming, knot-tying . . . all the good stuff). While this site is designed for Americans, it's got an impressive list of Canadian camps. Find them by clicking the Canadian Camps link on the left-hand side of the home page. Each camp listing includes, at the very least, a location, age eligibility, and contact info.

F.A.O. Schwarz

www.faoschwarz.com

A legendary toy store, now online: Once upon a time, parents needed to make a pilgrimage to New York's Manhattan Island to take the kiddies to F.A.O. Schwarz, the Toy Mecca. Not anymore; now F.A.O. is on the World Wide Web (which is to say that it's everywhere). At this toy store, Elmo is four feet tall; Barbie sports an F.A.O. Schwarz sweatshirt; and exclusive, beautifully crafted, and intelligent toys are the order of the day. Browse the fairy tale–like aisles by category and have a blast checking out toys that are often described as "deluxe" or "super-deluxe." The site has a straightforward shopping cart with lots of graphics, plus full descriptions of the toys accompanied by photos.

Although we think this is a site worth visiting and we *do* recognize the fact that F.A.O. has been enchanting the Little People (and their big escorts) for more than 130 years, to call this site "upscale" is an understatement for Canadians. Prices are in U.S. dollars and shipping is extremely expensive (40 percent of your total order cost). There's also a US$200 minimum order for everyone except Americans. F.A.O. is promising a change in policy on non-U.S. orders. We're waiting!

Hugg'ems Collectibles

members.tripod.com/~huggems2/
huggemsx.html

One-of-a-kind crocheted dolls: In all our travels around the Web, we've never run across a site before that welcomes you in through an actual door. (Well, it's a photo of one really, but it's still pretty homey). Hugg'ems is a Canadian site based in Nova Scotia, where you can buy a number of hand-crafted items online, including an array of crocheted dolls. Choose a dress colour, hair colour, and hairstyle, and a doll will be tailor-made for your little one. You can complete your order online, but despite its Canadian heritage, prices are listed in U.S. dollars (US$70 per doll). For those of you with the skill, make sure to check out the free downloadable patterns for both dolls and teddy bears.

Mastermind Online

www.mastermindtoys.com

Toys for the child with an inquiring mind: Mastermind is a special kind of toy store. You won't find your gun-tottin' action figures here, but you will find hundreds of toys that are at once cool, fun, and stimulating to the ol' gray matter. Here are just some of the categories of products available for sale online:

- *Brain Teasers.* Rubik's Cube may be the best-known teaser, but you can also find a host of equally challenging puzzles and unique games.

- *Dress-up Theatre.* Puppets and sets for the budding thespian in your family are included in this category.

- *Magic.* Rabbits disappear, coins drop from behind earlobes, and kids learn the science, theatrics, and showmanship behind a magic show with these products.

- *Scientific Explorer.* Whether the children in your life are botanists-in-waiting or prone to "experimentation," you can find something to advance their learning here.

Paramount Canada's Wonderland

www.canadaswonderland.com

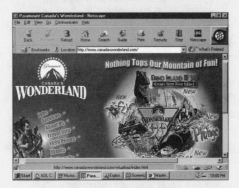

Wonders of amusement park wonders displayed online: It's got 180 attractions and 330 acres of land, and let's face it, kids go nuts for this place. Paramount Canada's Wonderland, located outside of Toronto, is a popular tourist destination for families from across the country. So if you live in Regina but are thinking of a trip out East, this site is very helpful. Check ticket prices, browse upcoming events and concerts, read about on-site services (like first aid and infant care), or take a virtual tour of the park via illustrated maps.

The Disney Store Online

www.disneystore.com

A central source for all the goings-on in the Magic Kingdom: Racking your brains for the perfect gift for your wee ones (or for their playdate playmates) — or, for that matter, anyone else on the planet? Not to worry. Mickey has things well in white-gloved hand. He and the rest of Uncle Walt's magnificent and uniquely ubiquitous characters are at your service. The Disney Store's *Gift Finder* can fix you up in no time; you can search for items by Character/Movie, Product Category, and

Age Group. Among the site's legion of features are the following examples:

- *The Pooh Gram.* A brilliant idea, conceived no doubt with very little help from that Bear of Very Little Brain.

- *Disney's Theme Park Passes.* Buy passes online and explore, endlessly, the attractions that all the U.S. Disney parks offer.

- *Design Online.* Customize/personalize mugs, mouse pads, baby blankets, and a ton of other merchandise.

As you may well imagine, the site is loaded with graphics. All in all, the Disney charm is wholly irresistible. You're gonna find yourself humming "When You Wish Upon a Star" in spite of yourself. We Canadians should take the time to read the shipping info in the *Guest Services* area. You'll see that prices are in U.S. dollars, shipping costs may be higher, and duty may apply to some products.

Zellers

www.hbc.com/zellers/home.asp

A Canadian favourite for family shopping goes online: You got kids? You need stuff? Surf to the Zellers Online site and breathe a sigh of relief. Here, you can buy just about anything a child could want or need, including toys (from video games to Barbie dolls), furniture (fun beds to wacky bookends), and an entire online catalogue of baby products (diaper disposal to slings to nursing accessories). While you're at it, take the time to check out the rest of Zellers site — you'll be pleasantly surprised by the breadth of products and services.

It's the thought that counts

We've found a great way to welcome folks to the online community — send them a greeting card. All electronic greeting cards work basically the same way: You go to a Web site, pick out a card, address it, add your message, and click the Send button. Your intended recipient gets an e-mail message that a card is waiting at such-and-such URL. All your friend has to do is go to that Web site and enter a code that was also in the e-mail. Presto, an instant welcome (and a brief tutorial) for the newbies among us.

American Greetings

www.americangreetings.com

Gifts of all shapes, sizes, and Simpsons: In addition to the traditional holiday greeting cards — rotated to match the season — that the American Greetings Web site carries, you find a lot more Homer and Marge, Beavis and whatsizname, and dozens of other cartoon-media superstars. You can create and print your own greeting cards, or you can send some very interesting animated greeting cards electronically. You also find electronic postcards featuring the aforesaid pop icons and their pals. Aside from a full range of cards, American Greetings features plush gifts, chocolates, flower arrangements, and even CD-ROMs so that you can make your own greeting cards right at home.

Bargoon.com

www.bargoon.com

Online auction house offers something for everyone: If you can't find it an online auction like Bargoon.com, maybe you're putting too much pressure on yourself to find the perfect gift, because with their growing list of categories, sites like this truly cater to every taste. At Bargoon.com, you can buy everything from clothes to garden furniture to art to unique collectibles. You might have to dig a bit, but the prices are right, and you can get stuff here that you won't find anywhere else. Best of all, new listings appear every day, so if you can't find any baseball memorabilia for your brother today, try back tomorrow! Bargoon.com is Canadian, so prices are listed in our very own currency.

Baskits

www.baskits.com

Gift baskets for every occasion: We are partial to this site because we're partial to gift baskets. For the receiver, there's always something unexpected under the wrapping, and after you've emptied it out, the basket becomes a gift in itself. For the giver, gift baskets are a simple yet personal way of wishing someone well. Baskits are just that: specialists in gift baskets. Choose from the main categories, including *Gourmet, Fragrance and Occasion, Active Kids,* and *Baby Gifts.* Within each category, you find a range of gift ideas, depending on your price range (under $50, between $50 and 100, or more than $100). We're hoping someone will deliver a basket called *Decadence Drive* to our door — it's teeming with chocolate products. Yum!

Diva Postcards

www.cyberwomen.com/postcard

A free postcard shop featuring postcards by women artists: While you're figuring out what else to give the object of your e-ffection, stop by Diva and check out the exquisite collection of women's-art postcards. Images of sculpture, drawings, paintings, photographs, and so on, by contributing artists are available. It's a varied collection of original work, some stark, some humorous, much lyrical, and all worth seeing and sending. The electronic postcard service is free. In addition to choosing the image, you can choose your message's typeface, colour of type, and, if you want, even add a character icon. This site is a wonderful gift to all of us from the cyberwomen of Diva.

FTD Florists

www.ftd.com

Flowers and gifts across North America in a hurry: The great advantage of FTD's affiliate system is that you can send and receive flowers pretty much anywhere in Canada or the U.S. without any headaches. Usually, the flowers will arrive by lunchtime the next day. At the FTD Web site, you can order from a vast array of flower arrangements, as well as gift baskets and stuffed animals. You can also find an electronic calendar listing a year's worth of occasions. (Did you know there's a "Friendship Day"?) You can even personalize that calendar to include your own special occasions. Try the florist finder to locate an FTD affiliate near you (by postal code or city name) or use the reminder service to avoid missing upcoming birthdays and anniversaries. The only drawback to this well-designed site? Orders are all placed in U.S. dollars, no matter where you're sending your Diva arrangement.

Galerie Inuit Plus

www.inuitplus.com

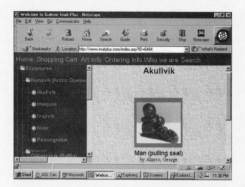

Inuit art made accessible: Inuit art is one of the few contributions by aboriginal peoples in Canada that has received the kind of attention it deserves. People around the world look to Northern artists for their unique worldview as expressed in sculpture, drawings, and paintings (not to mention song). If you're buying for someone with distinguished tastes, we suggest taking a stroll over to the Galerie Inuit Plus online. The range of Inuit sculptures and prints available for secure online purchase here is both diverse (originating in several different communities across Canada) and beautiful (like hand-carved soapstone pieces). The site includes extensive information verifying the authenticity of all the articles for sale, as well as interesting background on each of the contributing Inuit communities and their artistic tradition. A class act from start to finish.

Royal Canadian Mint

www.rcmint.ca

The people who print our money are selling online: It's true! Collectors across the country go ahead and cheer! The Royal Canadian Mint has a beautiful Web site where you can buy coins, watches, and jewelry of the very best quality, including limited edition collections. You can place your order online. Shipping costs $6 and takes about four weeks. Not surprisingly, everything at this site is clearly presented, including beautiful photographs. This is, after all, a top-notch site run by the federal government. Recommended for enthusiasts and window shoppers alike.

The Body Shop

www.thebodyshop.ca

Offering environmentally-sound body care products: We Canadians have helped make The Body Shop into something of an institution as far as gift-giving goes. Many of us (including both your co-authors) have received one of those fragrant, deliciously wrapped gift baskets containing things like berry-scented soap and foot lotions. Now you can order these and other goodies online at The Body Shop Web site. Search for a gift either by recipient (him, her, or child) or by price range (under $20 to more than $40). The *Smart Selector* cross-references these searches to show you the best range of gifts for the special person on your list. You can pay and have your gift shipped using the online form. The whole site is attractively laid out in colours that match the company's green leanings.

And don't forget the cat food!

Pets definitely fit into our definition of extended family. They love us unabashedly and need us unreservedly. The Web is a pet fancier's dream come true. Not only can you find a great number of Web sites devoted to shopping for animals, but you can also find no end to the sites offering support and valuable information. Not to mention the pet vanity sites with pictures of Rover's or Tabby's latest adventure.

PawsPlus

www.pawsplus.net

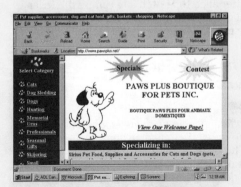

One-stop pet supplies shop: Now here's a site you can really sink your teeth into. (Ha!) Whether you're a pet owner, a breeder, a trainer, or even a veterinarian, you can find something for the animal in your life at this site. Among the offerings

here: food, supplies, gifts for your family pet, biscuits, and even odor control products. How 'bout a reflective vest for your hunting dog? Or try some "skijoring" supplies — that's a Norwegian winter sport in which your dog pulls you along on cross-country skis! An in-site search engine helps you pinpoint the exact item you're looking for. When you find it, just follow the simple checkout process, and your pet purchase is on its way. We can't get over the selection here. We think you'll like it too.

Pets in Pastel

www.islandnet.com/~theos/index.htm

Pet portraits for the true pet lover: You've bought your pet the perfect play toy. You feed her the very best in pet food. You walk her, hug her, and even let her sleep on your bed once in a while. So how do you go the next step to show your affection? How 'bout immortalizing her on canvas? That's the idea behind Pets in Pastel, a site owned and operated by artist and pet lover Sarah Theophilus, of British Columbia. The way it works is that you send Sarah a photo of your pet and any specifications, and she draws a portrait.

You can either mail your photos to her or e-mail them if you have access to a scanner. Then she sends you a thumbnail version of her portrait via e-mail for your perusal. If you're happy, she ships out the final product. If not, you aren't obliged to pay. A typical portrait run about $95 — a small price to pay for your pet's eternal image. Even if you're not planning to commission a portrait, you can browse Pets in Pastel's online gallery or send a free electronic greeting card bearing one of Sarah's creations. We told you this was for the *true* pet lover!

Stayin' Alive

We admit that the following statement sounds pretty funny: Get online and get pumped up with the great outdoors. After all, you'd think that the more time your average Web jockey spends plopped in front of a keyboard and monitor, the less time he or she would have available for exercises more strenuous than thumbing a spacebar. The truth is, however, a great number of fitness junkies are also Net savvy and see the Web as a terrific way to spread their message. The sites that we list in this section vary from those aimed at people for whom the body is a temple to those geared toward people whose body can handle only a Western University sweatshirt. No matter what your sport, however, you can find an outlet worth exploring on the Web.

Sports, Health, and Fitness

Okay, we were not what anyone considered "sporty" in school. So, we've come to appreciate sports and fitness a little later — does that make us any less crazy about health? The sites listed in this section display a bit of the passion that many sports enthusiasts feel. And in case you haven't noticed, health doesn't come cheap. It feels good to recommend some cybershops that are good for both your body and your wallet.

CFL Shop
www.cfl.ca/CFLShop/home.html

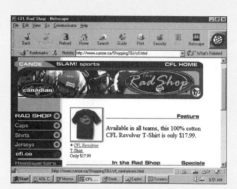

Get CFL collectibles online: Collaboration between the Canadian Football League (CFL) and Canoe, the CFL Shop, is the place to go for Canadian football fans. Here, you find T-shirts, caps, flags, jerseys, and even lighters celebrating your favourite CFL team. You can also link directly from the shop back to Canoe or go on to explore the CFL's Web site.

Discount Golf Warehouse
www.golfdiscountwarehouse.com

Everything for the golf enthusiast: This is one of the most *shoppable* Canadian golf sites we've come across. On a pure aesthetic level, the site's also very beautiful: Navigation icons are brightly coloured in sharp relief against a black background, making for easy reading. Choose from over 1,000 golf products for sale — through a secure server, of course. The list of categories here includes golf equipment, clothes, gloves, outerwear, shoes, bags, balls, and much more. Discount Golf Warehouse also has the gift-giver in mind, offering an e-mail gift reminder service and gift certificates for the golf nut in your life.

Excel Water Sports

www.excel-sports.com

"Everybody go surfin', windsurfin' Canada": Excel Water Sports specializes in windsurfing equipment. Whether you're a novice or an expert, you can find a range of boards, harnesses, foot straps, and accessories to suit your needs, and you can buy them online! There's also a photo gallery that will undoubtedly inspire you to get to the beach very soon.

GolfNet Canada

www.golfcanada.com

Canada-wide course listings and vacation packages: Planning a golf trip in Canada?

The GolfNet Canada site is a good place to start. The site keeps a listing of hundreds of courses across the country. You can also find accommodations or even book a vacation package. The *Virtual Pro Shop* has links to other golf sites on the Net.

Nature's Nutrition

www.naturesnutrition.com

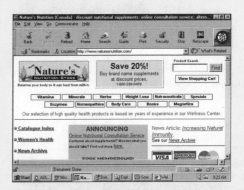

A holistic approach to health products: Nature's Nutrition runs a Web site that appeals to the health-conscious and the experimental among us. There are vitamins and health books, as well as minerals, herbs, and homeopathics for people who are looking for non-traditional ways to improve their health. We like the *News Archive,* where you can read up on some lesser-known (and often controversial) health products like Echinacea. If you're still curious, sign up for the free newsletter, and Nature's Nutrition will keep you updated on developments in the alternative health field and upcoming in-store specials. If you're serious about vitamins, consider using the Online Nutritional Consultation Service (it costs $25). Best of all, you can buy everything Nature's Nutrition has to offer directly from the site by using your credit card.

Powdermagic

www.powdermagic.com

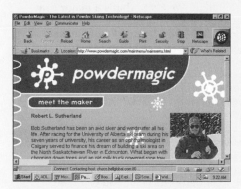

Innovative ski products: What directory of Canadian sporting sites would be complete without at least one site devoted to skiing? We chose this one because it is totally unique. Powdermagic is a company that makes a patented, wide single ski designed specifically for deep snow skiing. The company's owner and Powdermagic's designer is a man named Robert L. Sutherland, whose incredible story of innovation, tragedy, and recovery is told in the *Meet the Maker* section. There's tons of background info here on Powdermagic's design, but you can't actually buy the ski online. Instead, fill out the online order form and either fax, e-mail, or snail mail it to the company.

SportMart

www.sportmartdirect.com/store

Equipment and accessories for all your favourite sports: One of Canada's biggest independent sports retailers is open for business on the Net, and you're going to be impressed both with what you can find here and the prices. Buy a tennis racket. Browse through the bikes. Check out the footwear. If you order more than $49 worth of merchandise, your order is shipped free of charge within Canada. West Coast residents can expect shipment within about three days; it will take just over a week for purchases to reach you Newfoundlanders. Probably the best over-all Canadian general interest sports retailer we've found online.

Nature Lovers and the Great Outdoors

All we can say is there's a lot more to camping than we learned in Brownies. Take a trek though the sites in this section, and you'll agree. In fact, with all the equipment, training, and paraphernalia available, the rustic outdoors are looking decidedly high-tech. Don't forget the gas-powered microwave the next time you go camping.

Camper's Village

www.campers-village.com

Western camping giant offers gear for any camping expedition: Good luck thinking of something you *can't* find at Camper's Village online. The company, which owns two mega-stores in Calgary and Edmonton, has a head-spinning selection of camping gear for sale at its Web site. There's also a chat area where you can learn camping tips from fellow lovers-of-the-outdoors. Finding a camping tool (from cooking stoves to tents to accessories) is easy: Just choose a category and pinpoint what you're looking for by using the Get More Specific drop-down menus. Excellent site. Nice design.

Canadian Camping Associations

www.ontcamp.on.ca/other.htm

Directory for Canada's Camping associations: Before you go off to blaze a trail, this Ontario-based site is worth a visit. Here, you find contact info, as well as links to camping associations across the country. Use the site to locate accredited children's camps in several categories: day camps, residential camps for girls or boys, co-ed, and camps for special needs children. We found the *Commercial* listings very complete too. A good resource for planning your trip to the hinterlands.

Mountain Equipment Co-op

www.mec.ca

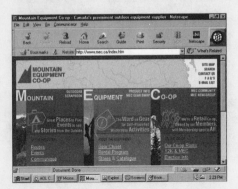

Outdoors knowledge hub: Probably the only thing you can't do at the Mountain Equipment Co-op Web site is buy outdoor equipment. We agree that's a major drawback, but if you do visit this site, you'll be compensated by a range of online services. (Just so we're all up to speed, the Co-op is a not-for-profit outfitter with stores across Canada. After you become a member for a small fee, you can shop there and even take part in the way the store's run.)

So what can you do at the Web site? Well, you can become a member, for one. You can browse the Co-op's excellent catalogue of outdoors gear. You can read about upcoming outdoor activities across the country or use the handy electronic checklists to plan your next backpacking, cycling, or kayaking tour. You can even swap your old gear for someone else's, using the electronic bulletin board. We're not going to let Mountain Equipment Co-op off the hook for their lack of online sales, but that's a pretty impressive list of services, don't you think?

Northward Bound

www.northwardbound.com

Simple site offers wide variety of outdoor goods: Northward Bound specializes in gear for kayakers, hikers, and canoeists. Aside from some practical stuff like stoves, sleeping bags, and paddles, check out the nifty gadgets for sale here including water filters, packing towels, survival whistles, and waterproofing kits. The online order form is simple to fill out, and this site, if a bit unglamorous, is delightfully uncluttered.

That's Entertainment

So, Fiorella, what do you feel like doing tonight?

I don't know, Marguerite. How 'bout a movie?

Sounds good. I'm just gonna log on and pick up some tickets for the 9 p.m. show at the multiplex.

You know, I'm more in the mood for some live theatre or a performance of some kind. Anything playing?

I thought I saw a bus ad for a Broadway show in town. I know a great ticket site that's got the best seats. . .

On second thought, how about if you just come over to my place and we catch a flick on the tube — do you know what's on?

Nah, the dog ate the TV section — but I heard about this Web site that gives you the TV listings no matter where you are in the country. We'll just. . . .

Marguerite, do you get the feeling we're spending too much time together since we started this book?

Yep. The writer's life is a lonely one, my friend!

Okay, it's not really that bad. Actually, we go out quite a bit, and we've learned how to find entertainment online when we need it. This section gives you all the ammo you need for a terrific night on the town or for hanging at home.

Goin' Out

Ready for a good time? Need help picking a destination? Restaurant reviews? Memorize them. The best seats at the best prices? Hunt 'em down. What movie to see? Well, you get the idea.

Cineplex Odeon

www.theatres.sre.sony.com/canada/

Find out what's playing and where: Cineplex has a pretty fancy Web site — meaning you'll need a better-than-average browser to view it properly. Some of the highlights include film listings and show times for several Cineplex theatres across Canada, The Store where you can pick up gift certificates (no online purchases for Canadians yet), the Hollywood links (via the Sony Entertainment network), and the Trailer Park, where you can watch a selection of movie trailers using a video player plug-in. (Yes, you can download the plug-in here.) Also, don't miss the Underground link, where you can view trailers for art films.

Cornucopia: Where Shall We Dine?

www.mnsinc.com/cornucopia/ resguide.htm

A huge selection of global dining experiences, organized by country and region:

Cornucopia's site still has links to a hundred times more restaurant listings than any individual dining guide on the Net. The site is geographically oriented, so you can select any of the regional links to find a selection of restaurants in your area. You also notice some interesting online-menu services and guides for dining on six continents (and not a few islands).

Entertainment Ticketfinder

www.ticketfinder.com

The one source for hard-to-find tickets to entertainment or sporting events: Entertainment Ticketfinder doesn't fool around. To begin with, it suggests browser versions of 4.0 or higher; anything less than 3.0 can't even access the site. Next, Ticketfinder charges a US$10 per ticket fee for tickets to non-sold-out events. Should you have money to burn, you can get tickets for the Super Bowl, the NBA Championships, the World Series, the Stanley Cup, and so on. Amazing, huh? But if you must go, Entertainment Ticketfinder seems to be your best bet. It issues certain guarantees and protects you from rip-offs. Ticketfinder also offers tickets to sold-out performances at La Scala and The Metropolitan Opera, ballet performances, major symphonies, Riverdance (an industry in itself), Cirque du Soleil (ditto), and award shows. (The Oscars, no way; but

the Tonys, the Emmys, the Golden Globes, MTV Music Awards, the Grammys, CMAs, and others? Can do.) This site is kind of exciting to look at, and if your corporation is paying — or if you're loaded and/or attending one of these events is a lifelong dream of yours — just knowing that attending *Any Event* (except, of course, the Academy Awards) is possible can be a real thrill. All ordering and pricing on this site takes place in U.S. dollars, so Canadian buyers beware!

Famous Players

www.famousplayersmovies.com

Major Canadian theatre chain online: Like its rival, Cineplex Odeon, Famous Players keeps a souped-up site with lots of bells and whistles. You need a later version of Netscape or Internet Explorer to view it correctly. At the site, you'll find an excellent search system for show times across Canada, as well as extensive info on special Famous Players theatres like IMAX (very cool) and the new SilverCity and Paramount megaplex theatres (super cool). The movie reviews are worth checking out here, as well as the online store and the TechTown downloads.

Ticketmaster Canada

www.ticketmaster.ca

Current tickets available for all manner of events: If you need tickets anywhere in Canada, you can purchase them here at the big daddy of online ticket-buying sites. This Web site offers direct access to the huge Ticketmaster database. Tickets to sports, concerts, museum exhibitions, arts, theatre, and family events are all available. Be sure to check the *On Sale Today* and the *On Sale Soon* listings to get a chance at the hottest tickets out there. Remember, thousands of people may be trying for the same tickets as you through Ticketmaster's server, so you'll have to be patient, and you may not get through before the event you're trying for is sold out. The Net can solve some problems, but the popularity of Barry Manilow — we're helpless in the face of it!

WWW Virtual Library: Museums Around the World

www.comlab.ox.ac.uk/archive/other/
    museums/world.html

A central jump-station for museum information: Where's the missing link? Couldn't find any here, but what we did find was an awe-inspiring collection of links to museums, galleries, archives, and exhibitions, with Web sites in more than 60 countries around the world. Areas covered include art, science, engineering, design, craft, and so on. You can also find a few art online museums (in case you decide not to go out after all).

Stayin' In

For all the joys of going out, staying at home has an equivalent pull. Especially when a must-see prime-time show is on. Or how about that movie you missed in the theatres that is — according to the Web — on the tube for the first time tonight. Want to pick up a hobby from your childhood? You'll no doubt be able to find a support group on the Web. Hey, you've got the weekend to go out, right? So kick off your shoes and pull that mousepad a little closer.

CBC Sports

www.tv.cbc.ca/sports/

Game listings and more from Canada's public broadcaster: CBC Television's sports division has a pretty basic site, but here you'll find the broadcasting schedule for the current NHL season (Hockey Night In Canada anyone?) as well as info on special sporting events. (The CBC has won the rights to broadcast the Olympic games for the next decade!) CFL fans can also use CBC Sports online to track football stats and watch for upcoming matches.

ESPN
ESPN.go.com

One of the most popular Web sites on any subject: ESPN is an unbelievably thorough sports site with great technical support, brilliant graphics, and knowledgeable and entertaining commentators. The ESPN site features live multimedia coverage of major sporting events through ESPN Radio, GameCast, and GameFlow, in addition to all the after-the-fact reporting and coverage. Membership carries weighty privileges, too. As an ESPN Insider, you get special access to some interactive features, as well as stats and discounts at the online store. You also get ESPN's top analysts and dozens of exclusive features, plus Insider-only columns with special event coverage. On top of everything else, ESPN is a gorgeous site to visit.

The Internet Antique Shop
www.tias.com

A must-see for collectors of any stripe: From antique advertising to Disneyana, from first editions to World's Fair memorabilia, the Internet Antique Shop has it all. An extremely popular site, the Internet Antique Shop Mall receives over 400,000 visits from around the world each month.

Across the board, you find superb graphics and descriptions, plus shopping carts in which to put all your purchases. The Internet Antique Shop is the ultimate cyberspace collectible warehouse.

TSN
www.tsn.ca

Sports nuts have a home here: If you're Canadian and you're a sports fan, you probably watch TSN — and if you like the TV network, you'll love this site! Watch video updates from TSN's Sportsbreak, read the latest news from the world of sports, sign up to have scores delivered to your e-mailbox every morning, keep track of scores in your favourite sport, and check listings for TSN's upcoming coverage. You'll also find a chat area and even an *Online Host* who provides commentary on the latest sports-related goings-on. This Web site is superior by any standard.

Yahoo! Canada Hobbies
ca.yahoo.com/Regional/Countries/Canada /Recreation_and_Sports/Hobbies/

An excellent launch pad for any hobby-related activity: Yahoo! has done it again. This URL is hobbyist heaven — the jumping-off point for Web-wide explorations of online resources related to your favourite hobbies, from amateur radio to textiles and writing, with plenty of stops in between — stops that lead you to cybernetic seas of information. Check out the Collecting category, for example, where you'll find a number of subcategories for things like coins and stamps. This site offers precisely the sort of Internet experience that makes you gasp at the immenseness of it all. You know, even if you don't include playing with the kids and/or pets, interpersonal communication, or an evening of romance, you can still find an awful lot to do without ever leaving home — and you can find it right here, through Yahoo! Canada.

Other Stuff to Check Out

moviesunlimited.com
www.birdhouse.com
www.canoe.ca/SlamGolfCanTour/home.html
www.cfl.ca
www.facets.org
www.goodmovies.com
www.kino.com
www.nhl.com
www.Velotique.com

Part VII
The Part of Tens

The 5th Wave   By Rich Tennant

"It's a free starter disk for AOL."

In this part . . .

Hey, got a few minutes? Let us feed you some fast facts. The Part of Tens is filled with the crème de la crème of online shopping. When you're ready to kick off your shoes and just breeze through some of the best justifications for shopping online, turn to Chapter 16. Not only will it give you food for thought, but also ammunition for the dinner table.

Already convinced and you're ready to shop — but you want the easiest route and the best deal? Then take a brief tour of the Web's bargain basement in Chapter 17. When you factor in the convenience of Net shopping in with the online deals, you're ready to walk out a winner.

Chapter 16

Ten Reasons to Buy Online

In This Chapter

▶ Motivation for buying stuff online

C onsider this chapter your facile explanation assistant. You're sitting around with a big group of friends — whether for dinner, a Tupperware party, or league night — and you happen to mention that you've tried — and liked — this online shopping thing. Uh-oh, you've done something no one else in your peer group has tried. You've gone out on a limb. You've boldly shopped where no shopper has shopped before.

Now your friends want to know why, for what, and how come. And all you need to do is read over this list of ten reasons that tell why shopping online, like eating oatmeal, is the right thing to do. Commit this list to memory, if you want, or use it to spur your own thoughts and reasons. Better yet, get the e-mail addresses of all your friends and send them an animated, electronic greeting card from one of the online shops — with a great big "I told you so."

It's Safer than Telephone or Mail Orders

What would you need to do to make your average mail order as safe as your average online order? When you're ready to put your order in the mailbox, you call up the armoured car service instead. Three burly looking gents pile out of the vehicle; one stays by the car, with gun drawn, looking from right to left, while the other two come up to you and demand to see some ID. They squint at your driver's license and then fingerprint you; the fingerprints go off for verification while the armed guards sit around and wait, watching your every move. While they're waiting, they take your order and put it in a 50-kilogram safe. The guards get the go-ahead (usually within 24 hours), take the safe with your order inside, and haul it out to the armoured car.

After everything is secure, the guards call for the police escort. Two squad cars and a helicopter follow the car cross-country to the mail-order company's headquarters. The two burly guys get out again and demand to see some ID from the company itself. They call in a team of lawyers to verify the business documents. Everything looks good, so the guards bring in the safe, spin the combination, and hand over the order to the shipping clerk. The shipping clerk gets out the scramble phone and calls the bank to verify your charge card. The merchant and bank exchange secret codes, and the bank eventually gives the thumbs-up for your charge. The shipping clerk, under the watchful eye of the security guards, takes your credit-card information and puts it in the big, time-locked company safe. After he squares everything away, the clerk calls the stockroom, pulls your order, and sends it on its way. The three armored-car personnel, the police escort, the lawyers, and the clerk look at each other and say, "Good job." The phone rings — it's another mail order. Everybody sighs and does it all over again.

Okay, so nobody ever accused us of being subtle. But because of modern encryption methods, digital certificates, and direct point-to-point communications, shopping online is way safer than mail order could ever be. And telephone orders? Don't get us started. . . .

It's More Convenient

Whenever anyone asks Joseph what he likes most about living in New York, or Toronto for Marguerite and Fiorella, we all say the convenience. Neighbourhood markets and delis are open 24 hours and just a few steps from our front doors. In a way, the Web is the ultimate Big City. Every store is always open; every neighborhood is perfectly safe to travel in, and the best shops are right at your fingertips. Literally.

You Can Shop Canadian

Remember those famous hosers Bob and Doug Mackenzie? It's hard to imagine that they — sitting near some ice hole fishing in Out There, The Great White North — could ever enjoy a fresh lobster dinner or don this winter's hottest trends in toques — that is, without first getting on a plane to get them.

These Northern bros are fictional but they serve as a good example of how spread apart we Canucks are, eh. While geographically, we live in the second largest country in the world, there aren't many of us — about 30 million spread across nearly 10 million square kilometres. Some of you live hundreds or thousands of kilometres away from other communities, let alone a department store, or the wonderful treasures that our regions have to offer.

Online shopping brings retail and Canada virtually and literally to your doorstep. If you're sipping lattes on the West Coast but crave lobster, check out Lobster Direct (`www.lobsterdirect.com`) to order those sea critters of the coast of Nova Scotia. Conversely, if you're in Halifax and would like to chase down that lobster dinner with one of those world-famous icewines coming out of the Niagara Peninsula, hop on over to Inniskillin Wineries at `www.inniskillin.com`.

You Can Shop the World

The world may be getting smaller, but that certainly doesn't make it any less densely packed. Every culture, every country has a flavour all its own. Granted, the best way to experience a far-away land is to travel there, but for more people, exotic journeys are few and far between. Sampling a distant country's wares, on the other hand, is a pleasure everyone can enjoy — everyone on the Web, that is.

The Internet is now (and has been for some time) global in its reach. After the computer infrastructure is in place, even the smallest company can sell goods and services over the Web easily and affordably. As worldwide online commerce grows, you can expect more and more companies to make their products available. Looking for an authentic timepiece from Switzerland or exotic rice-paper screens from Japan? Just take a look on the Web for these items and anything else from the global marketplace.

You Can Get an Instant Record

None of the authors of this book are the best record keepers around. Whenever one of us comes back from a shopping trip, we can never find our receipts until a couple days later — and then we discover them in our pants' pocket . . . after the pants are washed. So keeping track of what we buy and when and how much we spend is truly a catch-as-catch-can affair. Except when we shop on the Web.

Virtually every store or service from which we've ever bought online — from research to theatre tickets — has sent us an e-mail confirmation of our order. The confirmation includes each item on our order, spelled out in great detail; the cost of each item; shipping charges (if any); a confirmation number; and a customer-service contact — either as an e-mail address or a phone number (or sometimes both).

We generally file our electronic confirmations in a special folder each of us has created on our computers. That way, we can quickly find anything we've ordered by looking at the message headers. We can even sort them by date as April 30 rears its ugly head, so we can see what we bought last year that's tax deductible. (One of the major benefits of doing a book about shopping online is that everything we buy online is tax deductible! Research, you know.)

Shopping Search Engines Make It Easy

Generally, the second reaction anyone has to the Web (after the obligatory "Oh, wow!") is the complaint that, because so much is available, you can't find what you want. Search engines go a long way toward bringing the Internet down to a manageable size.

Apart from allowing you to do a regular search for a product, shopping search engines help you in two other ways. First, Canadian search engines like AltaVista Canada (www.altavista.ca) and Canada.com (www.canada.com) have done a lot of the legwork for you by setting up Shopping Guides on their sites that include links to merchants' sites.

Second, if you're searching for something that's not available in Canada, U.S.-based shopping search engines bring the right products to the forefront. Not only can they help you find goods and services anywhere on the Web, but they can also help you comparison-shop, especially for price — in American dollars, of course. Each of the various shopping search engines works differently, but some of them, such as ShopFind (www.shopfind.com) and Excite's Jango (www.jango.excite.com), give you a list of links showing the product, the vendor, and the price. Scroll down your search results, pick the best price, and you're on your way to getting exactly what you want at the lowest U.S. dollar cost.

Forget-Me-Not Reminder Services

We're not really forgetful or uncaring; we just get so darned busy that sometimes we can't even keep track of what day of the week it is — never mind remembering a special occasion in time to do anything about it. Several shopping sites online have developed reminder services to help out poor little schnooks like us and make us shine in our loved ones' eyes. Now, thanks to reminder services such as those on Sympatico's shopping guide, not only do we get the gift to the intended recipient in time, but the gifts we pick out are more intriguing, unique, and, well, better. Many of the reminder services offer specially tailored suggestions along with their e-mailed taps on the shoulder. And in true, hypertext fashion, all we need to do is click the gift suggestion's link, and we can order that gift right then and there.

Now, if someone could only come up with an online method of reminding us to feed the cat and water the plants, our lives would be complete.

Of Shopping Carts and Shopping Malls

One thing that's really annoying in real-world shopping is a complete joy in virtual buying. Ever made your way to the checkout counter with an armload of gifts or groceries and then realized that you forgot one essential item — or that a three-for-one sale's on and you're one shy? The question then is . . . Do you risk the wrath of the folks behind you in line by dropping everything and running down the aisles in hot pursuit? Or do you risk a parking ticket (or an irate baby-sitter) by turning your cart around, picking up the what-have-you, and then getting back in line — which, by the way, doubles in length in the time you're gone. We're not even going to talk about the embarrassment of realizing that you don't have enough money to cover the goodies in your cart. Does the phrase "I need to put something back" make anyone else's spine shiver? Getting through the checkout counter with everything you need may prove tough going in the real mall but is a thing of beauty and simplicity in the online stores.

Pile your electronic shopping cart higher than you'd ever dare at the local market. After you move into the checkout zone, you can easily add more of any item, drop something else altogether, or just totally return to shopping — all without losing your place in line, your time, or your composure. Shopping carts, in fact, are even more advantageous in a virtual mall, such as The Buyers Club (`www.buyersclub.com`) than in a real one. Imagine going from store to store at an online mall and seeing your shopping cart expand to fit whatever you put in it. And when you're ready to pay, you go through the process once — not once for every store you visit.

Variety, Diversity, and Novelty

The relatively low start-up cost for getting your business online, as opposed to opening a storefront in the world of cinder blocks and long-term leases, has been a boon to the tremendous range of products available on the Web. Now, if a market for goods exists anywhere in the world, someone can offer those items for sale online — and the seller doesn't necessarily need to go through a middleman, which naturally keeps prices down.

Speaking of prices, the Web can greatly level the playing field of market competition. Although a big international company such as Worldwide Wombats, Inc., can spend a lot more money on its Web-site design than can, say, Tommy's Homegrown Wombats, search engines list both of them. And the consumer can go for whatever wombat strikes his fancy.

Note: Just to cover our bases and make sure that neither Worldwide Wombats nor Tommy's Homegrown Wombats actually exist, we went to Yahoo! Canada and did a quick search for **wombat.** Although wombats aren't yet a hot e-commerce item (it's only a matter of time), we did find 101(!) listings devoted to the fuzzy marsupial.

You Can Save Money — and Make It

You know that warm and smug feeling you get whenever you buy something on sale? Or that pat on the back you give yourself when you end up pocketing a few extra dollars by getting rid of that old china set you still haven't taken out of the box since your wedding day? If you need such a pick-me-up, get to the Web. With the explosion of online auction houses like Bargoon.ca (www.bargoon.com), you have a way better chance to unload your stuff than you would with passers-by at your garage sale. And the overhead that merchants save when they open online — rather than on a street near you — means many sites are able to pass on the savings to you in the form of lower ticket prices. Items such as books and computer software, are generally cheaper on the Web. You'll also find some sites that offer coupons to shave even more off your bill. Heck, sometimes you won't even need your credit card: You can get things free such as music and greeting cards and . . . wait, why not just read the next chapter.

Chapter 17

Ten Things That Are Easier or Cheaper to Get Online

• •

In This Chapter

▶ Great buys online

• •

Any fisherman can tell you that you can have the biggest lake in the world right next door, but if it doesn't have any fish in it — or the right kind of fish — you need to get into your pickup and drive. Similarly, even if the Internet's accessible from anywhere on the planet and is always open, if it doesn't have the goods — and the good goods, too . . . the ones that you want — it wouldn't matter to you one bit.

In this chapter, therefore, you find ten categories of merchandise, products, and services that are easier or cheaper to get online than off — hands down. Now whether you need all this stuff is a question between you and your garage.

Doing the Software Download Shuffle

You're on the road at a sales conference with your trusty laptop in tow. One frantic call from the office later, you're scrambling to pull together a presentation for The Big Client. No problem, you assure the boss, you've got Map-O-Matic, the hot, new software that converts dull, meaningless spreadsheets into beautiful, meaningless graphs — guaranteed to close the sale. Powering up your portable computer, your heart sinks as you realize that you do have Map-O-Matic . . . but only on your system back at the office. Oh my, what software store is going to be open in this podunk town this late at night? Ah ha! You realize that you can purchase and download a copy of the program from any of the tons of online software stores or even from the Map-O-Matic Web site itself. Hot dog! You can make the presentation, satisfy the Big Client, and keep your job safe. Thank goodness for online software!

You don't need to be stuck in the middle of nowhere with a boss breathing down your neck to appreciate the benefits of online software stores. Maybe you just want to check out the latest game, so you download a try-before-you-buy demo. Or perhaps you need to get the latest version of the browser — the one that's certified as bug-free — because the last one crashes every time you hum "Oh Canada!"

In fact, distributing software over the Internet has become so accepted that only the rarest company does not have a download area on its Web site. Not only is online distribution a great way for companies to cut packaging costs, but it also gives customers a fast and easy way to get updates or to try out new software. The only major drawback is the download time — but compare that to the time that you spend trying to find a parking space at the local mall (where the only software store in town is located) — and that drawback backs right down.

To be sure, there are more U.S. one-stop sites offering software from a variety of developers than there are Canadian ones, but when it comes to downloading software, nationality isn't an issue — there aren't any borders to travel across. So if you are stuck buying software from an American site, you'll only have to deal with the American/Canadian exchange rate. That may add up to little in exchange for having your software NOW!

Tuning In to the Web's Top 30

There's a revolution going on in the music industry, and it has its roots on the Web. It goes by the name of mp3 — and it lets you download music on your computer, whether they're songs on today's Hit list or a favourite Golden Oldie. The term mp3 is essentially a file format that compresses audio files for downloading in such as way as to produce near CD-quality sound. Sites like mp3.com (www.mp3.com) or Lycos' search engine devoted to mp3 titles (mp3.lycos.com) have a listing of mp3 songs from artists or copyright holders who have given permission to let you download and play their songs. And some individual artists offer their songs in mp3 format right on their own Web sites. You'll need to first download a player — software, like Winamp, that lets you play the songs. For now mp3 music is free, but the music industry is scurrying to figure out how to distribute this format at a price.

Who Has the Information?

What better place to spend the Information Age than toddling down the Internet? Well, okay, aside from Hawaii. The very core of the Internet are the data, documents, reports, and other words of wisdom that thousands of scientists, researchers, and other pundits enter. Best of all, however, is the inherent searchability of the Web. After all, just because Alexander the Great had the world's largest library didn't mean that he could find the *Big Book of Battles* right when he needed it in a hurry. You, on the other hand, can use any of the numerous search engines online to help you in your hunt — no matter what the subject may be.

Not only is an enormous amount of information available for free on the Web, but a great many companies also want to help you find what you need. Sure, they're going to charge you for it, but what you're really paying for is your time, which, as we all know, is extremely valuable and better spent making deals than making copies.

Fly Me to the Web

Feel the need for speed? Or maybe a quick getaway? Well, whether you're an international jewel thief on the run or just a harried homekeeper who needs a break, you can find relief on the Web. Every major airline, whether it's Canadian, American-based, or from Hong Kong, has a Web site where you can check airfares, flight schedules, and ticket availability, and most sites enable you to book a flight online through them directly or through an affiliated travel agent.

Now, maybe you're a big fan of "hold" music, or maybe you just like the power of being served by "the next available agent." If that's the case, you're welcome to stay on the telephone for hours on end. Just leaves more bandwidth for the rest of us. One online ticket service that we start with whenever we're skybound is the Canadian version of Travelocity (`www.travelocity.ca`). By using Travelocity, instead of going from airline to airline looking for the best deal, you just send in your optimal travel dates and flights and the sites return *to you* with the lowest fare for those flights. We think that's something you could get used to.

Greetings from Afar

Friends we know keep a box full of greeting cards — holiday cards, birthday cards, get-well-soon cards, no-message arty cards — and whenever the occasion arises, they leaf through the drawer and pick out the most appropriate one. There was a good reason for it: Better to get a bunch of them at one time because just getting one is a waste. But we have a hard time justifying as time well spent the two or so hours spent driving down to the card shop, roaming the aisles, spinning the racks, getting the card, and hauling ourselves back home. But then again, we like to send cards that we pick out just for the person from a much wider selection than those in the drawer.

The solution? Online greeting cards and virtual flower bouquets. Thanks to selection and convenience both to beat the band, you can't go wrong by visiting any of the major sites, such as *Hallmark* (www.hallmark.com) or *American Greetings* (www.americangreetings.com) for greeting cards. Not only do they have a zippy collection of electronic cards that can be sent via email but they also offer electronic animated comics to keep someone laughing. Beats a drawer full of inappropriate cards any day. If you're feeling romantic but not very flush in the pocket, you can send that special someone via email a virtual bouquet of flowers — complete with a gushy poem — from a number of sites, including *Virtual Flowers* (www.virtualflowers.com).

Building Your Own Library

One of our favourite pastimes is spending an afternoon browsing through a bookstore and scouring the shelves for a best-seller or discovering a rare gem. Once in hand, we can cozy up in a chair and test-drive the book before actually paying for it. With booksellers taking to the Web, such as Indigo Online (www.indigo.ca) and Chapters.ca (www.chapters.ca), you can have almost the same experience right in your living room — or wherever your computer sits. In exchange for giving up the bookish ambiance, you'll get books carrying price tags that are significantly lower ("30% to 50% Off" signs are standard fare) than the ticket price on the same books sitting on the store's bricks-and-mortar shelves — savings that more than cover the shipping costs involved.

You Can Save the Trip to the Grocer's

Want to take a vacation but don't have the time? We'll, we've found nearly six days you can take back — the amount of time you lose yearly doing groceries, from driving to the grocery store, to pushing your shopping cart up and down the aisles, to packing and unpacking your car. Environics Research group says consumers spend an average of 156 hours a year grocery shopping, and suggests that you could cut that to at least 20 hours by buying online. Divide 136 hours by 24 and Hawaii here we come!

Oops! We got so excited we forget to mention it: You can buy groceries on the Net and have them delivered to your home! Most online grocers service local or metropolitan areas, such as Grocery Gateway in Metro Toronto (www.grocerygateway.com), where you can actually buy such things as milk and eggs, have them delivered to your door that day and then pay for items with your debit card. National offerings are also beginning to open cyberdoors. Yet you can order non-perishable foods anywhere in Canada from online stores like The PeachTree Network (www.peachtree.net). And most let you save even more time by storing your list of the regular purchases you make on the site. It's really only a matter of time when national chains get into the fray.

Playing the International Shopping Game

Hmmm, which of the alternatives in the following table are the easier ways to go?

- Fly to Turin, Italy, to pick up the latest dance music that's driving Italian teens wild. Visit *Discolandia Music Store* (www.discolandia.com), listen to the RealAudio samples, and order the top hits.

- Travel to Australia to hunt down a stuffed wallaby wannabe for your kid. (And suffer extreme jet lag.) Visit the *Wombat Australiana Store* (www.wombat.com.au) and order your stuffed Wombat, Koala, or Kangaroo. Have a g'day.

- Trek on over to Korea and scour the countryside for the sleekest in hand-painted ties. Drop by *Art Tie* (www.arttie.co.kr) and run your virtual fingers through the beautiful designs.

- Wade into the icy waters of Alaska to pull a 50-pound salmon from the Togiak River. Surf on by *AlaskaNet* (www.alaskanet.com) and order up smoked or kippered salmon treats — and stay dry.

We'll admit that nothing's quite like traveling the world for real; we're certainly not trying to talk you out of that joy. All we're saying is that if you don't have the money or the time to go globetrotting, you can always scratch your wanderlust with a few odds and ends from an international online shopping spree.

The Better Catalogue Way

What makes online catalogue shopping easier than offline catalogue shopping? One word: backorder. That's one word you never hear if you're shopping the online way because the Web-based catalogues are tied into the company's inventory. Whenever anyone orders an item, the item comes right from the available inventory. So if you go online and place an order, and a problem arises — for example, the product isn't available for two weeks — you know before you complete the transaction. And if you don't want to deal with it, you can cancel just that portion of the order.

'Tis Better to Give Online

Maybe the extraordinary variety of merchandise available on the Web is what makes it so perfect for gift giving. Maybe it's the fact that you can shop for someone the way that you want to shop — either searching for something specific or browsing the virtual aisles. Maybe it's because online shopping always involves shipping, so sending the package to someone else's home instead of your billing address is no big deal. Moreover, most sites are happy to gift wrap or throw in a card with a message from you.

But we think what really gives online gift giving the edge is that it can be so impulsive. Say, for example, that Great Aunt Elizabeth, the family's Elvis buff, has a birthday coming up. Your online-shopping-phobic twin, who lives across the river, comes upon a life-size figure of the singer, complete with a remote control that gets his hips a swiveling. But after weighing his options (and the figure) he decides that sending the gift is too much trouble and opts to keep looking. You, on the other hand, surf on over to The King Warehouse, the online Elvis memorabilia centre, and find the exact same model — ready to ship. You whip out your credit card, and before you can say "Chaaaargggeee it," you've picked out a nice wrapping paper and sent the gift on its way — with a message from both you and your twin, because that's the kind of sibling you are. Great Aunt Elizabeth is delighted with her new trophy and says "Thank you very much" by doubling your inheritance. See? Isn't online gift giving the best?

Index

• *C* •

• F •

● *O* ●

Notes

Notes

Notes

Notes

Notes

Notes

Notes

Notes

Discover Dummies Online!

The Dummies Web Site is your fun and friendly online resource for the latest information about ...For Dummies® books and your favorite topics. The Web site is the place to communicate with us, exchange ideas with other ...For Dummies readers, chat with authors, and have fun!

Ten Fun and Useful Things You Can Do at www.dummies.com

1. Win free ...For Dummies books and more!
2. Register your book and be entered in a prize drawing.
3. Meet your favorite authors through the IDG Books Author Chat Series.
4. Exchange helpful information with other ...For Dummies readers.
5. Discover other great ...For Dummies books you must have!
6. Purchase Dummieswear™ exclusively from our Web site.
7. Buy ...For Dummies books online.
8. Talk to us. Make comments, ask questions, get answers!
9. Download free software.
10. Find additional useful resources from authors.

Link directly to these ten
fun and useful things at
http://www.dummies.com/10useful

For other technology titles from IDG Books Worldwide, go to
www.idgbooks.com

Not on the Web yet? It's easy to get started with Dummies 101®: The Internet For Windows® 98 or The Internet For Dummies®, 6th Edition, at local retailers everywhere.

Find other ...For Dummies books on these topics:

Business • Career • Databases • Food & Beverage • Games • Gardening • Graphics • Hardware
Health & Fitness • Internet and the World Wide Web • Networking • Office Suites
Operating Systems • Personal Finance • Pets • Programming • Recreation • Sports
Spreadsheets • Teacher Resources • Test Prep • Word Processing

IDG BOOKS WORLDWIDE BOOK REGISTRATION

Register This Book and Win!

We want to hear from you!

Visit **http://my2cents.dummies.com** to register this book and tell us how you liked it!

- ✔ Get entered in our monthly prize giveaway.

- ✔ Give us feedback about this book — tell us what you like best, what you like least, or maybe what you'd like to ask the author and us to change!

- ✔ Let us know any other ...*For Dummies*® topics that interest you.

Your feedback helps us determine what books to publish, tells us what coverage to add as we revise our books, and lets us know whether we're meeting your needs as a ...*For Dummies* reader. You're our most valuable resource, and what you have to say is important to us!

Not on the Web yet? It's easy to get started with *Dummies 101*®: *The Internet For Windows*® *98* or *The Internet For Dummies*®, 6th Edition, at local retailers everywhere.

Or let us know what you think by sending us a letter at the following address:

...*For Dummies* Book Registration
Dummies Press
7260 Shadeland Station, Suite 100
Indianapolis, IN 46256-3917
Fax 317-596-5498

...FOR DUMMIES™

BESTSELLING
BOOK SERIES